Die-Hard Atheist:

from NDE Denier to Full-on Woo-woo
– Against my Will

by Louisa Peck.

Copyright 2023 by Louisa Peck

First Edition

Amazon Paperback

~ ~ ~

ISBN: 979-8-854-60345-4

DISCLAIMER ~ PLEASE NOTE:

While this book makes frequent reference to Alcoholics Anonymous, the views expressed and characters described herein reflect only the personal experience of the author and in no way represent the membership, meetings, philosophy, or program of AA itself. Except for quotations from AA approved literature, no part of this text is in any way related to the organizations of AA, Al-Anon, or IANDS. The names of significant characters have been changed to maintain confidentiality.

Cover art: Louisa Peck, *Self Portrait, 1988*

Die-Hard Atheist:

from NDE Denier to
Full-on Woo-woo
– Against my Will

Table of Contents

INTRODUCTION 1

CHAPTER 1: MY LIFE BEFORE 7

CHAPTER 2: MY NEAR-DEATH EXPERIENCE 15

CHAPTER 3: TWO "DARK" PARANORMALS I DENIED 43

CHAPTER 4: MY ANGEL SPEAKS – TWICE! 61

CHAPTER 5: SERENDIPITY ON STEROIDS 79

CHAPTER 6: HELP HER CROSS! 97

CHAPTER 7: DON'T GO! 119

CHAPTER 8: SPIDER MESSENGER THAT BROKE ME 127

CHAPTER 9: ACCIDENTAL MIND READER 149

CHAPTER 10: MY FATHER'S CROSSING 157

CHAPTER 11: VANESSA 169

CHAPTER 12: INTIMATE MIND READER 177

CHAPTER 13: INT'L ASSOC FOR NEAR-DEATH STUDIES 183

CHAPTER 14: GOING PUBLIC – SAFE AND UNSAFE PLACES . 195

CHAPTER 15: GUIDANCE FROM MY ANGEL 207

CHAPTER 16: DISREGARDING MY ANGEL 223

CHAPTER 17: MIRACLE IN THE WILDERNESS 229

CHAPTER 18: INTENTIONAL MEDIUM 243

CHAPTER 19: LIFE AS A HAPPY FULL-ON WOO-WOO 251

CHAPTER 20: LESSONS FROM EGNACIO (AND OTHERS) ... 271

CHAPTER 21: ON CONTEMPT VS. OPEN-MINDEDNESS 289

"One of the main functions of organized religion is to protect people against a direct experience of God."

> ~ *Carl Jung, founder of analytic psychology, heretic, and dummy*

"Something unknown is doing we don't know what!"

> ~ *Sir Arthur Eddington, astronomer, physicist, philosopher, and borderline dummy*

"Spiritual energy flows in and produces effects in the phenomenal world."

> ~ *William James, psychologist, historian, philosopher, and total dummy*

Introduction

The main purpose of this book is to convince you, dear reader, that the spirit realm is real, that it exists parallel to our material realm and impacts our lives constantly. I want to change your mind, not to my specific view, but to an open one that frees you to explore your own. You wouldn't have picked up this book if you felt certain there's no more to life than the physical and mechanical, yet the stigma connected with woo-woo (my affectionate catch-all term for acknowledgment of the spirit realm) is formidable and discourages us from looking into the origins of paranormal events. Sometimes it's hard to come out even to ourselves as fully believing that spirits, ghosts, and angels exist beyond the veil, as do dark forces. My experience – clinging fixedly to materialist atheism until an onslaught of paranormal events forced me to let go – has convinced me this is so. I know that the spirit world is here with the same certainty that I know my consciousness is.

You have a choice here to judge me – my *ethos* – as either honest and reliable or deluded and full of crap. If I'm dishonest, I'm making stuff up and/or exaggerating trifles for attention, jumping on the Near-Death Experience (NDE) bandwagon. Alternately, if I'm honest but just unreliable, I must be a dummy who repeatedly confuses mundane, explicable events with transcendent woo-woo manifestations. So also, by the same logic, must be all Near-Death Experiencers, people who claim to have visited an alternate reality while physically dead – many thousands of us.

Dumb people abound, it's true, or at least our gullible nature stands out sharply in this age of internet infancy. As I write this, we have Flat-Earther, QAnon, anti-vaxxer, and chem trail conspiracists, to name just a few. New groups will always crop up and support their claims with a few clicks of a search engine, currently termed "research" as in "I've done the research!" or better still, "Do the research!"

Credible science is easily cast aside.

But what about *gaps* in science – not so much of *what* but of *why*? Are the original explosion of the universe, formation of our Earth, and evolution of life thereon, including the billions of cells functioning to maintain your attention right now as you read – did all this immense orchestration and delicate balance *really* develop in accordance with principle "shit happens"? Einstein certainly didn't think so. The universe itself is a super-intelligence driving everything we know of and much more we don't.

I can't presume to describe that intelligence. I know only that it's infinitely powerful, intricate, and creative, manifesting simultaneously on countless levels – only one of which is our physical realm. I also know that, strange as it may sound, this same intelligence is Love. Intuitively, you know this. You see it every time you walk in the woods or contemplate a sunset.

But all that sounds pretty woo-woo, so maybe it's my dumbness talking. Maybe I just want attention, need to feel special and comforted, so I pretend, inflate, embellish.

You decide.

*   *   *

Forty-one years ago, I managed to kill myself at a snazzy Manhattan nightclub by snorting what I thought was cocaine in the chase for what I believed to be coolness – wrong on both counts. Naïve, shallow, and misguided, I should by all rights have died that night. But, for reasons I'll never understand, I was granted the gift of a second chance.

Can you guess what twenty-two-year-old Louisa did with this gift? I threw it away again and again, or at least tried to. Just out of Vassar College, I carried on exactly as before with all the drinking, snorting, smoking, trying to stockpile cool friends, and courting admiration from anyone who'd give it. Because I was a sane and sensible atheist, I flat-out rejected those strangely clear memories that stayed with me from the time when, according to others, I'd suffered a grand mal seizure followed by a three-minute cardiac arrest. That detailed experience *must* have been a hallucination, right? Sure, it *seemed* I'd traveled through landscapes, experienced intense beauty, and was subsumed in the bliss of infinite love while cradled by a powerful parent, but all these experiences *had* to be delusional symptoms of an oxygen-deprived brain.

Life had no point. God was a product of human culture – a conceptual invention and a cowardly one at that. I wanted to stick to facts: physical, material, Newtonian science.

And for thirteen years, I managed to do so – so long as I tucked away a few more inexplicable events as not worth pondering. Most NDErs reevaluate their lives in light of what they witness and realize on the other side. My only god, however, was coolness as exemplified in the popular culture of my time. I'd be a charismatic life-movie character known for her impulsive daring, much of which involved swallowing a legal neurotoxin known as alcohol and wallowing in the disease it fosters, as recounted in my addiction memoir. By the end I was driving shitfaced on a regular basis while toying with suicidal ideation.

Then, thirteen years after my NDE, I was given what amounts to yet another chance at life. My guardian angel blasted through my defenses and forced into my consciousness two telepathic messages: 1) *This is the last time I can help you*! and 2) *You do know right from wrong*!

This voice struck a chord. I "heard" him. And despite those many years of denying and locking away my NDE plus two paranormal experiences since, I did know, deep inside, that they had actually *happened*. My understanding – indeed my whole culture's – could not explain them. The message from this voice shook me to my core. From that day forward, I began a tricky dance of hypocrisy, *knowing* within my "closeted" self that the spirit world was real while insisting in my public persona that it was not.

Despite my thinking rather than because of it, spiritual energies continued to invade my life. After six more paranormal experiences, I finally reached a tipping point. More than 22 years after my NDE, I surrendered my intellectual grip on materialism and abandoned allegiance to every atheist scientist I wanted to respect: Stephen Hawking, Alan Turing, Carl Sagan. In the wake of what I call the 9th Weird Thing of 2005, I went woo.

Events I'll describe in that chapter moved me to give up my societally approved belief system and join the ranks of loony, whacky, simple-minded woo-woos. No one was with me when this awakening took place, except Egnacio, my guardian angel, and the infinite, sublime corridor he opened above me through the ceiling, removing for about twenty seconds the veil that blocks our perception of the universe.

To Egnacio, and to the god I sensed beyond him[1], I pledged that I would never again doubt or push away spiritual realities.

Since that afternoon, I've lived in a world unified and infused with meaning and beauty. I've attended many meetings and conferences of the International Association of Near-Death Studies (IANDS), as well as interviewed dozens of fellow NDErs to write up their stories for the Seattle IANDS newsletter. What I've learned from this community has complemented and contextualized what I myself experienced back in November of 1982. I can now decipher the key features of my NDE and its aftereffects with none of the confusion I plunged into when they originally happened to me.

Whenever I interview NDErs, I'm always careful to separate the raw input of what they actually experienced from the conceptual framework they've developed since, whether by reading, watching videos, or talking with fellow NDErs.

I plan to impose this same distinction on each pre-woo chapter of this book. Each story is, in essence, told twice: first as I originally experienced it and again as I reflect on it today. At the price of some redundancy, I'll be able to avoid retrospective conjecture in the first telling.

---

[1] I prefer a lowercase 'g' to differentiate god as the source of all intelligence/love from the anthropomorphized character referred to as "God" in various religions.

Chapter 1: My Life Before

Inherited atheism

I had a wonderful dad. With love and respect, I relied on him for explanations of how the world worked. The topic of God came up sometimes, and whenever it did, he explained that God was a fantasy primitive people had created for two important reasons: 1) they longed for a parent figure to comfort them, and 2) they couldn't otherwise comprehend natural phenomena. Some of these tribal myths and superstitions had evolved alongside human cultures and were gradually codified into mainstream religions – Christianity, Hinduism, and Islam. "Primitive" mythologies persisted much longer in Africa, Australia, and the Americas until those peoples were conquered and forced to convert to one of the big three.

Dad was a major fan of science. Sometime in the 16th century, the scientific revolution had transformed science all over the world by introducing models and replicable experiments.

My dad's own life had been similarly transformed when, after winning a full scholarship to Harvard University, he found himself swept from a small mining town in the Upper Peninsula of Michigan to the intellectual epicenter of Cambridge. His anger and contempt for the Catholic religion forced on him as a child, as well as wet kisses the priest regularly bestowed on him as an altar boy, seemed to intensify each year he was free of it.

I learned that, from the get-go, the church had caused nothing but suffering. Warlords used it to justify their privilege via divine right of kings while greedy church officials cooked up Hell to keep the peasants in line. The whole mess smacked of

The Emperor's New Clothes, everyone too afraid to call bullshit. From the horrifying Medieval and Puritanical witch-burnings to the ruthless genocide of Manifest Destiny, religion had inflicted harms that far outweighed any good.

I also learned that scientists and philosophers, the clear and undisputed good guys, could work in tandem to help all humans share the planet morally – both with each other and with fellow life forms.

It was an easy dichotomy to grasp.

My mother, however, demanded reverence – not for religion per se but for all the classical art, architecture, and music it had inspired in Western civilization. Every Christmas she'd trot out a tall stack of art books and give a mini-lecture to my sister and me. We had to look at many dozens of color plates showing the nativity, from Byzantine through the Renaissance, and we had to understand the stories they were illustrating. Why? Because they were important. Her solemnity around these presentations always puzzled me, given that all these famous Medieval and Renaissance artists were painting imaginary clothes on a butt-naked emperor.

God in nature

My father unwittingly contradicted himself by passing on to us his deep love for Nature's genius, its order and intricacy, which he viewed in terms of survival of the fittest. Really, if you're a purebred atheist, there's no place for wonder, awe, or, let's face it, *love* for natural phenomenon. From the vantage point of *The Selfish Gene*, nature is mechanical and ruthless. What is just is.

Yet, out on hikes in the mountains, my father might point out a tree and say, "Look how over the years it's reached further and further to the left to get at the light. Look how this one has spiraled from the wind." He'd point out the perfect dome of a spider's web, aerodynamics of swallows, refractions on atmospheric particles that created glorious sunsets. Notice, notice, notice, he was always urging. The facts were scientific, but it was his voice that carried a timbre of sacredness. Look how majestically it all functions! From the vast panorama of the night sky to a seed planted by a squirrel, this magnificent symphony of the universe, ecosystems, and tiny organisms moved him deeply, often to tears.

I reconciled the double standard: Nature is magnificent; God is hogwash.

Academic atheism

By the time I enrolled in my first philosophy class in high school, any talk of God made me barf. If you believed in God, you had to be a dumbass. I don't care if you're Plato and call it "the Good." Descartes, Berkeley, Kierkegaard, all of them were duped. The philosophers I loved were those who proved we could know nothing – mainly the Greek Skeptics and David Hume. By the time I reached college, Hume was my hero: he doubted everything we presume true about the world. Nietzsche I *wanted* to like, but he hated women (including me). Still, his famous one-liner, "God is dead," struck me as a cool "kiss my ass!" to all his contemporaries. To see the inherently meaningless nature of life, preferably while looking badass (e.g. James Dean in *Rebel Without a Cause*) took guts.

During my senior year at Vassar, I discovered the Polish-English novelist Joseph Conrad, author of *Heart of Darkness*. Conrad had once cherished a profound faith but gradually, over the twenty-year span of his work, abandoned it. In my hundred-page thesis, I placed him as a precursor to the Modernist revolution that, in a Dadaist sense, took a crap on an orderly, God-centered universe and acknowledged in its stead in a dark, uncertain one where shit happens and nothing matters.

Here's my favorite letter from Conrad to his buddy in 1897, talking about that very universe:

> There is – let us say – a machine. It evolved itself (I am severely scientific) out of a chaos and scraps of iron and behold! – it knits.... And the most withering thought is that the infamous thing has made itself; made itself without thought, without conscience, without foresight, without eyes, without heart. It is a tragic accident – and it has happened.... It has knitted together time, space, pain, death, corruption, despair and all the illusions – and nothing matters.[2]

Nothing matters. The universe is an accident. In *Heart of Darkness,* Conrad had the guts to puncture all the ways humanity had paper mâchéd over this stark fact – not only with religion but with morality, culture, and the social mechanisms that keep us all sane. Once we see through a hole in that nicey-nice shell and behold the starkly random, amoral nature of reality, we can never go back to pretending, as Marlow, the narrator, finds once he returns home. The novella was, I felt, kind of an epic variation

---

[2] Conrad, Joseph. *Letters to R. B. Cunninghame Graham*. Edited by C. T. Watts. Cambridge: University Press, 1969

on The Emperor's New Clothes, except in this case the fancy outfit wasn't just God; it was the foundations of civilization itself.

I dug it.

So pass the booze!

Given life's pains and uncertainties in a Godless universe, why not escape? My father passed on to me his favorite source of ease and comfort: it's called wine. Here, too, I followed in Dad's footsteps and threw in smoking to boot. Starting in college, every morning opened with a hangover. Some were minor and some staggering, but I could count on the fingers of one hand the number of times I woke without one.

Alcohol eased my loneliness. When, around age five, I'd realized our mother found any way she could to avoid spending time with my siblings and me, an inner shift began: I began to lack. Mom had desperately wanted *babies* as wifely accessories, but not four hyper kids morphing into awkward adolescents. The door to her room was usually shut, and we got scolded if we knocked on it to complain of being bored (i.e. lonely). "You're so uncreative!" she'd criticize, shooing us away.

At first, I looked to other authority figures for validation, teachers whose approval transferred to my parents. But no matter how many accomplishments I pumped into my leaky vessel of self-worth, I soon felt just as empty.

This experience is pretty classic for anyone who grew up in an alcoholic or otherwise dysfunctional home. Before I had steady access to alcohol, I escaped the pain of being me through a fetishized compulsive disorder described in my addiction memoir. Each dissociative episode brought temporary numbness, but immediately afterward I'd find myself plummeting into dark shame and self-loathing. Like most teens, I had no drama brakes, no sense that everyone struggles. Everyone, I was sure, would recoil in horror if they found out my secret, so I learned to compartmentalize. Whatever I didn't want to exist (i.e. my compulsive episodes) simply did not – except when they did!

Denial is a mainstay of alcoholism, both within the individual and throughout the family system. Much as I had seen my parents deny Dad's alcoholism, I lived as a fake and a phony, desperate to please everyone, never daring to be myself, and always wishing I'd been born someone else.

Then came my best buddy, alcohol. Wow! With just a few drinks, I was fixed! The world eased up marvelously and I could talk a long ribbon of wit for anyone. Throughout high school, I'd been labelled a geekish brain, so from college onward I hid my high grades. My compulsive behavior vanished. In that hazy crowd of peers who supposedly witnessed and were impressed by me, I developed a substitute god. Coolness, which now included being secretly brilliant, mounted the dais and ruled my world.

Unfortunately, that leak in my self-worth vessel persisted. No matter what I achieved, no matter how cool my exploits, the gauge rapidly fell back to "empty." Conrad's dark view of the universe appealed to me because it justified the sense of failure underlying all my accolades, both academic and social. If life was pointless and we were all gonna die anyway, why not try to make some sort of splash?

Dopamine: a reason to live?

Crush rush was one of the crutches I used to prop up my existence in pointless universe. In high school, I discovered the thrill of savoring the slightest interaction with cute, popular boys. Simply touching a door handle after they did, I seemed to pick up a bit of their magic charisma (otherwise known as an externalized locus of self-worth). Socially I was super awkward, too preoccupied with planning my conversational performance to actually *listen* to you or reply candidly.

Alcohol changed all that, too, so in college I became alarmingly able to *act* on my infatuations. Much of my addiction memoir recounts how drinking and infatuation intertwined to build me a false refuge, an illusory reason for being. The dopamine I got from feeling validated by cool guys was like brain-made cocaine. It revved me up with ambition, too – to bag whoever currently occupied the pedestal. Unfortunately, as soon as I clinched the prize, my idol would topple, losing their "magic" and turning into just another schmuck who occasionally farted. Each time this happened, I underwent an existential mini-crisis. Until, that is, I hit on a new crush!

Other external sources of temporary self-worth included vanity, friendships with the cool kids, showing up hot at the ultimate party, and of course, staying drunk and/or high. But the more I affirmed the freedom of meaninglessness, the deeper I sank into darkness and despair. What seemed to help me live was actually killing me.

I don't know a whole lot of contented, open-hearted atheists. Do you?

Chapter 2: My Near-Death Experience

What I Thought Then:

It's November, 1982. I'm twenty-two, six months out of college and living in Manhattan, where I've just found the coolest nightclub ever – the Peppermint Lounge. It's friggin' Mecca, somewhere in Greenwich Village, of course. The building's old. In the anteroom, a gruff bouncer nods us in. Someone accepts our ridiculously high cover charge and stamps our wrists under the black lights, music thudding from somewhere within. *This* is why I moved to New York! My date and I explore the three floors of dance music reached via a narrow staircase along an exposed brick wall. On this floor, the DJs blast buttrock; on the second floor is god-awful Country, but the basement is just right: New Wave, baby. Under the smoky crisscross of colored light beams, the churning crowd is spiked with key figures in leather, punk hair, and Goth makeup while the driving beats of Duran Duran, B-52s, Flock of Seagulls, Billy Idol, and Psychedelic Furs fuel the fervor. This DJ is choosing only the best.

I get a gin and tonic that costs an arm and a leg, but all is well. Black walls, glass floor lit from below, strobe lights fluttering everyone's movements at key parts of the songs. I can't wait to dance! I'm wearing a little black velvet dress I found at a vintage clothing shop, a look worthy of Deborah Harry, and my dark hair is chopped short like Pat Benatar's. I dance, vanity swelling with that secret feeling everyone's watching. I dance well.

My date is a best friend of my secret boyfriend from Boston, who recently broke up with me via super heartfelt letter because I'd hidden him with instructions not to call during a visit from my *real* boyfriend from New Mexico that I was sorta going to marry, except I even more recently broke up with New Mexico so I could upgrade to the secret boyfriend, except the secret one doesn't know that yet because I'm *waiting* two weeks between boyfriends, which seems the proper thing to do if I'm not a slut.

This best friend is a coke dealer – or was in college, anyway – which has a lot to do with why I asked him to come see me. Rumors float around that he has a drug problem, but he always brings cocaine and cocaine is just heavenly, so who cares? Booze is my bread and butter, but coke is luscious, beautiful cake. After a few songs, we take a break in a dim lounge area and snort the last of his vial from a small mirror. I'm all sweaty but sure I still look great, drawing on my cigarette with studied indifference. As we shout back and forth in each other's ears, our thighs occasionally brush and chemistry begins to build. Friends have rated this guy as handsome, though he's not my type. Would kissing the best friend of a soon-to-be-reinstated this time *not* secret boyfriend be a bad idea? I mean, if neither of us tells?

But what?! There's no more coke. Shit.

We ask around until someone points out a scrawny young guy in a beige leisure suit who reminds me of the clingy, suicidal character in *Saturday Night Fever*. He wants $50 for a gram. We test it by rubbing a little on our gums while he promises nervously that it's good stuff, good stuff. But it's *not* good at all, as we find out the minute we snort it. No high, and by now the guy's nowhere to be seen. I can feel my excitement, the magic of this place, that sense of invincible glamor all sinking to dullness as if someone were dragging their thumb on the vinyl record of my life.

I don't want that. So when my date chucks his snorting bill and pronounces the stuff worthless, I wonder, what if it's just weak? Didn't it numb our gums? There must be *some* high to be gotten from it. So I snort it all at one go, the whole pile.

On my way to the bathroom, I notice my peripheral vision is humming with orange speckles, sort of like what you see when you almost faint. Cool! Must be a side-effect from the coke. Why haven't I heard of this one? The bathroom line is backed up out the door, so by the time I'm close enough to check myself out in the mirror, my made-up face (which still looks good) is centered at the bull's eye of a churning target ringed with darkness and orange speckles.

"Wicked tunnel vision!" I think. For once in my life, I'm the coolest of all the girls around me.

But, wait. Something's wrong. Inside the stall, those orange speckles are closing in so far I feel claustrophobic – like I'm going blind. I can see only a small area directly in front of me. Trying to focus on the stall's graffiti, I realize can't read *any* of it. That can't be right. And now the air in the bathroom is all breathed up.

Something's wrong, really wrong. I bust out of the bathroom, heaving for air, only to find the open dance floor no better. This whole damn basement is all breathed up, and somehow I'm going blind! I find my date near the bar.

"What's the matter?" he asks, alarmed.

"There's no air down here! No air! Can't you tell?" I'm sucking in deep breaths, but it does no good.

Both he and the bartender tell me to calm down. The bartender hands me a glass of ice water – the last thing I want. Both urge me to drink, so I lift the glass to my lips.

BAM! Something hits me under the chin with such sudden force I wonder if I've slipped and struck the underside of my jaw on the bar. But it's way more than that! Wow! I'm shooting up in the air like a Brutus-socked Popeye, like I've been shot out of a cannon. All that nonsense – the nightclub, Manhattan, that pointless scribble of whatever I was doing down there as "Louisa" – recedes rapidly below me. I'm shooting straight up in the clean, pure air, climbing, climbing...

All around is the glorious blue sky, and beneath me is the ocean, pure and blue, stretching as far as the eye can see. As my upward trajectory slows, I get a playful thought: I'm good at movement, so I'm going to arch backward and open my chest and until I curve over in a swan dive, just like Esther Williams. And I do! It feels so good, and I'm so pleased, speeding toward the water's surface a few hundred feet below.

But wait a sec. Don't they say if you hit water from a great height, it's like concrete? Surface tension multiplied by speed and all that? But I'm not scared. I'm just game to find out!

SLICE!! I plunge deep into the ocean, so *that* worked out.

Beautiful bubbles rise around and above me. I look up to the dazzling, sun-dappled surface that's like magic, like joy, like music! But it's such a long way up, it might be hard to reach.

I surface effortlessly, so *that* worked out, too.

I see a shoreline perhaps 200 yards off and want to be there. Now I'm there, wading through the shallow waves, because I guess stuff just has a way of working out. This place is vaguely familiar, though I can't say why and it doesn't matter.

Down the beach to my left is a mesa or sea stack the waves have carved away from the shore, and standing upon it is a pastel blue, weatherworn house. That house! It's got to do with me! I need to get up there and check it out. The beach is rocky and dotted with barnacles, but that's no problem because I'm already at the base of what I can now see is a mass of boulders. But what's this? They're covered with something brownish-green and slimy – is it putrid seaweed? Yuck! Gross!

But I'm strong and good at stuff, and I mean to climb past this nasty slime. I make good progress, and soon I've reached the threshold of the house. Except somehow in the process of climbing, I've lost my body. I don't have one anymore, so my vantage point is only about an inch above the doorsill. That's inconvenient, but it's not going to stop me.

As I cross the threshold, I understand that we've all been here, all my ancestors. We've all passed through this same doorway, all gone through this same house. It's more like a waystation than a destination, and yet I can feel some of them present here, witnessing my arrival. There's one who's especially excited, my dad's dad – I feel his energy. I've never given him much thought because he died before I was born. When I was a kid his black and white portrait, relegated to a back shelf in Dad's closet, was almost inseparable from the scent of Dad's wool coats, but now he's someone, an individual, a presence rejoicing that I'm his granddaughter and he's finally going to meet me. All the rest of them are elated for me, too, proud of me, excited to welcome me.

Knowing all this in an instant, I'm gliding into the house, hovering just above the wooden floor, so close to the old floorboards I can see how their surface is worn to powdery grooves by so many of us having trodden here.

The room has only a large picture window that frames the ocean view; it's otherwise empty. But that's not right! A comfy armchair is supposed to face that window, the seat where all my ancestors have loved to sit and enjoy the beauty of the ocean. It's not here, and I'm too low, too small to take my turn. Oh, I *wish* I could see the view!

The instant I wish, I'm drawn forward, scooting, pulled by the sternum I don't have with that same weird feeling of a magnet – that power you can't see. I skim across the floor toward the wall under the window frame and – Oh my gosh! What? – I'm swooping up, over the window sill, and now I've launched into the open sky! How is this happening? I'm zooming ahead into the glorious, brilliant sunset. The low sun is casting a dappled path of gold across the water, and I'm flying over that path at fantastic, delicious speed! I feel the air skimming over me, the exhilaration of rushing forward through space as I soar into the heart of this glorious panorama.

But wait a sec: People can't *fly*! That is, except in dreams. Am I sure this is real?

More real than anything back there, answers a deep, resonant presence. I realize someone is *with* me, someone who overheard my thought and, I can sense, knows far more than I do. They mean more real than that place I was before – that Louisa business. And they're right. It *is* more real.

Meanwhile, the sun is swelling bigger and bigger as I approach it. I can see the varied gold and brightness of its corona. I'm on course to hit it, and fast! Is that bad? Will I vaporize?

Poof! I hit a mere filament and pass through. I'm inside the sun! That worked ou—

All is light.

Light is all.

There's no more asking, no more wondering, only love, love, love, love, love, love.

Love's only limit is how much I can absorb. Love is everything, permeating as warm light, saturating me. I want nothing – no sights, no sounds, no thoughts – only *this*, surpassing every love I've ever felt on the same scale as the Sun's output exceeds light from a candle.

I sense that presence again, the powerful one, like a parent. It has known and adored me always, one who has never forgotten me though I've forgotten it. The parent cradles me in unseen arms, treasuring me, flooding me with all-fulfilling love. *Little one, you are so loved!* That treadmill of living – the loneliness, the emptiness, the pain of being not enough – it's all gone, unreal, a bad dream.

Finally! Everything I've starved for all my life, it's here. I'm in it, I'm of it, I'm home. I love the parent so much that love seems to subsume all, the same way exposure subsumes a photograph. It's not a feeling, a transference of love from me to the parent. It's just what is.

But the light cuts to blackness.

You cannot stay; you're not done yet.

I hear this decision in telepathy, not words, as if one thunderous note of Beethoven could transform your entire future. I've lost the light. It's gone.

Noooo! I refuse to give it up! I'm furious, defiant, fighting with all I am. I'm gonna *show* the parent how wrong it is, how big a tantrum I can throw, how I'm more powerful than it reckoned. I mean to scream and kick the parent in the shins.

I sense the faintest, distant answer, loving but final: *Case closed, little one.*

I drop through darkness. For a moment, I don't know what's happening and feel terror, a sense that something horrible may ensue. But I'm not alone for long. Little stick figures appear like chalk drawings on a blackboard. Phew! These guys are nice. They're frolicking, swinging on chalk-drawn swings, tilting a see-saw, laughing. The parent, I realize, has left me this little diversion to pass the time until I can return to the light. And I *will* return! Meanwhile, though, I settle in the same way I used to for Saturday morning cartoons. The figures cartwheel and flip. They call out silly riddles and rhymes: How does a hippo light a hopscotch? How many fiddles make a flim-flam? A, B, C makes 1, 2, 3!

But one of the faces moves in closer, too close, its chalk circle filling like a dinner plate and obstructing my view. Hey, c'mon! I try to peer around it, but it's right in front of me and speaking less playfully.

"How many fingers? What's your name?"

Noooo. It can't be. With an onslaught of dismay, I realize what has happened: I'm back in the meat puppet. No, please no. Oh, *dammit*! This is how things used to work. He thinks we're *separate*. He's him and I'm me, so we have to create these burpy sounds with our breath that we pass back and forth like code. How stupid! How primitive! It feels like getting sent back to a kindergarten classroom – for the next 60 years or so. You can cut and paste. You can play with blocks or Legos or toys. Just don't try to leave.

But, okay. Dinner plate dude's thrown out this challenge, so I'll pick it up. I find the garage space down underneath my vision, on street level, so to speak, with the loafy thing that makes the shapes. I expel a sound: "Tooh!" That's how many fingers. Now he wants my name? "Lou-ee-sah."

I'm feeling pretty accomplished, I've gotta say.

Somehow, I'm lying on a floor. Those stick figures are now lots of people who can see me. The man kneeling by me thinks something quite serious is going on. How funny! I can pretend to be serious, too, but it's just a game.

Sit up, they tell me. Oh, there's my friend, my date! I'd forgotten him! He's so cute but clearly not having fun. I've been a bad date, it seems. They sit me up. Turns out my little cocktail dress is soaked and I'm sitting in a puddle of water. Did they throw water over me to wake me up? Now they want me to stand. My friend wants to lead me up some stairs.

I feel five years old – wonderfully so! Other people climb the stairs along with us. It seems to be the thing to do. I sort of remember the night club, the evening out. Everyone thinks something happened *here*, but they're silly. It happened *there*, in the magic place.

My friend and I sit on a bench with our backs to the building and he gives me my purse (my purse!) so I light a cigarette. A man in a white jacket has begun talking to my friend and I can guess he's a bartender. But then he wants to talk to me. He says

I was "gone" for three minutes or more. Gone means dead, which is extremely dramatic and embarrassing. He gave me CPR. That means his mouth was on my mouth again and again, but he's got to be in his thirties and he's kind of bald. How embarrassing! Won't he please go away? Now my friend is recalling how he, my friend, told him, the bald bartender, to stop because CPR wasn't working. He says I was grey and didn't look at all like me, but like a corpse. Corpse, huh? That's all very well, but the guy won't go away. Finally he does. I might have said, "Thanks," but I'm not sure.

After few minutes I'm bored and it's really cold out here so I ask my friend what we're doing.

"Waiting for the ambulance," he says. It seems a fine answer until I start to get a bad feeling.

"Who's it for?" I ask.

"You, of course! You were dead!"

I imagine an ambulance showing up – all that fuss. They'll take me to some pastel green hospital tiled like some huge lavatory late at night and everything will take forever. And then they'll call— my parents!

"I don't want to go! Please!" Now it's my turn to act very serious. "Don't make me go in the ambulance!"

My friend thinks, makes a decision, and, seizing my hand, runs with me to one of the yellow taxis lined up at the curb. People chase after us making a rabble. I grin because we've already slammed the door. "Drive! Just drive!" my friend tells the driver, and the car pulls away. People bang on the trunk with their palms. Bang, bang, bang!! I'm not sure why: maybe it's a game.

*   *   *

The next morning, I wake up and remember. No, it wasn't a dream. I was at the Peppermint Lounge doing the usual and then... and then a magic portal opened and I shot up into that place – that place where nothing was like here and yet I remember every detail so clearly, the beautiful bubbles, the gross seaweed, the fuzzy, worn floorboards. Oh, that joy of flying, that amazing, incredible light. Oh, that love!

My body hurts. I'm perfectly used to waking with hangovers, but I start recalling other things. People told me I had a seizure, that the balding bartender did CPR. The back of my head has several lumps. My knuckles and an elbow are bruised. These, indeed, must have come from flailing about. I wonder, for just a second, if I looked uncool. Ah, well! I'll never know.

When I sit up, I realize my whole ribcage is sore, especially around the sternum. That's from the CPR. They said my heart stopped. They said it was a big deal. Even so, I feel quite happy this morning. I really hit the bell on coolness. The prospect of having tea with my roommate, Elizabeth, a Vassar friend who puts up with my drunkenness, is delightful.

Out in the main room with its sooty, caged, eighth-floor windows, Elizabeth sits at the little table with its white cloth. She's made a pot of tea for me – so nice! – but her expression is, again, quite serious. The big deal. She focuses on me like a skeptical job interviewer. I know she's on the lookout for brain damage, but so am I. What fun! Brain damage!

Elizabeth makes me read aloud from the Sunday *New York Times*. Always up for a challenge, I forge ahead at the rate of a second grader, with some words appearing to me as such utter gibberish that I can't begin to guess – specifically the word "helicopter" in a large headline about a crash.

"Is that really a word?" I ask.

When she enunciates "helicopter," I know the concept, but this word, which has nothing to do with it, appears to be Greek. Such a nifty game! Guess the gibberish.

How I begin to tell Elizabeth about my journey into the sun, how I frame it, or how I feel while telling her – none of that do I remember today. All I know is that after the part about being adored by a parent comes a pause, an faltering eye-to-eye moment until Elizabeth asks, "So, was that God?"

Such intense awkwardness I feel, such embarrassment, confusion as to how to respond, because I'm pretty sure the answer is yes. I was sort of hoping to keep that whole matter at arm's length. But here's Elizabeth asking point blank. So I settle for a hybrid of sarcasm and truth: "Yeah!" I grin, nodding, "It was like... God!"

Elizabeth is clearly puzzled. This is November of 1982, and neither Elizabeth nor I have any names or concepts for my long, long, super-vivid memory[3] – except extended hallucination.

Maybe thirty minutes later, I'm alone in the bedroom of our tiny apartment. Elizabeth is on the phone with someone – she has a lot of friends. I can't say what time it is beyond that it's still Sunday. I'm on the floor leaning against my bed with an open notebook on my lap while my eyes stray to our little nightstand table, the lower shelf of which is quite dusty. I'm wrestling with how to think about what happened. Yes, I

---

[3] The term "Near-Death Experience," coined by Raymond Moody in his book *Life after Life* seven years earlier, has not yet broken into popular culture.

remember flying over the ocean and asking, "Is this real?" I remember how a deep knowing, like a voice but without words, answered, *More real than anything back there.* That thought wasn't mine. It was unsought and had a nuance of understatement. I recall my surprise and then my admission: this voice is powerful, it's speaking *IN* me not *TO* me, and it opens the core of truth.

Dreams – I've had countless dreams, even dreams where I could fly. Dreams progress through patchy mind-movies in faint, tangentially connected sequences that lack the vivid flow and impact of waking consciousness. This experience, however, had felt *more vivid* than normal consciousness.

If not a dream, then what else? What would Dad say about it?

Because if I *did* go somewhere real, then some kind of heaven exists. That means the one holding me was some form of God, so God is real, and religion must be right. How horrible!

In other words, if I accept the realness of what happened, I'll have to get churchy. How stupid and corny and Patty Duke. I'll have to start attending church, be "born again" like my older brother and sister, stop drinking and snorting coke and smoking weed and swearing and dressing hot and flirting and lying and screwing around – and change into a different person altogether. I'll have to chuck the quest for being cool, stop chasing fast living and magazine glamor – whatever success I've finally attained, after all those tortuous years of high school failure. For just a second, I see myself after a church service wearing a frumpy brown dress and hugging a Bible to my asexual chest while I chat up a bunch of fucking goody-goody peers.

No way – I can't do that! I *can't*!

A new scenario rescues me, something between a dream and reality: my brain shutting down. Without oxygen it was sort of like the supercomputer Hal 9000 in *2001: A Space Odyssey*. Hal, the space ship's computer, has gone rogue. It's being shut down by Dave, the hero, who's disconnecting the many memory units that power Hal's brain. The more he disconnects, the dumber Hal gets. "My instructor," volunteers Hal in his quintessentially rational but slowing voice, "was Mr. Langley, and he taught me to sing a song." As he loses more and more CPUs, Hal regresses to infancy, remembering only his source, the beginnings of his intelligence. He sings "Daisy," his very first program.

What if my brain had done the same thing? What if, deprived of oxygen, my circuits had gradually shut down, first indulging my longing for beauty and flight and then regressing even further to *my* very first program – love? My eyes are still on little table's incredibly dusty lower shelf as I arrive at my own theory: as a brain dies, just before it flickers out, it regresses to a primeval memory – the sun – and to the most foundational ember of consciousness, love.

That I can believe. Yes!

Dying brain – it's a purely physical answer, an awesome one that shoves aside my church-ridden nightmare. Yes. It was more than a hallucination, more than a dream, but less than real.

Except... what about that moment when the parent said, "*You're not done yet*"? How could a dying brain explain that? I was so stoked in the light, and it was so clear-cut, that shift to utter darkness and falling. How could I experience such a decisive turning point against what I wanted unless something else made the decision *for* me? And how could I not be "done" unless I was born to *do* something? I remember how *intensely* I wanted to stay!

Brown frumpy dress. Patty Duke. Bible shit. Some florid bozo I'd greet graciously as "Father Dingleberry."

No, no, never.

I slam that door. I double bolt it. I will hang onto my Hal explanation, even with the tinge of guilt it brings, and turn my back on the fucking church. Never mind that weird love for my ancestors; never mind my amazement at being sucked over the sill and the thrill of zooming through a sunset-flooded sky *more real than anything back there.*

I cannot do it.

I'm done with the night table, done with this wrestling. I close my notebook. Nothing has changed except that now I have a super cool story. I was *dead* for a while! Who can top that?

What I Think Now

I feel for my past self – her fear and confusion.

Everyone who undergoes a Near-Death Experience struggles with integration. People do so today even though popular culture provides a perfectly good term for it, allowing them to say to themselves from the get-go, "I had one of those Near-Death Experience things!"

The upheaval is still huge. Decades can pass before the person's thinking can get around the imposing roadblocks of materialist culture, before they're ready to disagree with the authority of both science and religion, before they can be vulnerable enough to be labeled wacko. It helps to know there's a sector of society that acknowledges what you experienced, but it's still hard to break down your own walls of conformist judgment and join them.

None of these ideas or terms existed for me in 1982. No person I knew of had ever talked about anything like my experience, so I had no way to understand it. I *did* know of grandiose nut-cases who claimed to have experienced the divine. I remembered Dad telling at dinner one night about a student who came in during office hours, asked to talk, and stated calmly, "I *am* Jesus Christ." It scared Dad, as you might imagine, to be face-to-face with a bona fide psycho. I imagined myself, if I shared what had happened to me, being similarly categorized. "I flew into the sun – I really did! – where a divine presence cradled me and knew me, but then told me I had to go back because I wasn't done yet."

Ri - ighhht...

My experience hadn't been physical, but neither had it been mental. It had transpired outside all frameworks of understanding. Having studied plenty of philosophers both ancient and modern, I appreciated the various lenses through which each presented rational experience, but I'd never quite internalized the fact that meaning itself – the meaning we employ in everyday life – is but a construct.

What does it mean to mean something?

Meaning requires situating one idea within a web of others – the same way our neural networks function. The more in-depth our knowledge of a given subject, the more intricate its contextual web of meaning. When I tried to situate my NDE among ideas I already held, the only ones remotely connected to it – *guardian angel, heavenly beauty, ancestral spirits, loving white light* – lay squarely within the lexicon of religion – which I then despised (and still kinda do).

On the other hand, as a budding alcoholic from dysfunctional family, I was really skilled at denying stuff I knew to be true. For instance, was it perfectly normal for me to phone the package store every night and order a pint or fifth of booze to be delivered before bed? *Sure!* If Dad became contentedly drunk night after night off sherry and wine, did that mean he was an alcoholic? *Of course not!* Did Mom suffer debilitating "tachycardia spells" (i.e. panic attacks) during which she seemed to wish I didn't exist? *What are you talking about?!* My family couldn't be happier. The simplest way to cope with any painful non-public fact was to deny it – so long as you also denied that you were denying anything. Many of you know the drill.

Denial was so much a part of my life that I went to it as a default. It was so much easier than trying to figure things out with no vocabulary, concepts, or tools. In 1982, my NDE felt like getting presented with an extremely difficult calculus equation when you haven't taken the course. You can just write "= 0" at the bottom and be done with it. Since you're grading it yourself, you get 100% credit. Problem solved!

Today, I know much more.

For one thing, I know my date and I were sold lidocaine, not cocaine. For years I assumed I'd overdosed on street coke, until a former drug dealer in AA explained to me that lidocaine, an anesthetic, was far cheaper to get than cocaine, so lots of dealers in the '80s cut their coke with it. Since I'd felt no high at all, my friend deduced I must have been sold pure lidocaine. A quick search for "lidocaine poisoning" lists exactly what I experienced: suppression of the autonomic nervous system resulting in bradycardia, seizure, and cardiac arrest. A few people successfully commit suicide every year by swallowing their topical lidocaine ointment. That shit is 5% lidocaine.

Also, today I know that mine was a "garden variety" NDE, one particular instance of an iconic experience shared by millions.

"Amnesiatic" is the term Eben Alexander uses to describe an experience like mine, meaning I forgot all about my current life as soon as I left my body. "Louisa" dropped away as a "silly" undertaking with that first thrill of shooting into the sky, so the idea that I'd died never occurred to me. I was more me than Louisa had been. People who have Out-of-Body experiences (OBE)[4] find themselves positioned right next to their body, whether standing beside it or seeing it from the ceiling. Not me! I was just outta there, navigating a symbolic landscape as a pure perceiver.

What does that mean? To understand the nature of "perceiving" symbolic stuff during an NDE, it helps to first deconstruct what's happening in our brains when we see, hear, touch, smell, and taste stuff through the physical senses.

The composite scenario our brains assemble from incoming sensory data seems to be simply *happening*, not as electrical patterns inside our skulls, but what's happening for reals right here and now. Strictly speaking, however, we can't directly experience anything external to us; we can experience only energetic *models* that exist solely in our consciousness.

Entire lobes of the brain are dedicated to translating stimuli on the surface of the retina and ear drum into a coherent

---

[4] OBE refers to Out of Body Experience, during which a consciousness perceives earthly surroundings from a perspective other than the eyes and brain of the body – often including sight of the body formerly inhabited.

hologram and narrative for "what's happening" around us. We forget all about photons bouncing off obstructions (sight) and compression waves of molecules in the air (sound), but in the objective world there *is* no light, no color, and no sound; there is only the phenomena of matter and energy in space and time. Think about it: everything we and other creatures, from whales to crickets, experience in physical life is a mental widget or placeholder that helps us approximate our immediate environment. The book or reader in your hand is a mental hologram compiled from retinal, tactile, and kinesthetic data. Not only does our brain's holograph lag a tenth of a second behind external reality, it's also inaccurate.

At the atomic level, physical matter is 99.9999999% empty space. Remember those atomic diagrams we've all seen depicting a nucleus and electrons as looking somewhat like our solar system? If the scale were accurate, the proportional distance of electrons from the nucleus, if the latter were the size of a golf ball, would be at least several city blocks away. And the electron would still be microscopic.

But even that's inaccurate. Electrons, we're told, occupy multiple positions at once, resembling both particles and waves. They don't exist in one particular location unless someone observes them, in which case they do. Since admittedly I have no clue how this can be so, here's a brief excerpt from an Ethan Siegel article in *Forbes*.[5]

> "When you have an isolated, room temperature atom, or a chain of atoms linked up in a molecule or even in an entire human body,

---

[5] Siegel, Eric. "You Are Not Mostly Empty Space." *Forbes*, 4/16/2020.

> they're [the electrons] not acting like these individual particles with well-defined points. Instead, they're acting like waves, and the electron is actually located *all throughout* this ~1 ångström volume, rather than in one particular point-like location [italics mine]."

The point is, what we assume to be "reality" is in truth a drastically dumbed-down *symbol* for an immensely complex set of ever-changing relationships. Our senses can bring us only a narrow range of stimuli – certain frequencies of light and sound, certain types of touch, taste, and smell.

Within those parameters, we're constantly bombarded with input we disregard. It's estimated that the human brain can process 11 million bits of information every second. But our conscious minds can handle only 40 to 50 bits of information a second. Our brains are designed to filter out everything not pertinent to our interests, which means – no exaggeration – about 99.9999% of what goes on even inside our little four-walled environment, let alone the universe at large.

Yet humans have built all their societal, cultural, and (until quite recently) scientific systems on the foundational assumption that the shared sum of these dumbed-down and incredibly selective mental holograms constitutes all there is.

But it *doesn't*. It really does not. It's merely theater – practical but grossly distorted – taking place within the Viewfinder toy of our skulls. We can never *experience* the outside world. We can only *imagine* it. That's what Kant was talking about with his distinction between noumena (stuff) and phenomena (our experience of stuff).

Whenever I think about that too much, I get a bit anxious, like I'm stuck inside a black box! But anyway...

We like to believe our scientific research somehow supersedes these limitations and delves deep in the nature of reality itself. But all research is conducted by humans, and, to borrow from Kant again, all humans are limited by the foundations of thought (time/space cognition) and modes of understanding (quantity, quality, relation, modality). Fortunately, you don't have to read Kant. All you need to do is concede that, if there are other ways of knowing, we sure as heck aren't going to know about them! Every researcher is an individual with a mind irrevocably steeped in the culture born of these categorical limitations. When they bump up against the unknowable (for example, electrons popping in and out of existence) they're stumped by information we can't understand because we lack the cognitive tools or intellectual horsepower to do so.

What about categorical noumena, such as the life force? We *are* the life force, so we can't *sense* the life force, much as we can't sense the presence of oxygen because it's inseparable from being alive. Again, we don't know what we don't know.

Consider this also: natural selection has favored organisms that possess the *least* energetic awareness of the spirit realm. Researchers have noted that, given a limited bandwidth for attention, any organism devoting sectors of that attention to matters *not* directly pertinent to its survival would be less likely to survive.[6] We'd be communing with spirit voices and

---

[6] See Hoffman, Donald. "The Evolutionary Argument Against Reality." April 21, 2016. https://www.quantamagazine.org/the-evolutionary-argument-against-reality-20160421/

unconcerned with death when the lions ambushed us. DOH!! Aware of heaven, we'd say, "Thanks, apex predator! I was getting hella tired of this survival gig, anyway." Meanwhile, humans *numb* to spiritual inputs while prone to constant fear and ready aggression would be most likely to survive and reproduce. Yep, that's us!

And yet, when I say "evolution" or "natural selection," I mean god. Apparently, god is doing something with us in embodied form and doesn't want us quitting early. What are we doing and why? To quote Sir Arthur Eddington, "Something unknown is doing we don't know what!" I believe life's purpose has something to do with expanding Love the same way god grows the universe and creates entities. I only wish I could report back to you after I'm dead long term: I'll understand much better then not only what's going on but why the living don't need to know it.

Also, when I say "god," I also mean *us*; I mean *you* and your cat and the trees and everything living. As one NDEr put it, "God is the cake mix, and I'm a lump in the cake mix." In other words, we're not separate, we're just god temporarily lumped. Another agnostic friend prayed in desperate times "God, who am I?" and was bowled over to get an answer: *You're me*! Embodiment appears to be something of a mission god wants us to stick with until we've at least moved up a grade. Witness: *You're not done yet.*

To sum up, every sentient being is constantly navigating in a sea of symbols. When we die, instead of our physical brains taking in energy via bounced photons and compression waves, our consciousness takes in energy *directly*. All energies exude a vibration, from the Big Bang to our every passing thought. These frequencies can be directly perceived by the spirit.

When we're just newly dead and still close to our earthly memories, symbols derived from commonplace *seeing* convey information most readily. That's why blind people are able to "see" during their NDEs and OBEs. Images on the other side can be likened to a puppet show or charades game suggesting events, options, and transitions with a simplicity we can easily apprehend. Every visual impression absorbed during an NDE is an icon representing spiritual realities via earthly metaphors.

For example, *tunnels* essentially connect us from hither to yon through a stretch of I-don't-know-what. That's why they commonly symbolize the transition from earthly to heavenly realms, though the tunnel's appearance differs for each experiencer. What matters is not the symbol itself but the concept behind it. For instance, many NDErs are shown a recognizable *boundary* and told by accompanying spirits that if they *cross that boundary*, they can no longer return to their physical bodies. The boundary can appear as a river or brook, walls of various heights and materials, doorways, window frames, gates, hedges, trellises, even simple painted line on a floor – all have been reported and all convey the same meaning: a thing to cross, a hither to yon, a change in where you're situated. Significantly, every single NDEr who returns to this life says they *chose not to cross* that boundary.

Symbolic Play-by-play of my NDE

When I think back on my NDE, I see symbols galore, but I'll try to keep this short. I soared up into the AIR, passed through WATER, waded ashore to the rocky EARTH, hovered over the WOOD floor of my ancestral house, and ended up in the sun's FIRE. What are these but the elementals common to ancient human belief systems?

The rotten seaweed I had to climb past symbolized my toxicity, all the ugly devices I'd picked up to cope with my insecurities: vanity, judgment, ego, greed, etc. In the spirit realm I needed to rise above these, so as I ascended toward the house, I did so. It's interesting that the process "cost" me my body, since at this stage of my life I was quite vain about it.

At the point when I crossed the threshold, I felt a huge love for my ancestors that had nothing to do with any earthly relationships. Honestly, I'd never cared a hoot about these people, even my grandmothers who used to visit. Yes, I'd vaguely heard of Dad's dad, who was pictured in Dad's closet and who'd died from a heart attack at 60, but that was it.

In other words, I had no reason to feel *so intensely excited* to be catching up with them, yet I could sense them watching me and rooting for me with love, and I eagerly reciprocated that love. The connection was based on our spiritual lineage, like leaves on the same twig of humanity. With a few exceptions, NDErs see, not their dearest friends or life partners, but parents and relatives – those sharing the spark of life passed down to them.

I think the armchair was lacking because whether I would stay or go back was still a toss-up. I was clinically dead back on Earth, but the Good Samaritan bartender's CPR efforts kept open the possibility of my return.

When I longed to see the beauty of the sunset, my angel pulled me through the next portal – the window frame – and toward divinity. Some might say the love I felt for the sunset's beauty raised my vibration enough to "unlock" the next level, but I honestly know nothing of vibrational and divine levels. I do know that up until that point, I'd been navigating by my own will, going wherever *I* wanted. But this was different. My angel took over, deciding what would happen henceforth.

Flying over the ocean sunset felt absolutely exquisite! That rush of forward motion, that thrill of slicing through space – it happens during spiritual "travels." I've heard others struggle to articulate its absolute deliciousness. This was my tunnel, my transition from hither to yon. I sometimes get reminded of it when I huff delicious cold air from a grocery store open-top freezer. I have no idea why.

As I flew, I remembered something, a way things somehow used to be, a contradiction. In that earlier era, I'd learned about how things worked and, namely, that flying was not possible. So the objection struck me: "Wait a minute! People can't *fly*! Is this real?"

I certainly didn't expect an answer. I had no inkling I was being flown by the being I now call my angel. To "hear" him answer my thought directly with *More real than anything back there* surprised me. In fact, he's always been with me. Frankly he's been on my case lately to finish this book. The difference was, on the other side, I could "hear" him telepathically with perfect clarity.

Inside the Sun, the light was a little taste of heaven. My father had taught me, and I'd often contemplated for myself, that the source of all energy on Earth is our Sun (except geothermic heat and lunar influence on tides). Every calorie we metabolize, every joule of energy we express in thought or movement was once combustion on the Sun's surface. In that sense, the Sun was my source.

In my attempts to dismiss my NDE as advanced hypoxia, the hardest thing to dismiss was the intensity of love I felt in the light. It filled me to capacity. It was a feeling at least twenty times stronger than any I'd had before or since, limited only by me. I knew the love itself was infinite.

I now believe that for a spirit to dwell in physical matter is super uncomfortable. Embodiment is an incarceration, no less. God takes something physical – matter – and infuses it with animation, metabolism, the "spark" of life. Gradually, through the process of evolution, god has cultivated us to possess increasingly independent consciousness. That's a lonely state.

Many NDErs get much farther than I did, so all their questions about the universe and purpose of life are answered. Everything makes perfect sense while they're there, but once they return to their bodies, what they understood as a spirit proves far too big to fit into the circuitry of their little primate brains. They report, though, that it has to do with contributing our tiny efforts to the cumulative power of Love.

But I digress.

Some spirits are given a choice: Do they want to stay or go back? God / their angels may warn that returning will be painful. More often, they lobby for the dying person to return, often showing scenes from a potential future where they're missed à la *It's a Wonderful Life*. Some obstinately refuse until god somehow persuades them. In my case, that decision was made for me.

You cannot stay; you're not done yet.

The rage and aggression I felt were the result of passing back through the membrane of anti-god that separates me from god – which I'll explain in the next chapter. I felt alone and falling because I was dropping to lower vibrations, which feels,

I believe, like a tiny taste of Hell. The chalkboard world seems a gradual re-emersion into the primitive realm of the living.

I awoke to a fully functional body despite having ingested a huge, more-than-lethal dose of lidocaine. I can't say why or how that happened. At 22, I'd loved no one outside my little defensive circle of family and friends, done little for the sake of anyone but myself. My only redeeming quality was a *desire* to do well, to please according to the totally fucked up rubric my family and culture had handed me. I always strove. As Thomas Merton wrote in his beautiful prayer,

> *"...I believe that the desire to please you does in fact please you. And I hope I have that desire in all that I am doing. I hope that I will never do anything apart from that desire. And I know that if I do this you will lead me by the right road, though I may know nothing about it."*

Certainly, I knew nothing about it.

Chapter 3: Two "Dark" Paranormals I Denied

The Ghost

What I Thought Then:

Five years later, life has rolled along, and I'm still drinking. I've finished my MA in English, making what I consider a big splash in the process – two prizes, a fellowship, a paid readership. But suddenly, there are no more hoops to jump through. I've married my once secret boyfriend, so now there's no one to chase, and we've moved back east again, away from my family and friends. At 27, the intellectual bohemian I imagine myself to be is facing an ordinary, conventional future that feels like dying – and I'm terrified of death, swamped with panic attacks.

I wake Sunday morning at a coastal beach house outside Gloucester, Massachusetts, with a crew of aerobics instructors – my coworkers – and their various boyfriends. We're here off-season for an overnight party. I've become crazily infatuated with Jenna, the instructor whose classes are over-the-top popular. Patrons take a number, they wait forever to jump into one of her classes. I, too, am waiting. Fantasy scenes of winning her love fill my mind constantly. But she's here with her frickin' boyfriend. Not only that, we're both intensely homophobic, as is society in general. My husband, immersed in business school, disapproves of my mindless partying with this fitness crew, so he's back home in Brookline, studying.

In the faint light of dawn, I can hear Jenna and her boyfriend squeaking their bed springs on the other side of the wall. The sound makes my romantic crush seem ludicrous. I can't get back to sleep, can't shut out the sound. Though I've had only a few hours' sleep, I can't stand it any longer, so I get up and tiptoe downstairs.

Brightly colored sleeping bags are strewn about the couches and rugs of the great room, and sounds of snoring fill the air. Beer bottles, ashtrays, and chip bags are everywhere. I make my morning tea, taking pains to be quiet and hearing a winter storm pelt the big windows. I smoke a cigarette. There's nothing to read, nothing to do, and I'm still in anguish about my foiled love for Jenna when I hatch a romantic plan: I'll go out in this storm and rage against fate, just like King Lear!

I find an assortment of rain coats in the back hall. As soon as I step out, the wind-driven rain hits my face, making me wince and question my plan. But I'm already out, so I head for the beach, toward the endless roar of the breakers. Everywhere the landscape is shrouded in mist and animated by gusts, the rain galloping in sheets over first the pavement, then, as I reach the beach, the expanses of wet sand and grey-green tumult of the ocean.

My mind defaults to imagined conversations with Jenna. I've walked for about fifteen minutes when I notice someone else as crazy as I am, someone braving this atrocious weather near dawn! He's cresting some dunes to my left, a sandy rise that borders a long stretch of marsh with no houses, lined at the back by trees. Except for his black boots, he's all in Mackintosh yellow: yellow jacket, rain pants, and hat. What the heck could he have been *doing* back there in the marsh? Bird watching? But he has no binoculars, nothing, and the storm's too overwhelming anyway.

As I get closer, I notice several things about him. First, he's old; I can tell by his gait and grizzled beard. Second, the rain gear he has on – that shit's not nylon. From the way it moves I can tell it's old school rubberized cloth, just like the big Mackintosh jacket my dad kept in our front hall closet when I was a kid. Lastly, his gaze seems fixed, as if he were staring at something straight ahead. Naturally, I look where he's looking, which is about the where the horizon *would* be on a clear day. But there's literally nothing to be seen out there beyond a smear of thick, heavy clouds and crashing gray-green breakers. Still, his attention sticks to a point so fixed, you'd swear he saw something.

At the same time, I'm thinking about his cool Mackintosh outfit. It looks like the real McCoy. Where could he have bought it? – jacket, pants, and hat, a full set! When I lived in Manhattan a few years back, I used to shop at vintage clothing stores on the ABC streets, so I imagine I can strike up some kind of vintage shopper's conversation with this guy. Our paths will soon cross on this wide-open beach, so I decide I'm going to compliment him and ask where he found his rain suit, even if I have to yell.

But the guy doesn't look my way, not even as we get close. He just keeps staring at the not-there horizon. Now I'm close enough to judge from his skin that he drinks too much and read in his expression that he's upset about something, in no mood for shoppers' banter. Now I'm within three paces, wind buffeting his beard, but he won't tear his eyes from the *not there* horizon. He crosses just in front of me, clearly not intending to talk, so just to spite him, I yell, "How's it going?"

One bloodshot eye shifts just a smidge in my direction before I step behind him. How odd! Not just odd – but rude!

Shouldn't two people out in such crazy conditions at least *acknowledge* each other? But no – this guy's too haughty, too cool for school. I remember how popular high schoolers used to "blow me off" when I greeted them in passing. "What an asshole!" I think, taking a backward glance in disgust.

But the beach is empty. I'm alone.

What?! Where did he get to?

He couldn't possibly have sprinted up a sandy beach so fast – too old. He must have dashed down toward the surf? That's the only possible explanation. He's thrown himself into the waves. Maybe he'd resolved to drown himself? I watch the water for a thrashing arm or foot, but there's nothing. With a clever air, I wait for his yellow rain hat to surface, watching a good twenty seconds. None surfaces. He is, in fact, gone without a trace.

What about footprints? Determined to catch this jerk, I stride back toward the point where our paths crossed. Not here. It must have been a little further back, a little further....

That's when it hits me: Mine are the only tracks on this beach.

That's not possible! He was *there*, I watched him from the moment he came over the dunes! I saw him clearly. He was a man. He walked. His face was individual.

The thought comes unbidden: a ghost.

I've heard ghosts walk the Earth when they refuse to accept some fact of their lives, as this man, who seemed to be watching a horizon from perhaps some other century, appeared clearly intent on seeing a ship, one that carried, perhaps, his dear friend or lover.

My brain assembles this new story. He was a ghost caught in time.

But I reject such nonsense swiftly. An essential rule has been broken: object permanence. The world is not playing fair. I was *not* hallucinating; I was calmly observing, right up to detecting capillaries in the man's skin. Maybe I walked further than I thought? Again I retrace that stretch of beach.

Meanwhile, on another level, my mind keeps refining the ghost idea. "He ignored you because he didn't *see* you, at least not in the conventional sense, or because he didn't expect you to see *him*. He's stuck in some trauma, some moment he cannot accept."

But notions like this only further irritate my rational mind. Ghosts do not exist.

By the time I get back to the beach house, almost everyone is up and our hostess is frying bacon. When I complain about this impossible thing that happened, she's quick to chime in that Gloucester is famous for ghosts. There's a huge plaque downtown, she tells me, listing hundreds of sailors who drowned. Everyone wants to hear my story. Normally I'd be delighted to be the center of attention, but instead I'm frustrated, upset at having experienced something *wrong*. Even Jenna's interest means little to me.

Why? Because either I'm fucking crazy, or I just crossed paths with ghost. Neither option works for me.

I resolve to simply shut the incident away. I won't think about it. Repressing that whole thing that happened in Manhattan when I my heart stopped wasn't easy, but I did it. Now I have *two* things to dismiss. But dismiss them I will.

What I Think Now

What's a ghost? And why can some people see them and others not?

I believe ghostly spirit energies are at once here, registering in space and time among us, and yet not here, not in our space or time. How is that possible?

Spirits inhabit a space-time inaccessible to the majority of living people. Their energy vibrates at a frequency most can't register, though mediums can. Many of us have seen videos of a medium relaying a loved one's characteristic turns of phrase and humor to the person who hired them, someone who sits in the same room yet perceives nothing, no matter how much they wish to. The medium has access to an alternate realm whether they like it or not; the loved one does not. All the mediums I know personally have feared they were crazy before gradually accepting their abilities.

Bruce Greyson theorizes that the brain has evolved some sort of filter that prevents it from recognizing spirit energies. This filter, he proposes, gets impaired by hallucinogenics, so rather than hallucinating, the person is actually perceiving realities to which they're normally blind. Other researchers, as mentioned above, have theorized that this filter evolved to keep our attention focused on strictly physical conditions influencing survival.

My theory differs from Greyson's based on my own experience of having passed through rage and fear states immediately before re-entering my body. I believe a filter exists, not in the brain, but surrounding our physical bodies like an energetic membrane. These are our auras, some of which operate at higher vibrations and others at lower.

Why do we have these? To make the cake lumps; to separate us from god and the spiritual soup in which we swim. In other words, each living entity is surrounded by a god-phobic sheath that distinguishes iy from the omnipresent god-energy of the universe.

In multi-celled organisms, individual water-based cells could not function in a water-based body without the hydrophobic membrane that surrounds each cell to repel what is not it. That's what initiated life on Earth, the creation of a hydrophobic substance – polymers – created when the bioelementals in pond water (carbon, hydrogen, nitrogen, oxygen, phosphorus, and sulfur) were hit by lightning. Miller and Urey's famous experiment[7] focused on the creation of amino acids chains through this process. Scientists have since pointed out the significance of the polymer byproduct that encased the tiny droplets of amino acids. "The origin of life occurred when a subset of these molecules was captured in a compartment and could interact with one another to produce the properties we associate with the living state."[8]

Similarly, we are god energy captured in compartments by spiritual membranes that distinguish us, allowing for free will so we can interact with one another autonomously. Our membranes are permeable from within. They allow us to send energies outward toward god – i.e. prayers – while not letting in spiritual influences that shape our choices.

---

[7] Wikipedia. "Miller-Urey Experiment."
https://en.wikipedia.org/wiki/Miller%E2%80%93Urey_experiment t
[8] Deamer, David & Weber, Arthur. "Bioenergetics and Life's Origins." National Library of Medicine. February 2010.
https://www.ncbi.nlm.nih.gov/pmc/articles/PMC2828274/

When an NDEr leaves their body and then re-enters it, they somehow damage their god-phobic membrane. While Bruce Greyson suggests that the "filter" within the brain is compromised by an NDE, I connect the increased psychic abilities of many NDErs with the fact that many of us feel rage as we re-enter our bodies. Remember how I went from intense love in the light to intense anger when I left it? Remember how I felt no fear when I was falling from a great height or approaching the sun, but I felt intense fear as I "fell" from the light? That's because I had to pass back through the anti-god ecto-aura or energetic sheath to get back in my body.

While I walked that beach in a depressed, denied, yearning state of mind, longing for something then impossible, I was vibrationally attuned to a similar energy in another spirit. The Mackintosh seaman from the 1800s and I were on the same dissatisfied wavelength, so his energy passed easily through my membrane. I assumed I was seeing him with my eyeballs the same way I might see anyone else. But I wasn't. I was perceiving him with my spirit, which my thinking transformed into sight as if he were physically there. As soon as I became angry ("What an asshole!"), my membrane thickened and blocked him out.

Two years later, after I'd left my husband for Jenna the aerobics instructor, we watched the movie, *Ghost*, which made me inexplicably angry. I felt the filmmaker had no business showing a bright light overhead to which Patrick Swayze's character was drawn. I recognized too many depictions stolen from my private, never-tell-a soul experience and publicized in this film for the whole world to see. It was both too accurate, and at the same time too different from my experience. The movie seemed to pry open a vault that I needed to keep shut.

I did *not* want confirmation. I wanted a Newtonian universe.

In the years since, I've met many people who have likewise seen or heard ghosts. None were aware of ever having left their bodies, yet the spirits reached their awareness.

One man told me he ignored his aunt's warnings as a young teen when she told him and his friend to stay out of a particular room because it was haunted. The teen and his friend brought in their sleeping bags and slept on the floor, ready for a good spooking. But each awoke with their own name whispered loudly into their ear by a voice that horrified them. The door opened, slammed, and kept on. The boys ran from the room and met up in the hallway with the aunt and her husband, who were, he said, upset that the kids had ruined their night's sleep. All four sat in the living room hearing furniture knocked over, things crashing to the floor, and the door continuing to slam. The boys listened in terror while the aunt and her husband, though concerned about "what he was breaking," simply waited for the racket to stop so they could go back to bed.

Another man was walking to his car in a parking garage when he saw a young woman standing in front of a car and looking at him. He thought she'd perhaps gotten locked out of her car, standing there as she was in business clothes. Because he himself was a tall black man (6'6") while she was a small white woman and the two of them were alone, he took his customary measures to avoid scaring her: he smiled and slowed down, but she stared back with no expression. He assumed she didn't like black guys. At that point, however, he crossed a support pillar in the garage that seemed to act as an eraser; the stock still woman never reappeared on the other side. She was simply gone.

A man I dated for about a year and a half owned a condominium in Port Townsend, an old Salish Sea port known for its ghosts. Having just moved to the area for a job, Reggie had never heard such nonsense when he bought his place. He also knew nothing of the building restrictions in the old town zone that outlawed new construction. What looked to him like a new condominium complex was actually a 150-year-old hotel extensively remodeled and refurbished. Several times as he sat in his kitchen facing his coffee maker, he saw a narrow reflected figure make its way across the chrome, someone crossing the kitchen from left to right. The figure apparently passed through the wall to his right. This happened multiple times.

He also heard a resonant dripping sound as if the kitchen faucet were leaking into a full bowl of water. This happened during the night. But every time he approached his sink and found it dry, the same sound would start coming from his bathroom sink. This, too, happened multiple times. Then, after he'd been there about a month, he woke in the night to see a man staring at him from the foot of his bed. A burglar, he thought, and sat bolt upright shouting, "What the fuck! What the fuck!" – with no effect. Leaping out of bed, he grabbed his glasses from the night table, but in the fraction of a second it took to put them on, the figure vanished.

Only later did he realize how antiquated the man's clothing had been, complete with tweed vest and derby hat. My friend didn't know this was typical fashion for the late 1800s, when the hotel was in its heyday. But he did know beyond a doubt that he'd seen a ghost in his bedroom staring at him. He instantly packed a bag and fled to a nearby hotel. In the morning, he called his mother and sister back in Georgia, telling them about the ghost and asking for advice on how to reverse the condo sale. They humored him, but the deal was closed. After four costly nights, he went back.

I was in his condo one night watching a movie when he hit pause and said, "Listen! He's doing it!" I was the first person to witness what he'd been putting up with for two years. I can't describe how clear the dripping sound was, almost amplified and obviously, unmistakably for anyone with two ears, coming from the kitchen sink. We got up, my friend practically bursting with glee: "Check the sink! Check the sink!"

I did. It was dry – but as soon as I touched it, Reggie bugged his eyes and pointed toward the hallway, grinning. The dripping sound now emanated just as clearly from the bathroom, as though that sink were full of water.

But I didn't go there. Instead I spoke loudly to the ghost: "Hey, look, I know you're bored, but this is a dumb game, and we're not playing it. Do you hear me? You can drip all you want, but I'm not chasing it, and neither is he."

The dripping stopped. Reggie was amazed.

He called me a few days later saying the ghost had scared the shit out of him again, standing just outside the bathroom door when he emerged from a shower. The man was dressed exactly as before, derby and all. He looked into Reggie's eyes, then vanished. Reggie followed my advice and called out sharply, "Get out of here! Leave! I don't want you in my home!"

I also advised Reggie to ask his neighbors if they'd seen the ghost, who certainly must haunt the whole building, but as one of few African Americans living in Port Townsend, he felt like he had enough going against him without labelling himself a lunatic.

"But think of the bond you can make if you find someone else he does the water thing to!" I said. "You can't be the only one who's seen him!"

"But what if I am?" he asked. "I'm already 'the black guy.' You're asking me to be the *crazy* black guy? No thanks."

Yelling at the ghost did help Reggie, though, if only by making him less afraid. I told him also to tell the ghost to go join god, but we stopped dating, and I don't know if he ever did.

As certain as all these individuals were of what they saw, heard, and felt, none of them had ever shared their experience beyond their immediate family. Even there, they'd met with smirks and ridicule. The only reason they told me was that I confided first. If I labelled them crazy, they could label me right back.

Foreknowledge of a death

What I Thought Then:

Five and a half years have passed since that ghost thing in Gloucester, an experience I avoid thinking about because it always brings me to two contradictory facts: 1) I observed an old man for an extended period of time and 2) this man left zero tracks in the damp sand.

I'm still a devout atheist with morals sinking rapidly. I've abandoned my husband (as codependent alcoholics are wont to do), published some short stories, won a nationwide fiction contest, landed a competitive full-time post on the English faculty at a community college, which I left after just three years because the hours interfered with my drinki – I mean, my career as a writer! Jenna, who has fallen in love with me, and I have bought our dream house. It's a log house "in the country," or unincorporated Thurston County, where I hope to write great things. Jenna earns the real money now, and I find work as a barista.

I'm on the phone with my mom one day when she tells me great news: my brother's wife is pregnant! Except it doesn't sound like good news; instead it strikes me as a dark knell of tragedy and despair. I *want* to feel happy. That is, in my rational mind, I'm excited for my brother to become a father. Except he won't. That's what the knell tells me. What my brother will experience instead is a darkness deeper than any I've known: the profound grief of losing a child.

Chatting with my mom, I keep my voice upbeat. Why am I entertaining such dark thoughts? I must be worried just the same way everybody worries about a pregnancy, right? That's very natural. Everything's fine.

Except it's not. The dark cloud of grief on my brother's horizon continues to gather intensity, growing more formidable with each week closer to their due date.

Like most alcoholic families, ours is not terribly close. Even though I live only thirty minutes from my brother, updates come almost exclusively through our mom. When she tells me the gender – it's a boy – I get another dark wave of knowing. When she tells me my sister-in-law has announced it's time to buy all the baby stuff – a crib, a car seat, and so on – my inner response is adamant: "Don't do that! Those things will never be used and they'll cause enormous grief when they have be gotten rid of. Who will dismantle the crib?"

I wonder what's wrong with me that I'm having these sick, pessimistic responses. I decide I must have had an initial, random concern that the baby might die, so now I'm having all these follow-up thoughts as responses to *that*, maybe out of guilt. The baby will be fine! What could go wrong? My sister-in-law is young and healthy. She had a daughter years ago. Check-ups show the fetus is thriving. There's absolutely no reason to anticipate problems.

Yet my dread comes to a crescendo the day before the birth day when my sister and I arrange a rare get-together with our brother. The three of us meet for lunch at a strip mall restaurant: Happy Teriyaki.

Happy Teriyaki?! Could anything be more ironic? Indeed, my poor brother is on Cloud 9. The birth is close; dilation is already starting. He's overflowing with love to give his newborn son, eager to meet him, anticipating fatherhood with joy. We get Teriyaki and appear happy, the three of us laughing more than we have in years. I'm sitting right next to him, concealing this awful, blaring knowledge: soon you'll plunge from this height into a bleak abyss that will swallow *years* of your life.

We leave the restaurant with cheery calls of "See you at the hospital!" and "Can't wait!"

I get in my car, which is parked an empty space or two from my brother's. He gets in his car. Can't I warn him? I've got to – I must say something! Can I jump out of my car right now and run over to his and rap on the glass and say… What would I say? "I don't know why, I don't know how, but your baby will die. It may be tomorrow or in several weeks, but his death will be like a sword run through your heart."

My eyes stay fixed on the center of my steering wheel even as my hands go through the motions of starting the engine. My brother has done likewise, and now he drives away.

There's no such thing as prayer, but I'm doing it anyway: *Please may he be okay, may all be okay. Please may the baby be healthy. Please may my brother be happy.*

The next morning, in my log house, the phone rings on the kitchen wall. I already know it's my brother calling to tell me the baby died.

"Hello?" I say as though answering normally.

Yet the next few moments are like getting hit by a freight train. He's at the hospital. His newborn son is dead. While he explains what went wrong, his voice full of desperation to somehow make it not so, I'm knocked literally dizzy. Two strong emotions collide in me like opposing tsunamis. First grief and compassion for my brother. It is so wrong, so awful that the baby he and his wife already loved so much has been torn from their lives. Second, amazement, a horrible confirmation that what I knew would happen has come to pass.

I listen, staring at the kitchen counter. Now, a third wave comes from an unforeseen direction: guilt. Here I am amazed at my knowing even as my brother is telling me the specifics of his son's death. All my attention should be with this tragedy, not derailed by the fact that I knew it in the same way I saw the ghost and journeyed into the sun. But derailed I am. I despise myself for play-acting surprise as though this unfolding catastrophe had never entered my mind.

How could I have known? Why did I know? What could possibly have been telling me this futurity over and over with a certainty usually reserved for things witnessed or conventionally learned? Time has wrinkled somehow; news of a dark future leaked to my present. Why didn't I warn my brother? Surely, I could have done *something* outside Happy Teriyaki. Surely, if I had the power to know, I had some power to prevent.

But now it has unfolded. Now it's a thing that happened.

I join my brother at the hospital where he's holding the perfect, blanket-wrapped bundle of their beautiful boy. It's a scene too heart wrenching for description. The baby's fate was set from the start: somehow his umbilicus, instead of forming as a distinct cord, fanned itself out over the amniotic sack. Ultrasounds did not pick up this abnormality. He was fine right up until the moment his water broke. When the amniotic sack tore, so did all his blood vessels.

It is I who, tears streaming, dismantle the crib.

At the funeral, I keep asking myself if I couldn't have done *something*. Yet I feel guilty for every such reflection that distracts me from pure grief. "If anyone knew I've known about this from the outset or that since it happened I've been wracking my brains for how, they'd consider me a monster. I'll never tell anyone."

For several years afterwards, my skeptic and knowing self argue like this:

SKEPTIC: Hindsight is 20-20. You were just worried, as family often worry about a pregnancy, and then jumped all over that feeling when the tragedy happened.

KNOWER: What I felt wasn't worry. It was my brother's *pain and loss*. It was like a big, dark cloud, and I knew it would be about the baby's death.

SKEPTIC: You just *feared* something would go wrong.

KNOWER: I lived in the penumbra of his future pain. The moment when I stared at the steering wheel was torture.

SKEPTIC: You've imbued that memory with significance retrospectively because of what happened.

KNOWER: Go fuck yourself.

SKEPTIC: Hey, I've got all the world on my side, loser.

What I Think Now

Almost every NDErs will relate to this form of inner debate.

As for what enabled me to foretell the death, I don't know, but I've heard from multiple NDErs that all moments in time are accessible on the other side.

Living in physicality, we can experience only an infinitely thin slice of *now*, looking down on the fountainhead of becoming, but our thinking inevitably places that infinitely thin slice on a linear timeline with memory going back and prediction stretching ahead. Our entire culture is founded in the construct of linear time. Clearly, this line is a metaphor borrowed from physical space, of physical paths and roads we've trodden since our ancient beginnings.

But outside these models, time remains a mystery. Is the future, in a sense, always existent? Did some of it leak through to me in this knowledge much as the past, in the form of the anxious Mackintosh sailor, had leaked through visibly? Perhaps my brother's grief was so powerful, and we are situated as such neighboring leaves on the same family twig, that some of his pain radiated into my present. I knew only of *his* suffering, not his wife's.

The first time I told my NDE and its aftereffects at a Seattle IANDS meeting (about twenty years later), a woman came up afterward and told me, "Don't feel guilty. We can't warn others when we know so little ourselves. I knew that two of my friends were going to be in a horrific car wreck, and when it happened, I felt guilty, too. But if we don't know when, where, or how, we can't go telling people, 'I'm pretty sure this horrible thing is going to happen to you at some point.'"

In the years to come, I'd have many more experiences with foreknowledge and clairvoyance. Yet I've never been able to use this "leakage" to foretell events. Often, what I foreknow is trivial, yet exact. For instance, I often know exactly what someone is about to say – though this is mind-reading as much as clairvoyance.

About five years ago I ruined a group game of "Catch Phrase," a spoken version of charades where players hint at a phrase on the game's screen known only to them. I was feeling a lot of love for everyone because we'd just prepared a meal for a homeless camp and were waiting while it cooked. Connections tend to happen better for me when love thins my anti-god sheath.

One teammate's thoughts were so synched with mine that I kept knowing his phrases instantly. Others noticed this pattern, put out as if we were cheating. For instance, when he said, "Uh... it's kind of military. Don't forget," I burst out, "Remember the Alamo!" The words came out by themselves. I'd seen his mental image of the tall, closed log doors of a frontier fort along the words he was trying not to say, though I myself had no idea that "Alamo" meant anything in the world beyond a car rental company.

Chapter 4: My Angel Speaks – Twice!

What I Thought Then:

It's 1994 and I'm 34. My NDE was twelve years ago and I hardly ever think about it. My mental health is not the best, I can admit inwardly.

Only when I'm quite drunk and with someone cool and artsy I'm desperate to impress will I trot out my NDE story. I tell it as something that happened while I was in a cardiac arrest, but not divine or anything. Some kind of neurological death throes in the brain is what I usually say with a shrug. Two things bother me, though. One is that, every time I tell the story in full, starting with that first thought that I'd hit my chin on the bar, every detail returns with perfect clarity. Even after a dozen years, it always feels like it happened yesterday, or like I'm somehow reliving it now.

The other is that afterwards I always feel like I've desecrated something. How silly! How can I desecrate something unless it's holy, and how can anything be holy when there *is* no God? Stupid shit.

I drink. A lot. I'm still living in the log house but now alone because, just as we were coming up on five years together, Jenna read my journal and found out I'm wildly infatuated with a cool boy from the espresso shop where I work (and to whom I drunkenly told the story at a bar). After I'd promised both her and our couples' counselor that I'd avoid all contact with him, Jenna almost literally ran into us downtown – as in came around the corner and faced off with me, him, and our friend Van so close we almost collided. So she kicked me out. I had to go stay with my brother and his wife for a week while she packed up and left.

In August, the cool boy and several other baristas who attend the local state college leave town to visit their parents. Jenna's still in the log house so I stay in a friend's apartment while he's gone – cool digs in a dilapidated building downtown. When it rains, water cascades down the staircase. Not sure why, but it's pretty damn Bohemian.

I decide to stop drinking for a month to avoid drinking myself to death now that Jenna's no longer around to act as a brake. I don't know how to drink *less*. I get a calendar where I highlight and then cross off thirty days dry.

I can give up anything if I know there's an end to it.

One morning when I'm especially happy to *not* be hungover, I'm walking with a coworker friend in the brilliant sunshine when we pass this pretty dyke who has a crush on me. She's a regular at the espresso shop, but right now she's futzing with her motorcycle. We offer a blasé, meangirls "hey" and, as soon as she's out of earshot, giggle and whisper about her. I feel great today, like I need nothing from anyone.

But then I get this crazy idea. You know what I should do? I should run back right now and tell the pretty dyke I'll take her up on that motorcycle ride she offered – the same invitation I declined a week or two ago, the one I made ruthless fun of with coworkers as soon as she left.

I should *what*?? Run back and say *Yes*? Why the hell would I do that?

Because it's sunny! It's summer! Think how beautiful the world will look rolling past, think how alive you'll feel in the wind!

The idea feels tantalizing, like the prospect of gulping cold water on a hot afternoon. I raise an index finger to pause my friend and say, "One second." I run back and say, "Hey, you know that motorcycle ride?" She's surprised, but we quickly set a date for it. When I run back to my friend, who looks puzzled, I laugh and say, "Why not? Why not?"

Neither of us has any idea I've just altered the course of my life.

Before I know it, we're dating. She's clean and sober – but, oh well. I'm doing that thirty-day thing. She brings me to an AA meeting for her third sober anniversary, where I'm both flabbergasted and horror stricken at the length of time these people have gone without a drink. Definitely *not* for me!

In a few weeks, my self-imposed dry spell is over and I take up where I left off – guzzling to blackout. When the cool boy comes back from vacation, I break up with the motorcycle dyke and convince him to rent a room in my lovely log house in the country. Sadly, after I throw myself at him more than once and he figures out I'm not the purebred lesbian he'd assumed, he ghosts on the room and eventually moves out. Now I can't afford my mortgage payments, not even with the newly recruited housemate I so dislike, a short Filipina bisexual sex addict.

I read a bunch of Bukowski. Fuck life. I'm disintegrating. Yes, I can see it, but not stop it. Honor, integrity, discipline – anything like that I once believed in is now flung out the window, and I hate myself more profoundly with each dull, sickened, inescapable hangover. I make it until about 3:00 p.m.

sometimes before a drink sounds delightful. I've got to stop, yet I have no choice but to get drunk again and dig even deeper into depravity, stalking the poor cool boy despite his new girlfriend, adrift in incomprehensible demoralization.

I journal about him obsessively, alternating fantasies and self-beratement. I call my ex-husband late one night, after seven years' silence, to ask his advice: Lissen, I've taken up again with this pretty dyke in hopes of appearing alluringly unobsessed with the cool boy, but she can't seem to tolerate my wild ways so she's broken up with me again. What should I do?

He answers something completely irrelevant: "Stop drinking."

What. Ever!

I get falling down drunk at parties and snort cocaine with kids a dozen years younger than me. I scrawl in my journal that this reckless depravity is the rock bottom truth. Good? Bad? They're nothing but cultural currency. Ethics? They've developed communally, no basis but hive survival. As Flannery O'Connor's Misfit puts it, there's "nothing for you to do but enjoy the few minutes you got left the best way you can... no pleasure but meanness."

I don't wanna be *mean*, specifically, but I'm all about not caring what happens – especially whether I live or die.

This one particular night begins like countless others. I go to a kegger near downtown Olympia, a ton of young people, loud music. The cool boy *was* there, I'm told, but he left. Shit! He might come back, though, so I drink.

I fall down multiple times. There's a goddamn step somewhere in the middle of the basement, where the keg's at, that keeps tripping me. Each time I'm going down, I hear that chorused "Whoa!" from everybody nearby – as if it matters whether one's body is vertical or horizontal. People make such a big deal.

Now it's late. My friends Megan and what's-their-name get in *my* car and drive me to a house one or two blocks up the street, where they put me in someone's bedroom. I'm supposed to sleep there on some stranger's bed. Driving's what I'm *not* supposed to do – they've taken my keys. No, no, no driving, Louisa! You're so shitfaced you can't even walk! But as soon as they leave, I decide, fuck this. I get up and stagger my way to the stranger's kitchen, where they've foolishly left my keys right there on the table.

Ha! Tell *me* what to do!

In the car, I'm able to figure out which key is the one but not able to find the thing. I stab again and again at steering wheel shaft, but the goddam ignition is nowhere. It's AWOL. I feel with my fingertips for about ten hours because it's too dark to see and my eyes won't focus anyway. Finally I get it and the engine starts. Yes! I'm such a rebel! No pleasure but meanness – I just don't friggin' care. I might die. That's fine. I'm so fucking tired of everything.

I'm speeding down the two-lane highway that winds into Thurston County, 80 mph in a 50-mph zone. Smack into a tree – that would be best. First prize is a Get-Out-of-Everything-Free card, and second prize I end up just crippled with brain damage. Finally no one will expect me to do stuff or be likable. "Such a shame," they'll say, "she had potential" – but at least they won't expect me to function. My parents – well, they have three other kids, right?

What's this? Here come reflectors for a skinny bridge over some railroad tracks. I see the diagonal black and white stripes, but they're tripled or so, so they blur across the whole goddam road. I just kind of shoot for the middle, sort of like bowling.

Whoosh! It's behind me!

A few minutes later, I roll into my driveway and marvel at my drunk driving skills, how I've made it home alive. The night is clear, the sky starry. I slop out of the car and, hanging onto the open door, look up, thinking: "Damn, I'm a bad-ass!"

But something hits me, hits my brain, my mental arena. ZAP!!! It's like a voltage shot into my consciousness, a bolt of intention powerful enough to blitz everything else from my head:

This is the last time I can help you! And you DO know right from wrong!

The blast of this knowing – out of nowhere – astounds me. It's like getting struck by lightning, but the lightning is *thought*. It seemed like it came from that starry sky, so admonishing it's as if somebody meant to physically slap my face: Wake up!

I feel shaken, bowled over, my billowing ego punctured.

I wonder in a sliver of thought: Is that God? Is it *you* who were with me in the light?

The next morning, I find the kitchen a mess and can't say how it got like that. A carton of milk – mine, not my roommate's – is sitting out warm on the counter. Oatmeal dribbled on the stove and half eaten from a saucepan. All this I must've done in a black out. Yet so clearly, so vividly, I remember that moment of whizzing between the bridge reflectors! So perfectly,

I remember getting shocked by that thought bolt, that pronouncement, that powerful knowing I did not make.

What the hell *was* that?

Who was that?

How could that happen?

In the weeks following, I can't get drunk enough to stop wondering. *You DO know right from wrong!* It comes back while I'm drinking, when I'm hungover, if I'm trying to impress people I know are shady. And trailing after the memory is a weird, implacable sense that, yes, someone *has been helping me*, saving my life time after time. And now they're sick of my stupid, dangerous games. Go ahead and die: they pretty much straight up told me so.

For me to hit rock bottom takes about a month. I've lost all fight, all rebelliousness.

I've sunk.

I give up.

I just can't.

On January 29, 1995, I resolve to take one of two possible actions. Either 1) buy a gallon of vodka and chug it down as fast as I can before I pass out and or 2) call the phone number a sober friend has scrawled on a scrap of paper when, as I exited her house, I mentioned being super hungover and conceded that I *might* possibly have just a tiny bit of maybe a slight potential drinking problem.

I know where the paper is, next to the wall phone. The allure of suicide gleams brighter, though, that absolute freedom of throwing in the towel. You've been rescuing and rebuilding a card house that keeps partially collapsing, and finally, instead of trying to prop it up yet again, you just flatten the fucker on purpose.

That's my life. I've tried and tried. No one, I believe, *really* cares about me, in part because no one's ever seen past that "like me!" tap dance I trot out to please every goddam asshole. I hate that fuckin' dance. I hate being *me*.

But I guess I have to call AA first, in part because, out here in Olympia in 1995, you can't really *buy* a gallon of vodka on a Sunday. Liquor stores are closed. So, fuck it. I'll call the AA number first and figure out the gallon thing second.

I call.

So much kindness from woman who answers floods me with feeling. She tells me a meeting time and place, yes, but it's her sweet voice, her grandma way of assuring me that, as I insist, this meeting will be far enough from town that nobody will know me. She calls me "honey," tells me "don't you worry!" I want to weep so badly, so gut-wrenchingly, but my eyes are broken.

At that first AA meeting of my own, I feel contempt for everyone as I'm clearly much too cool to be here. And yet... there's something in the room, some energy I can't put my finger on. It feels good and warm and safe, a lot like that grandma's voice.

Two weeks later, somehow I'm still sober and I've asked a woman to be my AA sponsor – the same one who gave me the scrawled phone number. She's a tiny young thing with a Great Dane twice her size that obeys her every murmur like some awed canine groupie. I, on the other hand, do not. She tells me that, if I choose to go to a vodka-slamming party thrown by my sister and her crazy Italian husband, she can no longer sponsor me. Fine! I simply thank her for her time – because I'm *going*.

I don't need a sponsor! I just won't drink. The cool boy's planning to attend, so I need to impress him with the profound inner discipline of my newfound sobriety. I shop for various aids to help me not drink – Tootsie rolls and M&Ms and lots and lots of near-beer. My two dogs, Tashia and Kelsey, are with me in the car, so on the way home I pull over at a watershed park to let them run. In an open field, I notice some kind of hill or knoll that looks artificially made. It's always been there, but today I find myself schlepping to the top.

I'm about to do something, something super weird and corny. I'm gonna to try what everyone in the AA meetings is always talking about – prayer. I watch the dogs, see the sunlight on the moving trees, and admit I kind of do want to live. There's no God, of course, but *something* shot that knowing through me, *something* implied it had "helped" me. So I think toward whatever that is: "I don't know what you are or what I'm doing, but I ask that you please help me get sober. I don't know how I can live without drinking, but I promise to try if you'll show me the way. Okay. Thanks."

Aren't you supposed to say "amen" so it sends?

"Amen."

Once I get home, I leave the driveway gate open a minute, and BAM! Tashia is dead. It all happens in seconds before I know what. Kelsey, my timid white Malamute-coyote mix, patches out of the driveway and tears down the road, her tail helicoptering with a fierceness I've never seen. She's chasing a big, two-trailer dirt truck, so I scream after her while Tashia is... Tashia is where?

I look behind me. She's lying across the yellow center line. I kneel by her, oblivious to what traffic may come around the bend. She's still conscious, my girl. She blinks her bright, shining eye, swallows once, and I realize her neck is broken so she can't move a muscle. A dusty tire track crosses the black fur of her ribs, and from the lower corner of her mouth trickles red blood. So red. It spills toward me on the slightly sloped asphalt, slowly, in pauses and surges.

The voice zaps me again: *LOOK!*

My eyes zoom in as if her blood were a river coursing in slow motion through network of canyons, a towering flood as if a dam has burst. *LOOK!* seems to split and unpack into sub-messages: 1) blood and metal and asphalt are physical things that conform to laws, 2) your blood will do this very same thing far sooner than you know, 3) cut the bullshit – now.

Tashia's eyes close. Her breathing stops. She's gone.

I'm still kneeling on the yellow line of a busy road, though there's been a lull in traffic. I lug Tashia's limp, 45-pound body to the side of the road. Now the dirt truck roars by once again, and I glance up at the driver through tears with no compassion, only rage in my heart. He passes a third time, continuing on his way.

I must choose. I can go into the house and call one of two people.

If I call the cool boy, I'll have a fantastic story with lots of emotion, and maybe he'll fall in love with me and I'll at last be cool.

If I call the motorcycle dyke, I'll fall back into that relationship, which, whatever else it may be, is *not* cool.

Standing beside Tashia, I'm seeing in my mind's eye something entirely unrelated to this train of thought. It's what – a Pied Piper? He wears colorful harlequin clothes and skips along merrily with his pipe, leading me and a gaggle of other cool-wannabes like characters from a fairy tale. This figure is the Pied Piper of Coolness, my current but unacknowledged deity. He promises this *next* party, this *next* drink or drug, this *next* feat of crazy-ass radical shit, will finally bring the grand prize of feeling cool enough. Just around this corner, this next party, next witty repartee, next outrageous display of wildness – "you will be *loved*!"

This glimpse is sickening – what an idiot I've been for so many years, deceived, gullible, taunted with a prize I'll never touch. He lies; he's evil; his game will kill us. Up to this very moment, I've been chasing his colors and melodies toward the precipice of death.

I know what I'm being asked: *Follow him no more. Drop him.*

But... but... my mind flounders, scrabbles. What else *is* there? What else can I *live* for? How will I know I'm gaining, or winning, or moving ahead?

Trust. There's something more.

So, with a huge inner heave, I trust. I release the harlequin, the cool boy, popularity, the vodka party, and all such snazzy shit to come. I will be no one. I will be dull. I'll sink into the boring, obscure loserdom of sobriety for all my days. Fine. I give up... again.

I wander back in the house and, overcoming one last reluctance, call the motorcycle dyke for only one reason: over three years sober, she knows something I don't.

Half an hour later, she's dropped off from the back of an AA buddy's motorcycle (hers is in the shop). We move Tashia's body down to my basement. Kelsey scratches and whimpers frantically at the basement door until we open it to let her in. She goes at once to Tashia but, scenting death, actually reverses her steps to back away.

The sober motorcycle dyke never leaves.

We go to AA meetings together.

We move first to downtown Olympia, then to Seattle's queer district.

We marry (not yet legal).

We have my son, whom I carry.

Then she finds someone new – but I stay sober.

Certainly, there's no need to tell anyone about this whole disembodied voice advice giver, is there? I've got to admit, though, it seems saner than I am!

What I Think Now:

Today I know everyone has at least one guardian angel, probably more. But we're deaf to them. Several NDErs I've interviewed stayed close to their bodies when they first left them, having an OBE during which they could see and hear people nearby. They recall trying their hardest to communicate with the living – in the case of Howard Storm, actually screaming at them – then gradually realizing that, frustrating as it felt, the living could neither see nor hear them.

"I noticed a lump in the bed where I'd been – a person. His face was turned away so I bent over to see it. To my horror, he resembled *me*! But I knew he couldn't be me, because I was *here*. I tried to talk with my wife, but she made no response. I thought she was ignoring me, so I got very angry. Then I went to my roommate. I screamed right in his face and still got no response." (Howard S.)

"I was looking at her but she wasn't looking at me; she was looking off to her left. As soon as she got down the stairs right in front of me, she took off to her left. So I followed to see what was going on, and after about three steps, I was confronted with my body lying there on the ground. I looked at that body and thought, 'Oh, shit! I must be *dead*!' It was a shock to me, because I'd always imagined there'd be some sort of bells and whistles, you know, some clear sign that you'd left. Nothing! All I'd felt was that sense of moving forward. I joined the people standing around the body. I was calling to them, trying to be heard. No one could hear me; no one could see me. After a while I thought, 'There's no point in staying here,' so I turned and went to look for my family." (Tony C.)

"Then the nurse came back in, and... I felt all her emotion; she was panicking, she was filled with fear and remorse. I knew it had been an accident, so I became immediately consoling. I almost went *through* her, wanting to say, 'It's okay, don't worry about it!' I could feel my own energy spinning with the effort, but I couldn't communicate with her. And I knew, 'She's a mortal, and I'm a spirit, and I'm unable to communicate with her.' I'd never thought about that kind of thing ever before, yet I *knew* it – like, green light means go – I just knew." (JoDee C.)

"I don't remember much about the paramedics arriving, though I knew people were asking me those questions, who are you, what year is it? I didn't care... In this moment, I could see figures *behind* those people, beings who were helping them help me. For lack of a better word, I'll call them angels – not physically there, but actively helping." (John B.)

The vast majority of NDErs encounter a spiritual being such as I did in the sun, pouring out love. Many can see them. Among those, many "recognize" the being(s) as having been with them all their life, knowing them more deeply than they know themselves because they've accompanied them, guiding and helping them, throughout not just *this* lifetime, but many.

Today I know the voice generating these telepathic messages was the same one who spoke to me as I flew toward the sun, the same one who held me in the light and who determined, *You cannot stay.* He is my dear angel, Egnacio, and he has spoken to me countless times since. I'll tell more about him as we progress.

At this time, I did not recognize his energy as masculine. I knew only that I was suddenly experiencing strong thoughts that ran counter to my own.

It's our god-phobic membrane that makes us "deaf" to spirits. The more anger, fear, resentment, and ego we carry energetically, the thicker the barrier and the less we can pick up. Leaving one's body during an NDE has, for many of us, an effect on this barrier like a tear in a membrane.

When I drove home drunk, my anti-god membrane was thickened by the self-deceit I was immersed in. I was full of fear, selfishness, and dark suicidal energies. For my angel to have communicated with me at that point, through that barrier, must have taken a tremendous burst of energy on his part. That's why I experienced it as a "bolt" or "blast." He must have bellowed into my consciousness with a power beyond what any normal spirit, like those newly dead NDErs quoted above, could muster. He is powerful, and he used that power to spiritually slap me.

Not until I'd told my story for IANDS Dallas-Fort Worth did an NDEr point out that the bent of my angel's communication was the "tough love" of Al-Anon. He was drawing a boundary, detaching with love, as must the loved ones of every alcoholic addict at some point when their assistance crosses the line between help and enabling. Don't give them money. Don't let them stay with you. Kick them out. Let them experience consequences. All this is bedrock Al-Anon stuff.

What my angel told me, essentially, was, "If you're so intent on bashing your brains out on a telephone pole, have at it! If you really want to throw this life away despite all your gifts and potential, I'll no longer prevent it." But he also underscored that I had all the tools I needed to save myself: "You do know right from wrong" means you already possess the inner compass you needed to navigate toward a meaningful life – if you choose to use it.

This message has enormous implications for the matter of free will versus fate. My angel was telling me that, while he'd guided me to the sober motorcycle dyke and saved my life multiple times, he was handing control over to me now. I was free to destroy myself.

I still remember that drive with perfect clarity, especially the moments of crossing the bridge. I remember the bolts of knowing with perfect clarity as well. But the time immediately after remains lost to me. Physically, my brain was in a blackout. The reason I can recall the drive and bridge so vividly is that my angel was *with* me. He guided my driving; he co-existed in my consciousness. Spiritual memories, like NDE memories, do not fade with time.

I further thinned my god-phobic membrane when I offered my first lame-ass prayer at the top of the little hill. I asked for *help*. When we do this and mean it sincerely, miracles follow. That's the cornerstone of the AA program. Apparently, I was able to muster a bit of sincerity, to open my heart to the spirit world just a bit. I remember that moment clearly, too.

Tashia's death saved my life. Its suddenness snapped me awake, woke me from the spell of addiction long enough for my angel to drive home his point: metal, pavement, and blood are real but your folly – this lifelong chase for coolness – is an illusion.

Sad as her death was, I believe Tashia could not have lived much longer, regardless. Both my dogs, Tashia and Kelsey, were rescues interbred with wild species. Kelsey was half Malamute mix and half coyote, which made her wily, intuitive, extremely shy, but loyal. She would become my first "higher power" because of her uncanny connection to Nature.

But poor Tashia was half German shepherd, half wild dingo. She once jumped out of the car window as we passed our neighbors walking their dog. Thankfully, I'd slowed to about 20 mph when she leapt. She hit the pavement, rolled several times with incredible rapidity, then jumped up and went to check out the dog. The shepherd in her would cower whenever I scolded her, yet the dingo would snap viciously at my finger as soon as I withdrew it, once even drawing blood. She decapitated my adolescent rooster (I never did find his head), getting blood all over her face. But most of all, she could not be confined. Around our 1.5 acres, I'd built a five-foot fence. She could somehow scale it or, given thirty minutes, burrow under and roam – she had to roam. Often she'd be gone past dusk despite all my calling and searching for her. Neighbors reported having seen her here and there on the roads. When I tied her up, she'd gnaw through the wire. When I got extra thick wire, it took her a while, and meanwhile she'd tangle herself up to the point that she could hardly move – this if I went into town overnight to drink.

I sold the log house. For the first few months of my sobriety, I lived with the motorcycle dyke and Kelsey in a tiny apartment in the heart of downtown Olympia. On rainy days, the only exercise Kelsey got was chasing her ball along the building's hallway or down its main staircase. On most sunny days, she got a walk in postage-stamp-sized Sylvester Park. I, meanwhile, now found myself within walking distance of several AA meetings. I ran into sober friends on the daily.

Tashia could never have tolerated those conditions, and I doubt I could have found another home for such a crazy, conflicted dog. But I also doubt I could have stayed sober living in a place remote enough for Tashia to thrive. I'd done my best for her for two years. In the end, I believe she sacrificed her life for mine.

Chapter 5: Serendipity on Steroids

What I Thought Then:

I'm about three months sober. Any time the word "God" comes up in AA meetings, I get grumpy – especially when the pronoun "He" goes with it. What they're calling "God" is really a human tendency toward group conformity: alcoholics join a "tribe" in which their new sense of belonging reduces loneliness (as I admit it's been doing for me). Instead of thinking "*I* mustn't drink," AA members can think, "*We* don't drink" – and voila! They find the needed impetus for self-restraint: conformity. They find they can do together what they can't do alone, as they like to say. So then, out of gratitude and loyalty, they conform even further by attributing that changed behavior to "God's" help.

For me, personally, going through the motions of joining AA is definitely helping. I'm coming up on ninety days without a drink, which utterly blows my mind. I'm slowly weaning myself off cool boy infatuation, too. At times I can see that he's stuck in that parade behind the Pied Piper.

My log house has sold with a $30,000 profit. I decide to travel to Greece for three weeks – alone. Why not? The motorcycle dyke, still an addict at heart, is super pissed that I'm not taking her with me. She'll be stuck at home watching Kelsey.

As soon as I've bought my tickets, an irrational urge keeps nagging at me to call my college friend Allie. Back at Vassar thirteen years before, we'd been best friends. In fact, I was half in love with her. Then, partly because I was scared by my own queer vibe, I became infatuated with a boy, my secret boyfriend future ex-husband, of whom Allie strongly disapproved because I was cheating on my "real" boyfriend, the New Mexico guy. All at once, I dropped Allie. I wanted no part of her guilt trip, so I just quit hanging out. She was deeply hurt.

Yes, I regret having done that, but thirteen years later, why am I having this weird, irrational urge to *call* her? I heard she joined the Peace Corps after graduation, but that's all I know. I have her Mom's number in Washington, DC, but when I finally give in and call it, the number's disconnected. Fine. I tried, right?

That should be the end of it, but it's not. Some weird thought, *Call Allie!,* harps at me even louder now, until I'm so sick of it, I call up our mutual friend from Vassar. She does indeed know Allie's current phone number. Allie now lives in Luxembourg with her South Afrikaner husband and two sons.

Where the hell is Luxembourg? It's some miniscule country landlocked in Europe. I call the number. In those days, transatlantic phone calls cost a bundle and lag a lot. My heart pounds as Allie picks up, surprised but also happy to hear from me. Phew! She holds no grudge.

"What made you call me?" she asks.

What indeed? I can't say, some weird voice in my head kept repeating and repeating *Call Allie!* So instead I say, "I just wanted to tell you I'm going to be only a thousand miles away from you for a couple weeks, so I'll be thinking of you. I'm flying to Greece!"

"You are?" she says. "That's so funny. *We're* flying to Greece first thing in the morning – in seven hours, actually! I almost didn't answer the phone 'cause I need to get up so early."

I grab my paper ticket and tell her when I'll arrive. Disappointed, she says, "Aww, man! That's the day we leave."

I'm sad, too, until Allie says, "Wait! We have a four-hour layover in Athens. When do you get in?"

I'll land one hour into that layover. We're squealing like little girls, not waiting for the transatlantic lag so everything crisscrosses and gets mixed up, but who cares? Before we hang up, we have a plan to meet at the airport for lunch.

Two weeks later, here's Allie in person, running up to hug me, her long black hair halfway silver but still beautiful, still the same girl who stole my heart. She shows off to me her super-blonde husband and their two tow-head little boys, then we leave to get lunch.

Face-to-face with her, I make my first AA amends; I own the wrong I did her.

Allie forgives me. Now it's time to catch up. I tell her about my brand-new sobriety and give her a copy of the prize-winning story I wrote about a character based on her. She tells me about the Peace Corps, how she met her husband, about their kids – and that her mom is dying from alcoholism. I remember really hitting it off with Allie's mother; I liked her because she was big on drinking, always "freshening" my gin and tonics, applauding my consumption, making the little jokes drinkers do. Dying, is she? I share what I know, that no amount of pleading or lectures, nothing but honesty and surrender can save a drunk. We cry together, holding hands across the Formica airport table.

"How can this have happened?" Allie asks. "The two of us sitting here?"

The chances are mind-bogglingly remote, we agree.

"I mean, this is obviously," she sniffles, "the work of our higher powers. Your calling me and my answering so late when

I never do that; your arriving here during our layover. I've never been to Greece before, have you?

"No."

"Well," she smiles, "there ya go."

We're as much at peace now as we were excited an hour ago. Allie's readiness to credit a higher power surprises me. She's super smart. She's practical. Certainly, I admit, phoning her was *not* my idea. Certainly, something greater than us wanted this reunion to happen.

Maybe I should try that prayer thing more often.

I catch a bus to downtown Athens. It's risky for an alcoholic with only ninety-some days to travel anywhere alone, let alone in a city where a slim, complimentary glass of Ouzo greets her from nearly every restaurant table. After what happened with Allie, though, I dare to ask "the voice" to help me.

"Please take this away," I hear myself saying time after time, never any less astonished.

My first night, I sense the magnetic pull of the hotel bar – its tropical plants, colored lights, and schmoozy music – but I set out walking two miles across Athens to an English-speaking AA meeting listed on my printout. I find the building locked, an old brick tower. First one then another alcoholic joins me, each seeming to pull a different foreign accent out of some unseen grab-bag, until the guy with the key shows up and they all unite to pitch him shit. He's not late, though. Half a dozen more members of this motley group gradually assemble in an upper room, where I recognize the familiar posters of Bill and Bob, the 12 Steps, Traditions, and slogans. Still, so many people who know each other! I'll just listen, not share. I almost wish I'd stayed by myself in my hotel room.

First to share is a weeping woman, her longish blond hair all messed up. Do I know her? She's a flight attendant, she says. *My* flight attendant, I realize. Upon landing in Athens, she screwed up her cross-check and inflated an emergency slide, delaying the plane's departure by several hours. She may lose her job. And she's inconvenienced so many people probably still stuck at the airport!

The voice hardly needs to nudge me. I share next. On the flight, she'd seemed pretty confident the plane wasn't going to plunge down in flames, whereas I'd never flown without getting wasted, so I felt a panic attack always on the horizon. To help myself stay calm, I intentionally observed her doing her job. Now I can recount every act of kindness she performed on that flight: that coloring book she brought the little boy two rows ahead of me; the confused old Greek lady she helped calm down. She was the only attendant on the flight who spoke Greek, I point out, so she was constantly responding to requests from coworkers in different parts of the plane. No wonder she was flustered by the end!

I find myself looking directly into her eyes across the circle of drunks. "You were the best flight attendant on that plane. They'd be idiots to let you go."

Practically everyone's tearing up. The weirdest thing, though, is what's happening in my chest. My heart seems to be physically swelling like the Grinch's. I want good things for this stranger. I, in a crazy sense, *love* her.

When the meeting ends, we all walk up the hill to a garden restaurant for dessert. Gathered at a long table among trellises laden with flowers, overlooking Athens' beauty in the low sun, these people pass around my tourist map and circle every must-see, cross out every dumb tourist trap. They're hilarious! We laugh together – alcoholics from all over the world.

When I confess I'm a little afraid to walk home two miles in the twilight, they share another round of giggles and guffaws. "Afraid of what?! You're not in America."

Next, my itinerary takes me to Delphi, site of the ancient oracle originally dedicated to Gaia, Mother of the Earth. If I had a goddess, Gaia would be she, and I'm at her front porch, so to speak, though the Greeks called it Earth's navel. What harm can it do, standing in this ruined temple whence steam once issued and a priestess spoke for the gods, to ask for Gaia's protection and guidance during my travels? This time, I even bow my head and close my eyes.

"Be with me, please."

BOOM! I get assaulted on the boat to Crete. I've somehow boarded the wrong ship, so I'm compelled to sit guarding my luggage until the concierges have checked in all the legit passengers. A kind-seeming Belgian man offers in German (which I speak somewhat) to store my stuff temporarily in his room so I can move about the ship. Then he wants to buy me a drink. I take only coffee, though he keeps urging booze. When I notice he's begun to "duzen" me, using the informal "du," I recall that this form is used, not only for loved ones and children, but for whores.

I'd like to fetch my things, I say. He discourages; I insist. Then, as I'm grabbing my bags in his room, he shuts the door. I just manage to swing my suitcase into the breach, and, as he moves close in to kiss me, his wet lips repulsively puckered, I yell out, "Das geht NICHT!" With a fierce tug I leverage the door and, burdened with three other bags, squeeze into the hallway, where I walk away fast, reverting to good ole' English: "Fuck you, asshole!"

About an hour later, as I sit trembling crazily on my pile of luggage by the front desk, the Belgian waffle and his friend pass by. He points me out, says a bunch in French, and they both laugh. I want to murder him.

Finally, after another hour, I've been assigned to a six-berth compartment. I'm luggage-free but now still seething with rage. I circle the ship's main level, hating, far too upset to even try sleeping. I'm shaking, heart pounding. Half of my route traverses the ship's long cocktail bar, its mirror-backed shelves lined with all my best friends. There's Jack Daniels, Absolut, Beefeaters. Hey, Louisa, it's us! Ain't you a badass no more? My brain's plan is this: down three shots of Jack neat, go back the asshole's room, and fuck that bastard up!

Somehow, I walk past again. I manage another prayer to Gaia: "Be with me!"

The voice speaks: *Don't throw away your life for that cur.*

I circle again. The bottles twinkle magically on their jewel-like shelves. Again the bartender smiles in greeting. But I've also noticed, sitting alone among the mostly empty tables, a young man. He's a white guy with long black dreadlocks. What better sign of an American?

He is Good, the voice says. *Go to him.*

What?! Wasn't that exactly what got me into trouble in the first place – trusting a man?

I circle again, pissed.

He has Goodness. Trust him.

So I approach this stranger's table. He's reading and has cast a large black sketch book on the table in front of him.

"Do you speak English?" I ask, hopeless but following instructions nonetheless.

He glances up sharply. He does not appreciate this intrusion. He says nothing.

I can't believe I'm doing this! My voice is shaking like the bleat of a sheep, but the voice pushes me, so I say, "I'm really upset because... a bad thing happened to me. I'm... all messed up and... I... I need to calm down. I really need to... calm down."

He's watching me, alarmed, more guarded than ever.

I sit down anyway and gesture toward his sketchbook. Now I know *exactly* what to ask. "Could you maybe, like, show me your drawings? I... That would help a lot!"

Now he outright scoffs, clearly put off by my urgency – the shaking hands, the bleating voice – which smacks of mental illness. Or I might be a con woman.

He shakes his head, his eyes askance. Nope.

Then I add one soft, little word, "Please..."

He looks at me differently.

I'm newly sober, I explain, and don't want to drink. Please will he show me his sketches?

He thaws just enough to nudge a corner of his sketchbook an inch or two in my direction. I feel hope blossoming. Whatever I felt for that flight attendant is here again; he's beginning to feel it for *me*.

"But, see, I need you to *show* it to me. I need you to, like, turn the pages for me, maybe tell me a little story about each sketch, like where you were..."

In those days, ASMR – autonomous sensory meridian response – is not a known phenomenon, though I know I have it. I know that whenever I listen to someone typing on a computer keyboard, or turning pages, or even making certain consonant sounds, I experience a tingly, super-relaxing sensation at the top of my head, down my neck, and into my body. It's sleepy yet not sleepy. I'm beginning to realize this feeling can quell my near-hysteria – without a drink. But I need this dreadlocks grunge boy to make the sounds.

Amazingly, he starts showing me sketches and, when I prompt, "Little story, little story!" even recalls anecdotes ("Um, okay. So, I guess there were a shit-ton of pigeons here, and this lady..."). But the miracle is not that every time he touches the thick, porous paper, pronounces a plosive, or curls a page over, my magic tingles spread, soothe me, melt away the rage. It's not even that he, Travis, brings me a soda and bowl of popcorn from the bar, causing me to weep, hears my misadventure and talks with me – candid, mellow, and funny – until I can go to my berth. Nor is it that I meet him crusty-eyed in line to disembark at 6:00 a.m. the next morning, which happens to be Mother's Day. Rather, the miracle that will save my sobriety (and hence my life) emerges from the fact that this young man *insists* on calling his mom. Never mind that the town of Chania is deserted on a Sunday morning: he *has* to find an international phone center and call to wish her happy Mother's Day.

I tag along, stopping any stranger for directions to help Travis track the place down. Once we find it, I go in with him, and while he's talking to dear old Mom, I get a little bored. I decide I may as well spend a little cash to call my motorcycle dyke back home, just to say hi. She picks up. Kelsey's fine, everything's great. As though it were funny, I start telling her what happened on the boat, but before I'm halfway though, I'm suddenly enraged again to full tilt, so humiliated and furious that I'm once again shaking violently: "That fucking fuckface! I wanna *kill* him!"

"Call the AA hotline," she says with urgency. "Listen! I'm not kidding. Call them *now*."

So I do. I peer at my fine-print photocopied listing and master my hand tremor enough to dial Chania AA. Someone answers, a man with a strong Australian accent.

"Alcoholics Anonymous."

In the midst of the words, "I'm... Louisa and I'm an alcoho—" I begin first to bleat again and next to start crying way too hard to speak, too violently to even sob out what's wrong. I'm trying my hardest, but I can't make words.

"Listen, dahling," says the Australian. "Just sit toight, okai? You're going to be foin, I promise. Stye roight whehr you ah. I'm going to hawp on a bus, and I'll be theh in fifteen minutes."

Travis sits beside me on the building's front steps, reluctant to leave though I've managed to stop crying. He needs to catch a bus, though, a few blocks away. I tell him I'm fine. So, with a brief, BO-scented hug, he says goodbye. We don't trade numbers; instead we promise never to forget.

Bruce, the Australian, first treats me to coffee and hears my boat story. Less than 100 days sober – this is not good, not good, he says, concerned: *Hungry, Angry, Lonely, Tired* – I've got all four of the HALT triggers. But Bruce hatches a plan to help keep me sober. He takes me on an impromptu tour of sober alcoholics in Chania, meaning we stop wherever alcoholics he knows live and work – about eight of them, all met in person. Each greets us with that understanding alcoholics share. Each learns I've got under 100 days and hears a brief recap of the boat story, often in French. They see danger. In response to Bruce's question, each tries to think of a good place for me to stay, though none have room themselves. Several suggest an American painter and his French-Canadian wife across town who have a guest room; so off we go, walking on the remains of an ancient Venetian wall across this vine and flower-filled city to an incredibly charming little house built of large stone slabs, something like the Flintstones'.

We find the couple home, so Bruce loses no time in telling them in French about me. John, with blue paint smeared on his hands and the tip of his nose, looks concerned; Gillian appears empathetic but speaks little English. They have two tiny kittens I play with while awaiting their verdict – because it turns out the guest room is already occupied by Gillian's friends, a gay couple from Quebec. Still, no one's willing to cut me loose; I'm too likely drink away the anger/trauma Bruce witnessed on the phone. Rooms for rent are available just down the street for five dollars a night. John, the painter, walks me there, telling me I can sleep there and spend days with him and Gillian. My rental room comes with a medley of delicious scents wafting from the adjacent outdoor bakery with its vast wood-fired ovens built of stone, a locus of activity with chatty locals constantly dropping off or picking up whatever they've made that needs baking.

Settled in, I go back to the Flintstones house. Like a lost child, I'm excited to have been adopted.

I can't imagine any place I'd rather be. Minimalist living, eclectic music, artworks galore, and fascinating people surround me. Flowers ramble and bob everywhere in the blinding white courtyard, where a bathtub and bucket-flushed toilet are concealed behind shoulder-height walls. John and Gillian feed me goat stew. A neighbor leans in the no-glass window with a large dish made from her garden zucchinis – in May! The Quebec gay boys, who speak about as much English as I do French, take me with them to a few beaches. Sober friends join us for dinner in a crazy array of languages: French, Russian, German, and, of course, Greek. So much laughter around the table, things that need no translation.

On the night when I turn 100 days sober, John rides me on the back of his scooter to an AA meeting, through the warm, sunset-tinted streets and hosed down, closing market. Maybe drinking is not the world's only adventure, I think. At the meeting, an older Finnish woman shares in broken English about her attempt to "make suicide," with vodka and pills; again I feel that odd swelling in my heart. What's happening in there? Why am I hugging these strangers?

Three days later, with big hugs from all, I leave to continue my adventures. Matala almost leads to romance; Santorini is a dream come true. But by the time I reach the island of Paros, I'm travel weary. I circle the entire island on a moped, but somehow I'm too lonely to enjoy it. I can tell I'm in trouble. I stop at multiple phone booths along the way, calling the AA hotline for Paros, but no one picks up.

Discouraged, I begin to feel grim, abandoned, sorry for myself. The clouds thicken and the wind picks up. I've already bought an "island hopper" ticket to leave Paros that afternoon, but now the waves are too high for the hydrofoil. The delay will be two hours, so I sit down at a dockside bar and get a Sprite.

I could order a beer.

No one would ever know.

Literally everyone around me is drinking. I'm an adult. I can make my own decisions. *Why* do I want to be sober, again?

Somehow, remembering the oracle, I pray: "Goddess, be with me."

Of course, nothing happens. Rather, things get *worse*. Two obnoxiously loud guys take the table right behind mine. They laugh and gab in classically gay tones.

The wind gusts. Now I'm cold. A shot of Jack would warm me right up! I wonder if they have Jägermeister.

Turn around and talk to those guys.

What?! Where did *that* come from? Those gay guys? I don't even know what they look like!

Turn around and introduce yourself.

Sorry. That's too embarrassing and just plain stupid.

Do it now. SPEAK TO THEM.

It won't let up. Just like with *Call Allie!* but closer together. *Now. Now. Speak to them.* Man, I can't even think!

Okayyyyy. Fine. You win.

I twist around in my chair to see two guys in their mid-thirties. One is overweight with glasses and a fringe of curly dark hair under his bald pate, the other one fit, tan, and blond with all-American good looks.

"Excuse me. Are you two friends of Dorothy?"

That was me. That's what I just said. Because I'm an idiot. There's a pause.

"Are we... what?" inquires the blond.

"Friends of *Dorothy*," I say with more emphasis, meaning *The Wizard of Oz,* meaning the iconic movie loved by gays, meaning "are you guys queer?" It's a stretch, I realize. Still, my buzzed hair and men's plaid shorts must tip them off, because they swap glances and smirk.

The blond is curious. "You mean, like ...and Toto?"

I nod, and he laughs outright.

"Sure we are!"

He invites me please to join them, so I just rotate my chair. There's a nearly empty glass of beer right in front of me now, the chubby guy's, so close I can smell it. Great idea, Mr. *SPEAK TO THEM!* How's this gonna help?

A waitress comes around. The pudgy guy asks for another beer, but the blond orders "another Sprite" – and so do I. Something about this overlap emboldens me to confess I recently quit drinking.

The blond perks up. "John, alcoholic!" he beams. "Eleven years sober!" He offers his hand and we shake. John, I find out, is a mainstay of Alcoholic Anonymous on Paros, one of "about seven" full-time residents who meet regularly. They also trade off covering the AA phone number – that hotline I was calling. "You mean Jessica didn't pick up *all day*? That's terrible!" His face shows he means it. "I'll pitch her some shit about *that*," he vows, mostly to himself.

A loudspeaker announces the boat delay is now extended to four hours, so John volunteers to show both of us – me and Michael – around town. He's an artist, it turns out, another painter. In fact he teaches art at a beautiful studio he'd love to show us. It's upstairs in an old convent.

I've heard of such an art school, so I dare to ask him, does he by chance know my friend Dorothy? Not the one from Oz. A Dorothy who studied art on Paros years ago. She used to send me post cards of... a beautiful convent.

"You mean Dorbie?! That's so cool! Yes, she was my student!"

He knows both Dorbie *and* Dorothy! We laugh.

Now John and I have so much to talk about, we can't shut up. Poor Michael's the odd man out. John's apartment, where he stops for his keys to the convent, is cute and tidy and crammed with art – both finished and in progress. The convent has that chalky, mineral smell of old stone construction. We pass under archways and climb to the studio where Dorbie took lessons – its wooden floor spattered with paint, tall, arched windows overlooking the town with the sea beyond it. Sun breaks through the clouds and angles in shafts to illuminate the room's space.

Finally, as 6:00 approaches, the sun comes out for real. We're waiting under graceful Eucalyptus trees near the port. The Aegean is calm. I remark on what a lucky coincidence it was to have run into John.

"Luck?" He furrows his brows and shakes his head. "Louisa, how often do you turn around and ask total strangers if they're, they're – what was it? – 'friends of Dorothy'?"

"Well. Never."

I can't tell him about the voice.

"And what are the chances of one of them being sober?"

"I guess.... pretty slim."

"Do you have any idea how many people are on this island? In the summers, ten thousand, twelve thousand. Out of all those fucking people, *five* of us, really, hold down AA. Me and a couple of friends, and I'm the only one here in town. You were feeling close to a drink. *Why* should I sit down right behind you? It's crazy! I never go to that place! I only went today because some friends asked me to meet Michael!"

Before Michael and I get on the boat, John looks me in the eye. "Louisa: a miracle is nothing short of miraculous," he says. "Don't be afraid to *see* it."

What I Think Now:

Not until years after I'd returned from Greece did I fully realize how crucial this experience was to fix my faith and sobriety in place such that I've not relapsed in 28 years. For many normal drinkers, to understand the compulsion of an alcoholic drinker is difficult, if not impossible. But think of those you know who have died or are dying of alcoholism. Do they *choose* to die, to be rotted away ftom the inside? It's not a matter of reason, of resolve, of discipline, of really meaning it, of kicking habits or forming new ones. It's a matter of sanity versus insanity. If an alcoholic takes a drink – even one little glass of beer – a switch is thrown in their mind, not in the frontal lobe, but in the amygdala, the lizard brain, the most primitive part of our limbic system that lights up this notion like neon: "A Drink Is a Good Idea!"

Nothing can challenge it. And another drink is an even better idea. Hence the saying, one is too many and a thousand not enough.

I didn't understand this when I left for Greece. I felt unsure about what was going on in my life: drinking was such a mainstay and sobriety such a new contortion. I'd always assumed that sober people were boring, glum, conformist, and uncreative, while drinkers were passionate, inspired, and alive with art and creativity. I'd relinquished drinking, but I was still romanticizing the passion and creativity I connected with it.

This trip introduced me to sober living as a beautiful thing.

My angel went to some trouble to connect me with Allie. I owed her an amends, and I made it. Drinking had been key to our college relationship, but she didn't drink anymore. Here I was able to sit down face to face and have a conversation with her more sincere than any we'd ever had – about how alcoholism was killing her mother. Here was Allie, whose intellect I so admired, saying this meeting was the work of a higher power.

In my few weeks sober, I'd always thought of myself as going to meetings to *get* support rather than to give. Planting my flight attendant across from me, she who had seemed so brisk and well-coiffed in flight now a mess of self-loathing emotion, taught me the other half of the equation. As the Saint Francis prayer words it,

> *Lord, grant that I may seek rather*
> *to comfort, than to be comforted;*
> *to understand, than to be understood;*
> *to love, than to be loved.*

Those words may seem hokey when we read them, but when we *live* them, they're anything but. In being useful to another, in helping to heal what is broken, we experience a sense of fulfillment, of doing exactly what we're here on Earth to do. I didn't think of it that way. Eating ice cream with my flight attendant, Kathleen, at that hillside restaurant in breezy Athens sunset, seeing her laugh and knowing I, Louisa, had offered her support so key to that happiness – all I knew was it felt really, really good.

The Belgian waffle who tried to entrap me in his room – he liked to drink. In fact, it was the several cocktails he downed on deck that emboldened him to try and shut the door. My response to anger had always been drinking. I was sooooo close! Yet as soon as I made the choice to go against my compulsion and follow my angel's guidance, I opened a portal to fantastically divine outcomes.

Travis led me to Bruce, and Bruce to his AA village and the idyllic home of an artist – the paint literally wet on his hands and nose, flowers literally burgeoning in his garden, Mozart literally flowing from his tape deck and kittens and goat stew and neighbors leaning in the Flintstones window – I'd landed in a Renaissance painting, in a world of all things Louisa deemed beautiful. Rather than inviting me for a single dinner and turning me out in the world, this AA village understood that I needed babysitting, so they kept me safe until they felt I was restored.

On the island of Paros, my angel asked me to do something ludicrous. I followed his guidance and, again, was ushered to safety, *again* with an artist, a creative and masterful painter, shown the very room I'd been jealous about when I read Dorbie's post cards years before. Fellow writers intimidated me, but painters inspired. Egnacio knew this.

For the rest of that trip, I talked to my angel in my mind.

How could I say now sober people were boring, glum, and uncreative? By the end of that trip, I'd reached a level of peace and contentment beyond anything a drink could mimic. I'd learned I could feel safe, relaxed, and at peace in the world while completely awake and alert. Everything's okay because, in essence, god's got it covered. I began to understand that.

Chapter 6: Help her Cross!

What I Thought Then:
I live in Seattle now, and I have a secret. There's this voice who talks to me sometimes. While it's doing it, I'm completely certain it's not me, not my thoughts, not my ideas. But afterwards, I always manage to talk myself out of that. I ask, "How do you know it wasn't your thoughts? Maybe it's your conscience. Maybe it's your subconscious." I *know* it's a distinct voice, but part of me is determined to deny that can be true, so I worry I might be crazy. Schizophrenic. Psychotic. Stuff like that.

At 37, I am still a hollow faker of selfhood. I know only acting, how to answer perceived expectations by donning various behavioral costumes. Who I am and what I feel right now – more than ever, these are mysteries to me. Fourteen years of drinking away feelings will do that to a person. It retards our emotional growth because the answer to every problem is the same: get numb.

I move into an old rental home on Beacon Hill with my partner, who soon sells her motorcycle. We bring in two male housemates, both of them regulars at a "solution-based" AA meeting called Drunks R Us. My partner and I tentatively attend. Young, heavily tattooed and pierced people in this meeting talk a lot about god. God, god, god. But they mix it with fuckin' goddamn fucks and shit like that. It's cool spirituality.

"I'm so fucked without God and sobriety and shit."

There we meet a handsome young recovered addict named Terry who comes by our house sometimes, though Kelsey, my coyote mix, cannot abide him. Normally a shy girl, she barks and lunges at him savagely no matter how much we yell and spank her, no matter how many treats Terry offers her. Terry agrees to reroof our rental house. He's gonna hire some guys to strip it down to the rafters. Our landlord pays him $7,000 up front for supplies and helper wages, all of which he takes with him when he skips town.

Coyotes, I tell ya! They know stuff! Terry did *not* have goodness. I privately wonder whether Kelsey hears a voice as well.

In 1997, I've been sober two years when I hear from my sister Adelyn that the breast cancer relapse she discovered a few years back has now metastasized not only in her bones but in her liver. Doctors have informed her she has about three months to live. She asks me to pass on the news to our parents as she can't tell them herself.

On the phone, I'm at a loss for words. "What I really hope," she confides in a wavering voice that wanders between confession and grief, "is to die of a hemorrhage. That's the quickest way, I've heard, and the least painful. Cancer throws together lots of blood vessel systems that are badly made, so they can just *break*, and then you go. I'd rather die that way than linger on in pain."

What's she *saying*? How do I r*espond*? I don't know who to be in this situation, a misfortune beyond anything I have the strength, honesty, or courage to navigate. I've never imagined anything like this happening in our family. I grope for some landmark of precedent but find nothing.

The shameful truth is that, for me, this talk of dying, of mortality, of having only so long "left to live" feels intensely awkward, somehow embarrassing. I know my response is self-centered in the extreme, and I'm deeply ashamed of it, but there it is! What I want most is for my older sister to remain the powerful, invincible, wrathful tyrant she was when I was little and to please insult me as an inferior the way she would before she became ill – claiming my lesbian relationship was not meaningful in her God's eyes, implying I'm stupid and superficial. That stuff I know how to respond to, how to play my role in the family. This new role thrust upon me, sister to a dying sibling, is uncharted territory.

So I book a flight to Washington DC. I'll go as soon as the college course I'm teaching wraps up, more than a month away. I continue to post sticky notes around the house that advise, "Call Adelyn!" but continue to hardly ever do so. It's just too scary. I should, but I can't.

One day, everything changes. Adelyn's hip, disintegrated for months by cancer the doctors have misdiagnosed as arthritis, breaks off in the socket, and for dubious reasons she's given a hip replacement.

Now her voice over the phone is meandering, faint, and childlike. She's in a hospital cot in her living room. "People think I can't hear what they're saying when I'm on morphine," she tells me, indignant. "But I *can*. I hear every word. They talk as if I'm not even here!" And then she veers off on another tangent related in ways only she can perceive, with me trailing after and struggling still, pathetically, to interject witty banter.

Soon she's been taken by ambulance to a hospital ICU. Swelling from infection has split her hip incision. Her body can't fight both cancer and infection for more than two weeks, as her doctor calls to tell us. I fly out the next day, leaving an ill-equipped substitute to cover my Modernism course.

The family gathers at Adelyn's home, where my heart finally breaks. Her children are adorable. Everywhere I see her losing battle to keep house, impossible as she grew weaker. Her Texan husband, it appears, has scarcely pitched in. The toys everywhere, children's books, and a training potty transform my view of her. She's a mama, gentle and adoring, as I should have gathered from all the pictures she used to send me enclosed in her letters, but I somehow couldn't banish my childhood fears of her. Now I curse myself for having been too chickenshit, too enmeshed in my own stuff to have flown out when she needed me, long before my teaching quarter even began.

We as a family gather around her bed in the ICU. It's a shock. I can scarcely recognize her. One can see her skull – the indentations at the temples, hollows around her once brilliant blue eyes, which stand out oddly globe-like. Those eyes now dance over all of us lovingly, the dysfunctional family encircling her, and her voice quavers with delight and apology that we've all traveled so far just for her – my parents having cut short their three-week fabulous vacation in Australia (did I mention being dysfunctional?). They landed in Sydney only to turn around and fly back.

My younger sister stays while Adelyn is transferred to a standard room, the rest of us returning to her house, where my father drinks to excess, as others deem only natural.

That night, my brother and I return to the hospital to keep watch. I secretly and shamefully feel I'm earning virtue points, somehow, by sacrificing a night's sleep, but at the same time, doing this feels right. The virtue part feels like ego static, similar to mental chatter one can't control, but the "right" feeling is weird. It's like a deep keel, an approbation from I don't know where. The plan is that Adelyn's husband will bring her children to see her the next morning to.... None of us can bring ourselves to use the phrase "say goodbye."

My younger sister, wrapping up her shift, has told me that earlier today Adelyn called out in a desperate wail, "I want my life back!" and "Dying of cancer at forty-one is the ultimate put-down!" She appears to sleep now as my brother and I sit down in vinyl chairs on either side of the bed for what will prove a long, difficult night.

Every time Adelyn's consciousness resurfaces, she cries out for her children, flinging her arms up. She *must* get to them! She must! Dying as she is, she forces her body to sit up and attempts to clamber from the bed, oblivious to the IVs and catheter tethering her. My brother and I have to physically press her back down, squashing her determination, assuring her as best we can that she'll see them soon, first thing in the morning, they'll be here, they'll visit. It's beyond heart-breaking. Adelyn refuses to comply until she grows too faint to resist, sinking back again, her sighs fluttering with anguish. Her eyelids close. My brother and I exchange glances as her words trail off into mutters, then silence, and we each sit back down.

Now she calls out for a priest. "Father! Father!" She's a devout Catholic, born again in her teens in rebellion against our dad. Again, my brother and I attempt to calm her with assurances that a priest will be on duty in the morning. She settles back, defeated, only to remember her children and start all over again.

Finally, thank god, she seems to sleep. My brother and I kill the light and slump in our respective chairs, I on her right side and he on her left. We try to doze. After a few hours, I've sunk into a pleasant, dreamy state when something arrives to wake me.

My eyes open. The clock reads 4:00 a.m. The first thing I see is that almost nothing has accumulated in urine bag attached to her bed. Her body's shutting down. At the same time, but from a wholly different part of my consciousness, comes something potent with meaning, something I'm trying to identify.

What is this excitement stirring inside me and infusing the room? Something's gearing up, something major, gathering power like huge turbines slowly accelerating, immense jet engines engaging prior to take-off. Something incredibly wonderful – but what?

I know: the Light is approaching. The same Light, the one that subsumed me fifteen years ago with all its tremendous bliss and love, it's— where?

Seeping through the base of the window into the room like a slow mist.

Impossible. Ridiculous. Nothing's there. Just an ordinary hospital room at 4:00 a.m.

I close my eyes, determined to sleep. But the fog, the strange fog – it's coming in, and it's joyful. The time is now. The time is now.

Nonsense. The doctors gave her two weeks to live!

But what are these nitpicking thoughts of human doctors next to the power, the reality of what's unfolding? As if the window were open a crack at the bottom, although it's not even designed to do that, light is seeping across that threshold, over the window sill, then dropping down, skimming across just above the floor like a fog rolling in from the ocean. It gathers, pooling, swirling above my sister's body. Within it are innumerable sparks of brightness. Tiny lights. Zillions of them.

To the part of me that recognizes it, the Light brings joyful anticipation. It's coming for my sister! Countless tiny points of light swirl above her, a galaxy with its center just above her stomach. My spirit perceives that each light is *someone* – a spirit, a being. Angels, ancestors, countless divine beings of light who know my sister far better than I do or anyone else does, loving her better than anyone here on Earth. They're gearing up to bring her home.

I know this. I know it in my core, with a clarity deeper than thought.

Earlier yesterday, I tried to apologize to Adelyn for the lousy job I'd done as both a sister and aunt, but she stopped me with the single word "Don't." This morning, though, when I spoke on the phone with my sponsor, she urged me, "Tell her everything. Hold nothing back."

Now those remembered words "tell her everything" seem to expand, to reference far more than my thoughts or emotions: *Tell her everything you know from the other side.*

Something's blocked; something needs to shift, and I'm the one able to help. Pain weighs on Adelyn's heart. "The ultimate put-down," she'd said, but by whom? God? All the wounds from her childhood, times she was bullied, our mother's endless nagging about her weight, rejections, inadequacies, self-loathing – they're taunting her now, pointing to death as proof she's not loved. But those voices are *wrong*. Adelyn needs to know this, to cast aside her burden of victimhood and embrace love.

These thoughts – they're not coming from me. The voice has been silent for almost two years. I've all but managed to explain it away as subconscious undercurrents. That was serendipity in Greece, all of it. And luck. Lots of luck.

Help her to cross, the voice urges me now – and I recognize it as the same, always the same voice, that same feeling, same energetic cadence. It highlights Adelyn's fear, her painful doubts about god's love, and conveys that they're preventing her from crossing to the other side.

Help her! You've crossed! You can tell her.

I know exactly what the voice wants. I can share with Adelyn that she has nothing to fear or grieve, that dying is every bit as wonderful an experience as birth. But I can't! This is crazy shit! What, I'm supposed to go tell her some cliché like "heaven is real"? Besides, she's not conscious – I'd be talking to myself!

The voice highlights words from her phone call weeks ago: "I hear every word…" Touché, voice, I think. But still I resist. I'm in public. I can't go obeying my invisible voice.

Do it NOW! the voice urges again and again. I keep willing myself to shut it out, but it's right back in my mind's centerstage, louder than ever: *Do it NOW! NOW!*

But... what will I say? How can I describe the Light?

Only begin. Now. Right now.

Okay, I sigh, resigned. I'll do it.

I stand up, cross to her bed, and kneel by her head.

I take her hand and begin in a murmur close by her ear.

"You've had a wonderful life," I tell her, and from here, like silks from a magician's sleeve, the words keep flowing. Everything she's done, I say, she's done beautifully. She brought beauty into the world through her love of music. Her amazing intellect, she used it so well. She created three beautiful children and gave them a beautiful, love-filled home. And here, remembering her faith, I know what I'm to say:

"Jesus sees all you've done, and he's proud of you. But now," new ideas come forward, "your body doesn't work anymore. It's broken, and nothing in the world can fix it, so Jesus will bring you home. His love will be all around you, warm like sunlight but all through you, so much love!" I can almost feel it now with a joy that fills my voice. "You'll be in light that's so warm and bright, surrounded by love. Oh, and you'll feel so safe and loved, Adelyn! *Everything* will turn to love! Jesus loves you *so* much! You're his child, and he loves you more than words can tell. I love you. We all love you."

With that, my words cease as suddenly as they began. I linger a bit in case there's more, but I can sense I've done what was needed, awakened some spark in Adelyn that will kindle on its own. What comes next is between her and the galaxy of a million sparks. They are in concert.

I sit down again in the vinyl chair. My brother, who's awoken at some point, glances owl-like from me to his clearly unconscious sister. We sit in silence.

Twenty minutes later, Adelyn sits bolt upright, letting out a brief cry of pain. I see something I never dreamed possible: blood is spurting from her nose as if from a spigot. It sprays in sync with her pulse. The sight is utterly terrifying.

My brother and I full-on panic. Gone are all thoughts of the light. We dash out in the hall crying, "Help! Help us, please!" I run to the empty nurses' station and back, terrified both at the shock of what I saw and my utter helplessness. By the time a nurse steps into the room, the blood has stopped and Adelyn's body lies limp.

"Mrs. Trevor!" the nurse brays into her face, getting her name wrong. "Mrs. Trevor!" She slaps rapidly at Adelyn's hand. Me, I want to club the bitch. While she's fetching a doctor, my brother grabs the bedside phone and tries frantically to phone Adelyn's husband, but without success. He dials again and again. We yell at each other. We yell at the phone. Adelyn remains still.

Finally, into the room walks a pretty, pristine little doctor who applies her stethoscope. "She's hemorrhaged," she informs us curtly. "Her heart's still beating, but it'll stop once it runs out of oxygen." Folding her stethoscope, she steps back neatly.

We all stare at Adelyn's dying form on the bed. No one does anything. Rage howls in my chest that no one's even *trying* to save her! I understand there's no hope and yet I want to grab that doctor's skinny little neck and throttle her for that way she said, "it'll stop."

But the next moment, something – abruptly and completely – erases my rage and simply *replaces* it with peace and wellbeing. It's like someone turned a roaring locomotive, with just the touch of a wand, into a spring duckling.

"All is well," fills my mind. But it's not the same voice; this one's coming from elsewhere. I now become aware – or I should say *consciously* aware, because the second voice has been competing with panic for some time – of Adelyn. Her essence is hovering overhead, her energy, her presence, looking down on the room's activities. What I mean is, throughout the entire fiasco of my brother and me screaming for help, running around and trying to dial phone, I had stereo perception, a bit like looking through a spyglass without closing the other eye. My peripheral awareness sensed Adelyn's spirit trying to soothe us.

She was telling us not to be afraid, that she was fine, she was wonderful! – but I didn't hear her until now.

Adelyn's love has a specific quality, a specific pitch or flavor I'd recognize anywhere. I felt it whenever she was around what she loved, during the times I helped her cook or those awkward moments of Christmas or birthdays when we hugged, or even when she spoke about her various crushes and boyfriends. Most recently, I've felt it in her powerful love for her children, that vibration of Adelyn-love charging the space around her. Now I feel it, potent, distinctive, and communicative, coming from… from…. *above* us, somewhere near the ceiling. It's Adelyn-love, loving not only my brother and me but also the prim little doctor and the braying nurse. She loves *all* of us, everything. She *is* love.

Her happiness, her light continues to fill me. All dark emotions evaporate in brightness and I'm filled with a joy so brilliant it's all I can do to conceal it – which I *must*, because nothing could be less okay. Death in our culture is a tragic, horrible, cruel fate. What can I do with all this love? It's humming in my every cell, so wonderful, so amazingly bright!

Can light be in cells? I wonder. Aren't cells physical? So how is it *in* them right now? I feel every cell vibrating, cells in my legs, cells in my stomach. It feels awesome! I can't remember ever being so sure that everything is wonderful, everything is peace and goodness, sitting not ten feet from the empty shell my sister has just vacated.

I recall my despair when I lost the light – *you cannot stay* – when everything cut to darkness, the tantrum I threw. But Adelyn gets to stay! In fact, she gets to go *further* into the light, and I know she will. Already she knows a joy and intelligence and harmony greater than our brains can conceive – that far I did get. And she's giving me a little freebie.

She's telling me something, giving me a knowing, something exceptionally important to her. *Explain to Darius. Do not leave him out.* Her two-year-old, Darius – no one's going to unpack for him why she's gone. This matters! She will tell me what to say. Inwardly I agree to do whatever she asks. The sense of purpose I feel is similar to that keel of rightness I felt when I agreed to overnight at the hospital. It's as though I'm on a track, gliding, with goodness as my North Star.

Back at the house, I speak briefly with my younger sister in the front hall and then look for Darius. He's playing with small toys under the dining room table, a strain on his face as he purposefully ignores poignant wails of keening from the next room. I kneel to his right, sensing Adelyn just to my right, and deliver the words she gives me: "Darius, your Mama loves you *so* much, with all her heart. She wishes she could stay here and be your Mama; that's all she ever wanted to do! But she couldn't. Her body stopped working, and she can't be in the world anymore. She had to leave it. But she still loves you *so* much, Darius, so very, very much! And she'll love you, always, wherever you are."

He listens with a scowl of concentration, his eyes on a small white Storm Trooper he keeps bending back and forth.

"Can I hug you, Darius?" I ask.

He shakes his head no, eyes still down. He's angry, but I sense that he's in the midst of absorbing what's happened in his own two-year-old way. I've given him the puzzle pieces he needs.

Today I am no atheist. The voice is real and it used me to help Adelyn, who has transcended her body and is free. It feels like I'm daring to connect the dots in an ancient papyrus comic book, and they make a pattern as familiar as a crayoned house by a tree under a smiling sun. Archetypal, cliché, hackneyed, and yet it's real. It's real. It's real.

But I also know never to speak of these occurrences to anyone, as they'd only hear me twisting a devastating, painful tragedy into something about *me*. I also know I won't be able to sustain this connect-the-dots image going forward because it conflicts with the reality by which I've tacitly agreed to live. It's today's experience versus every fact I was ever taught by every figure I ever respected. Today doesn't stand a chance.

At the funeral, despite everything, grief overwhelms me. Even if Adelyn is in the light, she's been taken from us here: I'll never see her face or hear her voice again, and the loss is too awful, too much to comprehend. I can't remember a time I cried this hard. Dirt falls on her coffin. The grave is a few miles from the family's rental house under a cherry tree in bloom. Despite her tremendous scholarly accomplishments (having permanently revised Western history's account of written music), all she wanted engraved on her tombstone, beneath her name and dates, was the single word, *Mama*.

What I Think Now:

The first time I told my story at Seattle IANDS, when I got to the part about my sense of Adelyn hovering somewhere near the ceiling, I faltered with embarrassment and apologized, "I know it sounds like some corny movie or TV scene, but that's where her energy was coming from."

Seattle IANDS' founder, Kimberly Clark Sharp, was moderating. She motioned me to pause and turned to the audience. "How many people here have also sensed ceiling hoverers?" she asked. To my surprise, perhaps half a dozen of the sixty attendees raised their hands. "And how many have themselves hovered?" A different set of people raised theirs. Turning back to me, she explained with perfect simplicity, "We hover near the ceiling. That's just what we do."

She was right! In the years since, I myself have interviewed several "ceiling hoverers," NDErs who saw their body in an OBE. Here are a few excerpts:

> "And I realized, 'Oh my gosh! They're giving me a *choice* to go back...' I look down and the bed's re-eally far away, and there's this scrawny, bald, little gray body on it, hooked up to oxygen – just barely making a ripple. So I was kinda like, 'Hunh! Really?' Because it's so peaceful where I am, surrounded by love and in this amazing presence." (Maureen B.)

> "The room had been cold, but now I felt this warm air blowing over me, through my crazy long hair, and I was lifted out of my body to an upper corner of the room, watching this team do CPR on my body. I thought, 'If that's me down there, who am I?' A presence beside me responded in my consciousness – to me it was feminine. She said, 'José, your body's like a car

with a million miles on it. We can't fix it, so you need to say goodbye.'" (José H.)

"All of a sudden, I could see! I was looking at all the faces around me, the medical people working on me. I rose a little higher, thinking I was just trying to get a better look, but then I realized my spirit was moving without my body. I purposefully looked straight down, and there was my body! That was a jolt! It was blue and lifeless. When the doctor drew out the arterial blood, she said to all of them, 'Her blood is black.' I could feel the energy of every person in that room just as clearly as I could see their faces. Everyone gave up. Nobody immediately stopped what they were doing, but there was sadness, a disappointment and hopelessness in the room." (Kris W.)

"I found myself looking down on my body on the operating table surrounded by hospital staff. I was so baffled! 'How can I be in two places at once?' I wanted to tell the medical staff there was really no need for all their concern. I was fine! I just needed, I thought, a few answers about the two bodies." (Norma E.)

"I started to hear my girlfriend's voice, sounding upset. I was able to look down to see her and her stepmother kneeling with this lump or blob between them on the beach. For a moment, I thought I was looking down from the

> loft of the house where we'd been staying and they were in the living room below." (John B.)

Today I know hovering abounds for OBErs, and if the OBE happens indoors, they hover near the ceiling. At the time when Adelyn left her body, though, I'd never heard such an account. I distinctly sensed she was above us, near the ceiling tiles, but I felt batty for knowing it, and later batty for saying it.

Less commonly noted is the swirl of sparks pooling above a body in preparation for the crossover. In September 2012, I gave a bookstore reading from my addiction memoir, during which I read this part of my story. Most of the audience was made up of people who knew me from AA. But I didn't yet know the man who approached me afterwards to tell me that he, too, had undergone an NDE from necrotizing fasciitis, a.k.a. flesh-eating disease, nine years earlier. He'd picked it up while "slamming" meth amphetamines intervenously. David R. was thrilled by my account of the "fog" – the mist of swirling of points of light I'd sensed pooling and circling above my sister's body. He knew exactly the phenomenon I was describing because he, too, had seen it.

I recently interviewed David about his experience:

> "About a week later I had a dream and I told my mother, 'I'm going to die today – I know it.' She assured me it wasn't my time. But later that day, while I was lying in horrific, unstoppable pain, I began to see this misty, white, swirly kind of fog moving around the room. It had a million sparkly lights inside it, and I watched it kind of wind its way toward me. All of a sudden, it

swooped behind me and I felt a pull upward on the back of my neck to lift me. I was sitting up in bed, but my body was still lying behind me.

"All at once, this black evil came pouring out my mouth like smoke, like disease, like filth, just like the flies in *The Green Mile*. It was all the addiction, the death, the terror. After that, I had no pain for the first time in my life. I felt great. A voice asked me, 'David, what are you going to do? Are you going to live, or are you going to die?'

"I looked over at my mother watching her son die – the clappers, the resuscitation efforts – and for the first time – I... I'm sorry – I realized she'd given me life, and that I was disrespecting it. I felt enormous compassion for her. She was so kind!

"In that moment, I understood that for years and years, all my priorities had been backward. Out of all my supposed 'friends,' the only ones at my side were my mother and sister – because they *loved* me. It was such a profound moment! I couldn't hurt them by leaving, so I chose to stay. Then, back into my body I went! And there was that horrific pain again, absolutely excruciating. But I now understood: I was *not* a victim. I'd done this to myself."

One of only three people to survive this virulent strain of flesh-eating bacteria, David redefined his life after this experience. He climbed Mount Rainier – twice! – which is how

I came to know him, moved to Bali, and used funds from his design business to feed thousands during the pandemic.

The "sparkles" in the fog, he agrees, were angels and ancestors who pulled him from his body just far enough to purge him of whatever demons possessed him. Cleansed of those, he perceived the truth, that the power of love is paramount.

As for the message Adelyn wanted me to send to Darius, I feel confident she could communicate with me easily in those moments just after her crossing, channeling through me to Darius, much as Egnacio had channeled through me to her when I knelt by her bed.

One question remains for me today: If my sister was going to find her way to heaven anyway, why was Egnacio so urgent? Why did he keep stressing, with increasing urgency, *NOW!* – as though time mattered?

It makes me wonder about the nature of dark, negative, self-destructive thoughts that can block us from god's love. David's had to be vomited out. Perhaps darkness can gather momentum if allowed to prevail for too long. Perhaps as long as she was *choosing*, in the intense grief of losing what she loved on Earth, to conceive of God as bullying, the universe could not, because of free will, receive her. Egnacio may have been urging me to rekindle her faith swiftly so that she could open her heart and enable the upload her countless ancestors – the sparks – were ready to initiate.

That's all just me guessing. I don't know... yet.

* * *

For those who've experienced the like, here's a brief note on the painful friction of being woo-woo in a materialist culture. I'm not saying, "Wahh! Call me a wambulance!" I'm just saying, it's lonely and confusing to sense and know what others consider ridiculous.

When I first came back to Adelyn's house, when I first walked in the door and before I'd even approached Darius, I was aglow with the light, floating in amazement, and recalling the moment when I'd said, "Okay, I'll do it." I understood that in that moment, I'd turned *against* consensual reality, materialist science, everything I'd ever been taught by humans. I had no confidants then – it was just me and Egnacio, known to me then as only "the voice." When I'd dared to trust that he was real, that the Light and "galaxy" of sparks pooling above my sister was real, and that these countless spirits knew far more of what was occurring than any human doctors did – in that moment I'd had the lonely courage to align my *actions* with the spirit world and carry out what Egnacio was urging me to do as a physical being my sister could physically hear.

When my younger sister greeted us at the door, I longed to share what I so strongly felt. But no one in my life knew I experienced Weird Things! As far as everyone was concerned, I'd had some sort of hallucination long ago from cocaine overdose, and that was the end of it. So I couldn't catch her up that this voice spoke inside my consciousness. I couldn't say, this morning I dared to *act* on what the voice told me, as I did two years before in Greece, and the voice was right again! I couldn't explain how I'd felt Adelyn's love and joy spilling over from the other side and that maybe, just maybe, I'd helped her cross – which I intuited to be among major deeds of my life.

So, unable to say any of that but filled to the brim with feeling, I said only, "I was so brave" or maybe "so strong!" I don't recall which, because my mind was on Darius. But those words, in light of my younger sister's reality that I'd basically sat around while our older sister died an incredibly horrible death from cancer, convinced my younger sister that I was an incorrigible narcissist. Years later, in an emailed bullet list of reasons I was a terrible person, she cited it near the top, and only then did I remember what I'd said in the front hall.

Today, happily, my sister accepts that I experience Weird Things that I believe come from the spirit realm, and though she's not a hundred percent onboard, we've healed our relationship – which means the world to me.

I did for some reason try to share what happened that day with my family at a dinner about five or six years later, and I got an email about how I "glowingly described her death in a way that made my blood run cold." So I shut up about it.

Years later, when my addiction memoir first went up online, my brother insisted Adelyn's hemorrhage in the hospital had been bloodless. He accused me of adding a "gore" element to sell more books, owing to my being a terrible person. I know not only what I saw, what terrified me at the time, but also what I strongly feared in the moments after the nurse and doctor arrived – that more blood might spill if her body were moved at all.

Today, happily, my brother and I have a decent working relationship and, despite his certainty that I'm a deluded, half-baked wacko, I'm pretty sure he doesn't believe I'm a terrible person.

As anyone knows who has experienced spirit energies or crossed to the other side, families are the toughest audience to share with, because they think they know us best, though they base their knowledge on who we were as children. Whether it's in the name of science or religion that they decry our experience, sharing with family is no picnic.

Chapter 7: Don't Go!

What I Thought Then:

It's about 11:00 in Seattle on a Sunday night, 1999. I exit the freeway northbound at Mercer Street near downtown and come to a stop at the red light. I'm waiting to cross Fairview Ave. N., zero traffic in sight.

The light turns green. At the same moment, something tells me, *Don't Go!*

What a dumb thought! I'll ignore it.

DON'T GO!

I realize it's not a thought; it's that voice again. Even though I've not heard it since Adelyn's crossing two years before, I'm learning to recognize it faster, to distinguish it as "the voice." Tonight I'm getting that feeling when you think there's someone in the back seat, but there's not.

DON'T GO!

Green means Go, but this voice has never been wrong and I can tell how emphatic it is. Should I obey?

The rearview mirror shows no cars behind me. No one would care if I just sat here a bit. Nobody would know about it except me and the voice.

I obey. Against every reflex, I keep my foot on the brake and watch the light shine green for a full second, not going. Another second, still not going.

This is crazy! I ask the voice, How *long* don't go?!

WHOOSH!!! Like a rocket fired from behind a building to my left, a white sedan streaks down Fairview, a silent missile at

100mph. It shoots through the intersection exactly where I would have been.

I'm dumbfounded.

For one thing, I've never seen anything move so fast, and without sound, so unlike the movies with all their sound effects. An instinctive sense of catastrophe flushes in my gut – except that I'm okay. I'm sitting right here in my car – not out in the intersection where I'd have normally been.

You saved my life, I think to the voice. I falter, awkward in this new relationship, but venture to say out loud, "Thank you!"

Am I really sitting in my car *talking* to an invisible voice? You bet your ass! I'm not *killed* because of this thing!

Nothing happens. Even so, I don't move my foot from the brake for another couple of seconds. I'm too stunned, too afraid of danger from some car in pursuit or who knows what. Now I hear a police siren, joined shortly by a second, and then a third. A chorus of sirens. This entire experience has taken about twenty seconds.

A similar incident transpires a few months later when I'm behind the wheel of an ancient VW bug we recently bought from our mechanic. The front defogger works only in theory, the rear one not at all. It's downpouring, "a dark and stormy night," and I'm crossing the West Seattle bridge, needing to change lanes across the bus lane to reach to my far right exit lane. I have no way to see what's behind me, everything totally fogged up. I've got only about a half mile to get over, so I signal to merge into the bus lane.

Don't go!

How annoying. You, again? I think. You'll make me miss my exit!

DON'T GO!

I can't be listening to you! I need to get home.

DON'T GO!

I'm thinking fast. This voice has never been wrong, and last time, he saved my life. I should just suck it up and miss my exit.

Okay, fine! I huff.

But just as I switch off the turn signal – *WHOOSH!!* – a bus, a gigantic-seeming two-section one, blasts past me. The little bug is blown left and then – *WHOMP!!* – water floods my windshield like a tidal wave, so heavily that, for a few swipes of the toy-like wipers, I can see absolutely nothing.

"Holy shit! Holy shit! Holy shit!" is all I chant in toneless panic. A few more swipes of the little wipers and the red tail lights of the bus gleam in front of me, the words "OUT OF SERVICE" emblazoned on its back panel. Away it fades into the heavy rain.

My body's shaking, heart pounding, but even more strongly I feel shame at my initial bratty response. Shouldn't I know by now not to question this voice?

Okay, I get it! I burst out mentally. You're *real* and you *know* stuff, and for some reason you want me to stay alive – though I have no idea why. I'm upset, but thank you! I won't ever doubt you again!

Again, I speak out loud: "Thank you."

Even as I say this, however, I can feel my skeptical mind squirming, itching to come up with a way to dismiss what's happened. I'm making too much of what any normal person would shrug off as a close scrape. Blindly switching lanes is always a dumb idea, so I thought better of it. Why imagine the counter-thought to be a "voice"? Talk about making a big deal of a routine experience!

But the skeptic is not me. It's just a knee-jerk reaction in my thinking.

Say what you want, I tell it, I know the voice is real. How could it not be? Didn't it just grab my attention twice with DON'T GOs, totally out of the blue and counter to my plans? It's *somebody else*. I know what back and forth thinking feels like. I know what conflicted feelings feel like. I know what having a new idea feels like. This feels nothing like any of those. It feels like a *voice*. So shut up.

At the same time, I know from experience that my skeptic is a formidable opponent, armed with the clout of society at large. It's a mental conglomeration of all the societal conditioning I've absorbed over the course of my lifetime, humans being by nature both social and conformist. This conditioning persists in every waking moment, whereas my paranormal experiences are highly intermittent – every few years. So already I can anticipate that, sooner or later, I'll shove these divine warnings back into the shadows of my don't-think-about-it vault and resume being a normal person. Whatever that means.

What I Think Now:

I have no idea what it is that Egnacio wants me to accomplish, but clearly he sent me back to do *something* and he's not letting me screw that up yet again.

Every creature that lives is attended by spirits. That I know. Whether such spirits are a divine splinter of the same life (a split soul, as some call it) or an entirely different entity – that, I do not know. Maybe part of the snail is embodied while another part in touch with divine energies hovers outside it. Maybe I am a mortal splinter echo of Egnacio; maybe I'm a partial reincarnation of him; maybe he's my higher self. There's only one problem with those theories, though. Every time I've asked him, he's responded, *Nahhh...* It's an angelic *nahhh*, kind of like, dumb question. I've pestered him many times: What are you? Who are you to me? Was I your child? Have we ever been in love? Or are you just assigned to me, like Clarence in *It's a Wonderful Life*?

He responds with a mix of, You'll remember soon enough, and virtual head shaking. He calls me "Little one." He'll say something like, Little one, just be human! It's far too complicated for you to understand while stuffed in a tiny brain.

Every single person has spirits galore hovering about them, but we're generally deaf to them, as noted earlier. The more I've heard from Egnacio, the easier it becomes to recognize his voice. He's my proxy to god – my intermediary. But he gets loudest when I'm about to do something stupid.

One day after I'd been attending IANDS a few years, I made plans to visit a friend about ninety minutes away in Olympia. As I was getting ready to leave, Egnacio gave me a dark feeling about the freeway. It grew darker as I prepared to leave the house, until finally I stopped on the front steps of my house, afraid. Keys in hand, I asked, Should I *not* go? I listened. The dark feeling persisted. So I prayed, Please, Egnacio, can you protect me on this trip? Can you keep me safe? I love Jesseca and want to see her.

The darkness lifted a little. That's all.

I'm an idiot, of course. On the drive down, I was cranking tunes as the brilliant springtime sunshine came out, feeling awesome, so I forgot all about that dark feeling, all about my pause, my prayer, and Egnacio. The car started getting toasty, even with the windows down, and my car had no air conditioning. My fuzzy zip-up hoodie was making me sweat, so I decided to take it off as I drove – something many of us do when a passenger can assist with the wheel. Despite being alone, I was doing fine, going for it incrementally, when I tried to jerk my elbow back in the sleeve and at the same time jerked the steering wheel hard to the right. The car swerved hard right, scaring me. I overcorrected hard left, swerved out of my lane, and overcorrected again even *worse*, my arms hampered by the jacket – panicking, losing control at 70 mph.

Then, all of a sudden, the car straightened out.

It just quit pulling back and forth – I have no idea how. All was smooth sailing.

Clearly "the thing" had happened, what the dark foreboding had been about, but the outcome had been averted.

In multiple NDEs I've heard, people were shown an endlessly bifurcating paths of futures they might choose, decisions they might make. Crashing was in many of my future paths, but Egnacio was able to nudge me toward one where that didn't happen, perhaps with the help of my prayer.

Of course I thanked him and apologized and slobbered all over myself with remorse. I could feel Egnacio's patience, always patience, like a good parent with a toddler. He did acknowledge having fixed something for me, as if to say, As much as I love you, Little One, you can be kind of a handful at times.

I believe that when we ask, when we pray specifically and genuinely, we create an energy the spirits can work with. Not necessarily *carry out*, but work with. All genuine prayers emit energy. We unlock possibility.

Here are some examples from my interviews of prayers showing up on the other side.

> "I said, 'I do! I want to keep going!' So I started flying toward the light of God, and I got really excited because the light was love beyond words, pure joy, pure contentment. At the same time, I felt the prayers of my family – my aunt, grandmother, and mom and dad – like webs pulling me back toward my body, which was wayyy back there. I felt, 'No, no, no! You can't keep me back!' and I broke through their prayers." (Tricia B.)

> "There were figures, shadows, all facing me. The more I looked at them, the more my awareness zoomed in first on one then another. Each time, I could see them as an individual person. I knew, I could hear, I could feel that they were praying for me. I could *see* their prayers, and each prayer became the light of a candle flame." (Leena Z.)

> "I was still with my guide but now in a different, smaller room. He said, 'Look: these are the

prayers of the people who've been praying for you.' Off to one side, I saw all these prayers represented as black and white musical notes. I couldn't hear music, but I saw how the notes were linking to one another, rising up toward where we were... I could see my daughter's prayer that I not die linking itself to the other prayers. That's when my emotions from this life returned." (Karen T.)

"[In my life review] I could see instances when I'd prayed and the way each prayer had been answered. I was surprised to see how unaware I'd been when the answers had shown up. I could see that my prayers worked sometimes to my advantage and sometimes against me. Things I'd asked of God often became obstacles to the [deeper] objectives I'd set for my life." (Norma E.)

Prayer may explain this last rescue, but at the time when I was waiting at the stoplight or about to merge in the VW bug, prayer was nowhere on my radar. Prayer was still corny and embarrassing and I did it as little as possible – except if I was forced to meditate by a zealous AA sponsor or working the steps with a sponsee so that we prayed together. At this point in my life, I still wanted the Weird Things to stop happening and leave me alone so I could believe only societally approved ideas.

In other words, these rescues were purely Egnacio's doing. He has his reasons, and some day, when I get to rejoin him, I'll know them. Man, how we'll laugh!

Chapter 8: Spider Messenger, the Event that Finally Broke Me

What I Thought Then:

It's the spring of 2003. I'm almost 43 and my son is has just turned two.

Being a mom is tough – way tougher than I could ever have imagined. Turns out moms aren't moms. They're just ordinary people like me who find themselves with a baby to take care of. My motorcycleless partner has become someone I take care of, too. I've walked her to the Seattle Community College admissions office and helped her through the terror of signing up for classes with the GED she earned in jail. I've paid her tuition until she could start receiving scholarships, but even then I've continued to pay for rent, groceries, and transportation year after year. I've edited/rewritten all her college papers. Education has proven a rare exception to her classic addict pattern of constantly seizing on new fads and then abandoning them. A model codependent myself, I resentfully do 90% of the laundry, cleaning, fence building, and maintaining the yard. I cook dinners under the gun because otherwise she orders takeout.

But— when I birth this baby, our son through an anonymous donor, something shifts in me. I can't keep pouring all my energies into *her* needs; I must devote them to my boy.

I taught tech writing through my entire pregnancy, taking only three weeks off campus to teach remotely and give birth. That was so I could keep my medical insurance. It was exhausting, the whole thing. After the birth, I was always dashing to my office to pump during the mid-class break.

The deal my partner and I had was, as soon as she finished school, she'd find work and I could be a stay-at-home mom. But before she even graduated with her BA in history, she announced that she intended to get a PhD in History and become a professor. I said, fine, but you're going to do that through night school because it's your turn to support us.

She really, really disliked that boundary.

I watched her sulk through her graduation ceremony as I sat in the audience holding the baby and holding my ground. Eventually she found work as a paralegal at a bad-guy law firm. I'd written her resume and cover letter, and soon she was reluctantly helping horrid corporations defend themselves after irresponsibly maiming and killing innocent people. She hated it.

What a lucky break that recently an AA acquaintance, the wife of a big deal guy in the program, has heard her woes and said she might be able to hire her at the big law firm where she, the AA acquaintance, directs human resources. I've written a new resume and cover letter, and now we've landed the new, better job.

Really, I have zero time and energy to give a crap about whatever Weird Things used to happen. I mean, I know they've *happened*, crazy stuff, things I can't explain, but does that *really* mean there's no rational explanation for them? Am I *really* going to contradict the conventional wisdom of billions of people and over three centuries of post-Enlightenment science to say, "Yeah, maybe the world obeys Newtonian laws of physics for *you* guys, but *I* have a magic voice in my head that talks to me! *I* saw a ghost and knew the future and get warnings from that voice! Why? Because *I'm* special!"

Am I really gonna claim that? Not so much, no.

What do researchers say about the brain's filtering system? About how the human brain can process millions of bits of information every second, but our conscious attention can deal with 40 to 50 bits per second? What if therein lies the explanation for all my Weird Things? Let's say that my brain's information filter was damaged that time I died for a bit, so now on random occasions, information I don't recognize as known comes through – and I mistake it for a "voice"?

Something like that! Accessing information hitherto unretrieved within the brain. A cordoned off part of my brain. A freaking broken elevator in my brain! Basically *anything* but believing in paranormal shit.

Anything. Because I just can't go there.

Except when I'm desperate. Foxhole faith. Like after thirty-six hours in the birthing room when my son, with the umbilical cord wound twice around his neck, was pulled out by suction, his head a dark purple, and did not cry, made no sound for a few seconds, more seconds, more seconds... and I felt myself falling into darkness. I was plummeting into a black pit. I willed, *Nooo!* and somehow, like a Marvel superhero defying gravity, I felt my fall slow to a hover and I heard... first a bleat and then a cry. My son's cry.

But, oh, come on! Stop it! I was just scared out of my gourd the way every mom of a stunned newborn is, and maybe fainting, but then everything worked out – right? And of course after what happened to my brother's baby, I would create this "dark pit" narrative.

Silly me! Silly imagination! Life is just life.

But one night, I have this dream:

I'm visiting my brother and sister-in-law, sitting in their living room. On an end table is a house plant, some densely needled evergreen. And among its branches, we all become aware, lurks an absolutely enormous spider. The thing is gargantuan! I think, "How horrid. But this huge spider is here and not going away. If we don't deal with it right now, it can hide anywhere in this house. And yet it's too big to squash. Just way too much guts."

I ask someone to bring me a glass and, when they do, I manage to overcome my heebie-jeebies enough to somehow knock the spider in. But instead of righting itself, the spider lies there on its back, holding perfectly still in the bottom of the glass. As I peer down at it, I see on its belly an intricate pattern: interlocking triangles of beige, dark gray, and light gray. How wonderful! I'm moved in spite of myself – such a perfect geometric design! To think that every detail of this world, even something so lowly as a spider's belly, is created with such intricate artistry: diamonds of orderly precision!

I wake up, but the dream stays with me. While my partner gets ready for work, between warming a bottle and dressing our two-year-old, I tell her the dream and even try to describe the pattern on the spider's belly. That she's hardly listening is obvious. She's all excited about going to her new job.

Now it's later, around 10:00 that morning, and I'm running late to deliver some stupid activities binder – a three-ring notebook I never should have accepted – to a fellow mom in my son's toddler co-op. This business of being a mom is just too much! Why am I always harried, exhausted, and frantic compared to regular moms? Finally I've gotten everything together: diaper bag, snack bag, toys. I've hoisted my son onto my hip so I can also grab the stupid binder and scrape my keys off the counter when I see—

What the hell is THAT?!

In the next room, directly over my chair at the desktop computer, I see stuck to the ceiling something like a black marble, almost a black ping-pong ball. I take a step closer, peering with my forty-three-year-old eyes. Another step.

Can it be? Shit! It is!

It's an absolutely gigantic, monstrous spider with the legs drawn in! The thing's humongous! And I'm *terrified* of spiders – absolutely terrified. I've never seen one so absolutely tremendous, except that one at my brother's house. But, no – that was a dream. Still, what a weird coincidence! To dream of a huge spider last night and then see one this morning!

Now what?

I'm already running friggin' late. The normal mom who's expecting this binder is gonna judge me. The *last* thing I need is something like this! If I could just pretend I hadn't seen it and leave anyway – but no. The spider is here in the house. If I don't deal with it right now, it can hide anywhere.

Wait a second... I had those same *thoughts* in the dream. How does *that* happen? And what else is weird, why would a spider choose such an exposed spot to hang out, in plain view and smack-dab over the place where I sit at the computer? Why would it *do* that?

I'm staring.

I'm here for you. You know why.

My heart quickens. *Do* I know something? I seem to experience this moment at two levels. On the surface there's my frazzled toddler-mom who just wants this crap over with, and underneath is my deeper, calmer self who senses this exchange is profound. That part of me absorbs the message. Fate. Future. Choices. I can find *courage*.

Don't freak out, I coach my frantic self. In the dream you were brave. So you can be brave now.

To my son, sitting astride my hip, I say, "We can't leave just yet, honey. There's a great big spider Mama has to deal with."

"Big pydoo?" he echoes, turning his blond head.

I point with my keys hand, allowing time for his gaze to follow the line of my finger. With toddler gusto he affirms: "Big pydoo up high!"

I set him down, not taking my eyes off that... creature. I get a glass and post card and then, hardly able to believe what I'm doing, step up onto the wobbly swivel chair directly beneath it. Squinting, I raise the glass over my head. The spider does nothing even as the rim approaches, until at the last millisecond, like a spring-loaded umbrella, it shoots out eight legs. Too late! I've got it sealed off. The post card does its work and – plink! – the spider falls to the bottom of the glass.

Wobbling, catching my balance, I keep the postcard in place and climb down falteringly. I check sideways through the glass, but why am I even doing that? Jeezus!! It's like a turtle, a black crab. SPIDER, SPIDER, SPIDER!!! Teeming with heebie-jeebies, I jet through the house, out the front door, down the front steps, deciding as I go that this thing is so huge, I can't drop in my yard. No, siree! I walk down the sidewalk as far as the neighbors' rockery before finally shaking out the glass into a bush.

The spider plops onto the shrubbery – a juniper, as it happens, with dense green needles – and lands on its back. But instead of righting itself, it just lies there, belly up.

There, on its belly, I see a pattern. It's a design of interlocking triangles, beige, dark gray, and light gray, that compose a perfect geometric arrangement: Diamonds of orderly precision, even on something so lowly as a spider's belly.

There's a message here: god has crafted every detail of this spider, of this world, of this universe, with artistry and intention, all the way down to molecules and atoms and particles.

But the harried mom part of me can't fathom this stuff. I step back.

What – am I crazy?! Do I have some kind of skipping phonograph needle in my brain that makes it *feel* like something's happened before? Some kind of déjà vu, faulty apprehension? But I remember not only the dream itself, but *telling* it to my partner this morning! I described this very pattern out loud, this design of interlocking triangles, and now here it is again in real life! How the hell does that happen?!

My heart pounds. This can't be what it seems – there's a trick. Helplessly, I glance about for cameras, observers, anything. My eyes check – what? – the sidewalks, the tops of nearby utility poles for what, some kind of – I don't know what! – cameras, scientific equipment, in case I'm the subject of some psychological experiment, some kind of in-your-brain Candid Camera. Anything.

But there's only my familiar street, and certainly no scientist can plant images *in your dreams*. Full bore my brain scrabbles to explain, to make connections, find answers – but it feels like trying to pluck a needle from a haystack while you have on mittens.

Now a new thought forms: my little boy is alone in the house.

I crouch as near as I dare – to look, really look. That is the pattern. And it's undeniably beautiful. As if on cue, the spider now rights itself and begins a crab-like retraction into the bush.

It's gone. With a parting glance up and down the street, I run back indoors.

My child, still sitting on the kitchen floor, looks up cheerfully. "Big pydoo, new home?" he asks, using our phrase for such matters.

"Yes," I say breathlessly. "Mama gave the spider a new home outside."

Up we go! I grab him, snatch up the effing binder, the diaper and snack bags. Yep, another one of those Weird Things has just happened! Dream lived out. Something told me to find courage and I found it. Something told me nothing is meaningless. That's all I know.

A year passes. My partner, incredibly, has an affair with the AA lady who offered her the better paralegal job – a lesbian affair with this Republican, Catholic, married lady in her fifties who says "Gosh!" a lot. My partner is never home, angrily insists they're just friends, spends all her paychecks courting this woman so we're broke and dozens of checks bounce, yells at me that I'm crazy for being jealous.

Then she leaves me.

They're in love, her email tells me, and have been carrying on together from almost the day she got the job.

I am destroyed. I want to die. My cherished little family – Mama, Mommy, and baby – is obliterated. I cry with gut-wrenching pain every day and night. Booze and suicide call to me like sirens from my past. I want to drink, to take drugs, to ruin myself – but I have my little son, this beautiful soul whose future depends on what I choose now.

So, with the help of a sober friend who reaches out, I resume going to AA meetings, which I've abandoned amid the constant hurry and fatigue of motherhood. Old friends welcome me back. I make new friends. I get romantically obsessed with a man. I land a job as a glorified secretary, put our son in daycare, and commute across the lake every day despite the flood of tears that blurs my vision and ravings no one hears. Months pass before I can make it through a single day without crying.

But such a day does finally arrive. I build the foundations of a new life.

It's now the November of 2004, about a year and a half post-spider. A friend from my early sobriety days has invited me to her 50th birthday party. I've not seen Franny in over a year and she lives on the opposite side of traffic-choked Seattle. Despite an excellent array of reasons to decline, I decide I'll go. I'll attend this party and wish her a happy birthday. On the way there, I get that feeling of rightness again, of following a North Star.

But from the moment Franny opens her door, her long, silver hair flowing past her shoulders, I'm sure I've made a mistake. What was I thinking? I know only one other person there and my son, now four, is the only kid. Franny finds some toys for him, and he's chosen a spot to unpack his "briefcase," where he keeps notepads, books, and crayons, so I'm able to socialize a little, sitting on the hardwood floor.

The conversation turns to clairvoyance, and I realize I actually do have an entertaining story to contribute.

"I had a clairvoyant dream once, but it was about the dumbest thing! A spider. Like a huge, huge spider." To Franny and a few others I tell the dream, describe the pattern, and explain how I encountered an insanely large spider the next morning, how I saw the same pattern on its belly. "It was a totally clairvoyant experience," I laugh, "yet about something completely pointless!"

"Spiders aren't pointless."

This remark comes from Franny. She's calm and serious, the most woo-woo person I know. In her mid-thirties, she recovered from Stage 3 breast cancer by following up her double mastectomy with only a three-month meditation retreat at a wheatgrass farm in Puerto Rico. It worked. Twenty years later she's fine. More recently, during the darkest days of my dying relationship, she treated me with light and aroma therapy.

Now she's interpreting my experience as she sees it: "That must have been a spirit messenger. Something was up. Hang on – I've got books."

From her extensive woo-woo library, Franny pulls out two embarrassingly stupid volumes on spirit guides and animal totems. She leafs through them and speaks soothingly as the others drift to nearby conversations. Her voice calms me. It's while she's reading aloud that I understand – whether in my gut or my spirit – that this is the reason I've come here: it's so that Franny can step in and convey the sense of what happened. Spiders, she reads, are connected to the three Fates of Greek mythology who spun, measured, and cut the threads of each lifetime. Distinct phases within our lifespans may also be spun, measured, and cut. Spider may visit to announce the end of one stage and start of a new one.

She's pondering. "Didn't this spider show up around the time you and J— broke up?"

"No," I say. "This thing happened in April or so, and we didn't break up until September." Remembering, I add, "September 11, 2003. It was my own twin towers."

Now Franny's reading from an animal totems book. Apparently, the spider is a powerful icon of female creativity and blah, blah, blah, woo, woo, woo. It's related to the alphabet cause of something to do with its web. Who writes this crap? Seriously, a *spider* totem? Are there flea and tick totems, too? I listen politely, trying to comment as if it weren't nonsense.

But on the drive home, Franny's words – or the books' words – continue knocking at some closed door in my brain. September was when my partner left me, but April *was* the month when she betrayed me – becoming infatuated with her lesbian-curious AA acquaintance at work. It occurs to me also that, when my relationship with her began, I was staying in the home of my brother and his wife because my previous partner, Jenna, had kicked me out after reading my infatuated journal entries about the cool barista boy. I remember describing the motorcycle dyke to my brother and sister-in-law as swashbuckling leather butch, seeing their faces gradually register "bad idea" as I bragged about how enamored she was with me. Even so, at some point during my stay with them, I chose that path. In short, the dream spider had shown me the *start* of our relationship's thread, and the real-life morning spider – *I'm here for you. You know why* – came to cut the thread as my partner began her affair.

Now I've got to find out more. As soon as my son is down for his nap, I sit in the wobbly swivel chair and Google first "life thread mythology" on the desktop. The monitor shows me images of the Three Fates, some on ancient vases, others in ancient frescos, measuring and cutting threads. This spinning and cutting threads theme has appeared as a trope in multiple mythologies. After going down several Google rabbit holes, I stumble on this passage from Ted Andrews' *Animal-speak*. Unexpected words jump off the screen, truths I've not admitted for years, not even to myself:

> "If spider has come into your life, ask yourself some important questions. Are you not weaving your dreams and imaginings into reality? ...Are you focusing on others' accomplishments and not on your own?"

I'm stunned. Yes, gradually, without knowing it, I'd devoted all my energies to my partner's life, fulfilling *her* dreams, not mine. I didn't know how to break the cycle, so it was broken *for* me. I see this now. My pulse quickens.

> ...Do you need to write? ...Spider is the guardian of the ancient languages and alphabets. Every society has had myths about how the different languages and alphabets were

formed... This is why spider is considered the teacher of language and the magic of writing. Those who weave magic with the written word probably have a spider totem."

This is too much. Since childhood, I've been one of those people who must write. Before this relationship, I published ten fiction stories in five years. But once codependence swallowed me up, I had no time for it. Only after she'd left me did I begin to write again, first melodramatic poems about the Republican Catholic married lady as a snake, then little stories. And now I'd just submitted one for publication.

I'm here for you. You know why.

Every detail intentional. Diamonds of orderly precision. My gaze, leaving the monitor, rises toward the ceiling, to the spot where the spider had crouched in the open. *This* was the spot the spider chose because *this* is where I wrote – or was *not* writing.

"In the dream you were courageous. So you can be courageous now."

My defensive walls crumble, and in flows the knowledge that it's all god – everything, everything that is, every life and flower and barnacle, every happening, beauty, and loss – and I find myself overwhelmed. Somehow my soul's eye sees past the spider's place, through the ceiling, beyond the evening sky. A portal to outer space opens above me revealing the universe, the brilliant, starry universe that extends infinitely above me, below me, and out in every direction. All of it, every particle and wave of its making, I realize, is crafted in "diamonds of orderly precision." All is one. All is god.

Simultaneously, I sense the voice confirming: *You've done well, little one. We rejoice for you!*

I'm too honest in this moment to do anything but embrace it. This voice is *someone* – not a quirk of my psyche. This spirit and others I can't hear have been here all along. They witnessed the worst of my pain, me crawling on the carpet as my son played "horsey-back," tears and snot dripping from my face, despairing but nonetheless neighing for my little boy, cherishing his innocent toddler laughter and knowing I must, I *must* show up for him. Every staggering step I've taken to regain my footing – they have seen it.

The light fills me. I am loved. Now for the first time in my life, without conditions, without a doubt, without a shred of recalcitrant cynicism, the doors of my heart and mind fling open wide. I thank god for my life, for its love, for its guidance. My upturned face is by now streaming with tears. In a ragged, ugly-cry voice, I sob out loud:

"I know… that you are."

The voice responds. I sense joy but also – could it be? – someone is cracking up. There's love in his amusement at my intense drama, my profound human fervor in seeing what's been there all along, plain and simple.

We love you always, little one. And, you're right! We can do real stuff!

Real stuff. Yes, they can do real stuff.

I see that, despite every miracle and paranormal gift god has provided me, fear has always won out – fear of appearing foolish, self-aggrandizing, abnormal. It's fear that's fueled my cynic, fear that causes me to recoil into the safe shell of "normalcy." It's fear that's walled out curiosity and wonder.

What my fellow humans might think of me has carried more clout than my own lived experience. But at my core haven't I always known this simple truth – that every plant and organism and even inert substance exists is part of the whole, part of the unity I can now call god? Of course I have! Everyone has!

Even so, I realize that this portal of awareness will constrict again, that what I grasp now will again become vulnerable to the labels of delusion, woo-woo wackiness, crazy talk – all of it throttled to silence by the grip of "common sense." Some kind of vow or promise is in order now – not for god's sake, but for my own.

So I say it out loud, my emotionalism punctured, my voice calmer: "I will never, ever doubt you again."

I see myself down the road making statements abhorrent to my skeptical self; I anticipate my societally conditioned, eye-rolling cynic demanding I conform, dismiss this craziness, the voice, the knowings – all of it! But I have unmasked those voices as fear. I pledge now that, no matter how difficult it feels to maintain this stance, I will never again let fear gain the upper hand.

I envision a shingle nailed above my mind's door something like Lucy's "the Doctor is IN" sign. Mine has always read, "Louisa Peck, Clever Atheist." That's who I was raised to be, taught to be, needed to be.

I now pry it off and break it over my knee. In its place, I nail up a brand new shingle: "Louisa Peck, Woo-woo Weirdo."

So be it – for the rest of my life.

What I Think Now:

Well, I've kept my word. And it did prove exceedingly difficult, especially at first.

Like all "coming out" processes, the first stage is simply coming out to oneself. That is, in the same way that, if one is queer, or alcoholic, or simply no longer believes in those family precepts with which they were indoctrinated, they must first acknowledge this fact to themselves. Only once they've accepted this truth can they begin to live it – first in their inner self-image, and later, perhaps, in their social persona.

At this point, I was far from ready to tell anyone else what I believed. But I'd become willing to acknowledge to myself what I knew of the spirit world and that its existence was an undeniable constant – not a passing fancy.

What I've learned since from the NDErs I've heard speak or interviewed, those who were shown more than I on the other side, is that free will is a huge deal. It's inseparable from our purpose on Earth. We can't know as humans why we've come into physical form or what we're here to accomplish – and I certainly don't pretend to. Nevertheless, I *can* conjecture it has to do with separation from god as an opportunity for us to individually choose to embody and expand the power of love.

In spite of free will, I see myself with a guardian angel who has repeatedly nudged me toward a better way of life. In fact, it was Egnacio who nudged me to *begin* that relationship years before with the motorcycle dyke. She was sober in AA while I was adrift in alcoholism. Egnacio also knew the power of my codependence, that in relationships I always changed myself to suit my partner. In this case, he leveraged that codependence to save me from the grip of alcoholism.

Egnacio later knew that my partner and I had finished fulfilling the roles we were to play in each other's lives: I'd enabled her to get her BA, she'd gotten me sober, and as a couple, we'd had our son. Perhaps Egancio also saw that, as a heavily codependent woman, being abandoned by the one I loved would try my lifelong weaknesses and push me to the brink of relapse. I would need to tap a deeper courage than ever before and, in finding my courage, I would rescue myself.

All things are interconnected. How easily, then, could Egnacio nudge the spider, an obvious emblem of my fears, to play the role of messenger. When I asked in thought why it had done so, it was Egnacio via the spider who answered, *I'm here for you. You know why*.

Once I'd passed through this upheaval and emerged in life's flotsam beyond it, I was directed to share my story with Franny as someone who might explain the spider's relevance. In that social setting, I could access only my skeptical view of Franny's books and beliefs. But once I was alone, everything she'd said began to ring true, and once I opened my heart to it, the truth rushed in and overwhelmed me.

I recall being quite surprised and even a bit undercut when Egnacio cracked up. Angels have plenty of humor – trust me. What they don't have is drama, particularly anguished drama. For me, making a lifelong acknowledgement that the spirit realm was real required a huge, deep transformation. To him, I was like someone lifting a paper bag from over a jar of peanut butter and sobbing, "Oh my *god*! It's PEANUT BUTTER!! Oh, from this day forward I shall always know it's PEANUT BUTTER!! Never again shall I doubt or deny its peanut buttery essence – no, no! Let them ridicule me as they may!"

Egnacio, in turn, was like a normal person just back from the store saying, "Yup! That's peanut butter all right! Right there on the counter."

It's what is. That's all.

Angels don't feel much in the way of strong emotion. Emotion's primarily a limbic thing. They feel compassion as they witness life reviews alongside the near-dead individual who regrets their misdeeds, because compassion is a subset of love. But most of our heavier emotions are of the body, and they fade from us when we leave it. Nancy R., whose NDE is relatively famous, recalls her angel sighing in answer to a question about emotions, "It's been a long time since I was human!"

I think, I wonder, I imagine that angels kind of miss it – having physical senses and strong emotions. I think for this reason my emotional drama always appeals to Egnacio as classically human, adorably naïve. He views me much as adults see a toddler delighting in peak-a-boo: look at them learning object permanence! Egnacio perhaps smiled, Look at her learning to see beyond fear! He was rejoicing: the spider message had done its work well, and I would live better because of it. But my dramatic reaction? It was just over the top!

Following my "transformation" to full time woo-woo, I began to theorize that perhaps that my NDE had something to do with my various paranormal experiences and knowings. Other people, I'd heard since *Ghost*, had gone on journeys similar to mine and claimed they'd crossed over. In fact, to cross over and come back actually had a name: Near-Death Experience.

Around this time, the phenomenon of NDEs was becoming a blip on the radar of mainstream media. I knew nothing of the research already well underway by Bruce Greyson, Kenneth

Ring, P.M.H. Atwater and others. I'd never heard of the U.S. based Near-Death Experience Research Foundation (NDERF) founded in 1998 by Dr. Jeff Long or the Canadian Spiritual Emergence Research and Referral Clinic set up by Dr. Yvonne Kason. Still, all these pioneers were exerting an influence.

When I interviewed Dr. Kason in 2022, she described the years following her NDE from a plane crash in remote Northern Ontario – not her first or her last NDE, by the way.

> "For many years, I lived a double life, publicly as a medical faculty member at the University of Toronto, and privately as a mystic – studying, meditating, even going to India to get guidance from Gopi Krishna. It all came together in 1990 when I was invited to speak on Kundalini awakenings at a conference put on by the Spiritual Emergence Network in California. Facilitating a sharing circle there, I heard nightmare stories from Spritually Transformative Experiencers (STE) who'd been mislabeled, pathologized, dismissed as crazy, condemned by their church, locked in psychiatric wards, subjected to electroshock therapy, and rejected by their loved ones. They were crying; they hugged me. That 'MD' after my name meant the world to them, just to finally meet a medical doctor who believed them.
>
> "I was walking on the beach afterwards when I had another transformative experience, my 'calling' mystical experience. I was 'called' to

> come out of the closet and start advocating for people who'd had such experiences. I had to speak out because the medical profession and public were doing harm by labelling Experiencers crazy. So I went back to my university department chair and said, I'll resign if you want, but this is what I plan to specialize in. My guardian angels must have touched him, because he not only consented but even gave me some pointers on how to set up what became the Spiritual Emergence Research and Referral Clinic."

Kason and her university clinic caught the interest of the Canadian media. She made frequent TV appearances, bringing NDEs into the public eye. Raymond Moody, meanwhile, had published six more books, following up *Life After Life* with further research. So the term NDE was now out there, and I heard it.

Aftereffects, however, I had yet to hear a whisper about. As far as I knew, I was the only NDEr to whom Weird Things happened on the regular. It sounds silly, but if no one else is talking about how they've witnessed things like old fishermen vanishing from beaches or soundless voices in their heads telling them what to do or what's going to happen, it *does* seem that no one else is experiencing them! I still felt a strong need to remain closeted; I still feared being labelled crazy. This deal I'd made beneath the open portal, this vow not to deny god's reality, was purely between me and Egnacio.... and, of course, god beyond him. I didn't have to share it with any humans.

As a side-note, ever since a spider took part in my awakening, risking its own gutsy death and patiently displaying its belly, I've lost my arachnophobia – or at least most of it. Common web spiders and Daddy Longlegs I can even scoop up inside my cupped hands. They run around and tickle – that's all. Jumping spiders are too quick for me to catch, but they somehow remind me of little clowns. Hobo spiders I do squish or feed to my chickens. A few times I've calmly held even smallish wolf spiders who ran off a sheet of paper into my hand, but anything bigger than an inch across still triggers the heebie-jeebies.

I mean, come on!

Chapter 9: Accidental Mind Reader

What I Thought Then:

It's spring of 2005. I'm 45 and I've been directing the Writing Center at the University of Washington for almost two years. The online sign-up system I'm having built hasn't launched yet, so we still rely on the good old clipboard for appointments. Students wanting to reserve time with a writing tutor have to either call or stop by to get their name written down for a selected time slot.

In walks a young woman who says she'd like an appointment. Someone has left the clipboard on one of the tutoring tables, so we go to it. Standing to my left, she tells me the time slot she wants, so I turn to that page and hover my pen above the line for her name.

"Wendy," she tells me, and waits for me to write it.

But somehow my brain jams. I cannot think how to write Wendy. I'm wanting to write it, but my thoughts feels like I'm trying to touch the wrong ends of two magnets together, until I push through to WRITE! A thought flashes that "L" is far easier to write than "W" because my name stats with "L." Good. Somehow, I write "Lee."

Wendy starts. She asks sharply, "How did you do that?"

Not why, but how.

"I'm sorry," I falter, drawing a line through "Lee" and writing "Wendy."

"No," she insists. "How did you *know* that about me?"

She points to the crossed-out Lee. "That's my last name," she says, anger in her voice. "But I hadn't said it yet!" Now she glares at me. "That's how you spell it, too, with the double E. How did you *know* that?"

I realize a Weird Thing has just happened. I've accepted them, but that doesn't help me explain them to another person. I tell the truth – that I couldn't think how to make a "W" and my name starts with "L," but even as I say it, I see I'm only enraging her further.

"That makes no sense!" Wendy all but shouts. "I've never been here in my life!"

Of course it makes no sense! You're in my Weird Thing!

That's what I *don't* say.

By now I've retraced the letters of "Lee" several times and drawn a fat comma between that and "Wendy," as if repairing the entry might somehow pacify her. By now the whole thing appears a childlike mess. My goal is to calm her down, but I myself am pretty tickled that I've accidentally read this young woman's mind. She won't stop demanding how I knew her name, so I finally speak the truth.

"My mind must have just picked it up because you were thinking it."

To Wendy Lee, this is an outrageously stupid lie. Clearly someone at the U.W. has been spying on her. I blundered by writing what I knew, tipping my hand.

Wendy storms out. I can't help smiling.

A tutor named Charlie has wrapped up his session but caught wind of Wendy's rancor. He's writing up the session notes when I decide to share.

I show him the crossed-out "Lee" and say simply, "I must have accidentally read her mind."

"Huh!" he says, smiling. "Wow, that's crazy!"

This is the second time in my life I've shared about a Weird Thing, the first being the Gloucester ghost. At that time, I was just as angry as Wendy.

"I think she thinks I've been spying on her," I say with amusement.

"But you haven't?" Charlie checks. "You just pulled 'Lee' out of the air?"

"Yeah," I say, beginning to realize how I must sound but sticking to my guns, even knowing Charlie is a born-again Christian. "This stuff happens to me sometimes."

Charlie shakes his head and we both resume business as usual.

I'm on a roll, though, so I email a friend and tell him what happened – just because!

A week or so later, Wendy Lee shows up for her tutoring session. She and I don't speak, but I catch her more than once giving me the old stink eye from across the room. That lady's a spy!

A little more than a year later, I'm reading on my couch before bed. Unexpectedly, a face pops into my mind. It's an old high school acquaintance, David Soluck. I didn't really know him in high school, and it's been thirty years since we graduated. But now I see him so clearly as he looked back then, his long hair parted down the middle, his large eyes, and the lip fuzz mustache he sported senior year. I wonder how he's doing and regret not having been kinder back then. I was too obsessed with popularity to really see anyone.

The next morning, I'm checking Myspace (Facebook is not yet a thing) when I see a new message – from David Soluck, who is indeed a grown man now, practically unrecognizable. I think happily, another Weird Thing! He wrote just last night to say he was looking at Myspace when came across my page. He shares a little of his life and asks what I'm up to. The time stamp of his message is a few minutes after the time I saw his high school version in my mind's eye.

I write back and tell him what happened the night before, how I saw his high school self, lip fuzz mustache and all. He writes back to say how proud he was of that mustache!

It's 2007 and I'm driving up a steep street on Capitol Hill in Seattle, Olive Way, when the face of an old AA friend pops into my mind. This is someone I haven't seen for almost five years, not since I quit attending a particular meeting he frequented. Tim is a robust man, likeable, reserved, and gay. Not only does his energy spring to mind, but I also know I'm about to *see* him. Specifically, he's going to be walking down this hill I'm driving up.

Oh boy! Another Weird Thing! I love these! I can't wait!

That's what part of me thinks. But my inner skeptic, still alive and well in my mind's back seat, rolls its eyes.

I spy a pedestrian walking down left sidewalk. It's a tallish, robust, bearded man – Tim, just as I remember him! I'm gleefully excited until, as he gets a little closer, I realize, actually it's *not* Tim.

My skeptic lunges forward. That's right! It's just a normal guy who looks enough like Tim to be easily mistaken by some woo-woo loser intent on confirming she's able to know things before they happen. If you hadn't noticed your mistake at the last second, you'd be driving along now convinced these Weird Things are real and imagining you had some special power. All this woo-woo is garbage! You need to give it up!

Right then, I see someone striding down the right-hand sidewalk. As he gets closer, I see Tim Smith for real, not just seeing but sensing his good Tim energy. I'm so ecstatic and flustered, I manage to honk my horn, but sort of too late, when I've almost passed him.

You-know-who is vanquished. Silenced.

It sounds crazy, but I actually taunt my own inner skeptic: What do you say now, smartypants? That was Tim! We both *know* it was!

Not a peep.

Once I get home, I find Tim among my Facebook friends (yes, we've moved on to that) and message him: "Were you by chance walking down Olive Way at about 1:15 today?"

"Yes!" he writes back. "I got out of class at 1:00 and was going home for lunch. Was that you who honked?"

Tim has a big heart and an open mind, so I take him into my confidence. I write back about the whole experience – knowing I was about to see him, the fake Tim that set off my skeptic, and then he himself, how seeing him knocked my cynic right out of the boxing ring.

"That's so cool!" Tim writes back. He expresses no doubt. He doesn't suggest perhaps I saw him from a distance without knowing I saw him or that my thoughts of him were merely coincidental. He believes I picked up his energy through telepathy.

So, at long last, do I.

What I Think Now:

Here we go again with that torn god-phobic sheath. I certainly could never read thoughts before my NDE. But since I passed through the membrane twice, leaving and re-entering my body, it don't work so good no more. That's why I've been picking up "leaks" from the spirit world – why I saw the ghost, knew my brother's grief, and was able to hear Egnacio's intentional warnings and urgings.

Sometimes I wonder whether this "tear" actually exists in space, in the spherical aura that surrounds me. Both Wendy and Tim were positioned to my left – as have been other minds I've since accidentally read. David Soluck, however, was in Wenatchee, 100 miles away as the crow flies and, for what it's worth, slightly to my right. Yet his thoughts about me were specific and strong enough to come through clearly.

Thoughts, we must conclude, are energies. They're far more than mere synapses in the brain. Wendy's thought of "Lee" as she waited for me to write "Wendy" was powerful enough to block my own thoughts: I could not write anything else. My mind, like a radio, was forced to play what she broadcast. I even recall feeling relieved once I wrote it, though it wasn't what I meant to write.

It follows that what we customarily think is indeed important. We can generate good or bad energy depending on the thoughts we entertain.

Each individual being, whether human, animal, or plant, also broadcasts a unique energy field of its own. In the case of Tim, I sensed only his Tim-ness. I had no clue what his thoughts might be. But my affection for him was awakened. This seems to suggest that our energies of aliveness and love are closely intertwined.

My inner skeptic suffered a major blow from each of these episodes, but particularly the one involving the fake Tim. It seems to me now that Egnacio set up the whole thing to sucker-punch that part of my psyche. Really, that an individual so resembling Tim should be walking down the hill at that moment, so I would see him and be fooled just a few seconds before seeing the real McCoy – that was no coincidence.

Sadly, my inner skeptic has not died, not by a long shot. Even today as I write this it's still back there saying, Are you actually going to *publish* this? Aren't you a professional? Why must you tarnish our reputation? Why can't you be normal?

I imagine most woo-woos – mediums, psychics, even remote viewers working for the government – experience similar thought static. The only break I get is when I attend conferences held by the International Association of Near-Death Studies. In that environment my mind is, for a few days at least, free from these signals. What a relief to be surrounded by people who know as well as I do that the spirit realm is real! It's as obvious as a jar of peanut butter sitting right there on the counter.

Chapter 10: My Father's Crossing

What I Thought Then:

It's now 2008 and I know I have gifts. I've told my boyfriend and a few trusted others about "the voice." I theorize that it is somehow related to my NDE.

I'm sitting at my parents' kitchen table when their bedroom door opens and Mom wheels out Dad in the wheelchair he's needed lately. Mom tells me his lungs are a bit congested though he's otherwise doing fine, speaking in a kind of baby-talk she often uses when taking care of him. For some time now, he's been falling and unable to get up. Mom and Dad cheerfully call 911 every time this happens as, in their minds, the firemen are just up the street and not busy anyway.

I know in that moment that Dad is dying. I don't know anything about heart failure or alcoholic cardiomyopathy symptoms. I just know we have little time left with him.

I text my out-of-town siblings that Dad needs to go to the hospital and that they should come. Dad goes to the hospital, gets diagnosed with heart failure, and is sent home for hospice care. Even though doctors tell him point blank that he's dying, he won't accept the idea, which bothers him remarkably little. His alcoholic history of knowing better than doctors dates back three decades to the time he developed gout. How silly of them! They're always nagging about that. Same thing here: what do *they* know? He comes home and stays in bed on oxygen.

On Sunday June 8, when he's hungry, my sister and I wheel him from his bedroom to the kitchen table and sit with him while he eats what will turn out to be his last meal with us: a toasted cheese sandwich and tea.

"Did I really almost *die?*" he asks incredulously, as if such an overly-dramatic idea blows his mind and he's obviously fine now. In the safety of his own kitchen, with my sister and me flanking him at the table, it does seem hard to believe. My sister and I only exchange glances. Neither can speak the truth: "Dad, you're on hospice care. That means you're dying *now*."

Overnight, Mom sleeps upstairs while a caregiver watches over Dad. I've gone home already, where, that night, I have a dream. Here it is as recorded in my journal:

> "I'm sitting at Dad's usual spot by the fridge and he walks in looking very young and bright. He sits across from me and teases me somehow, though I hear no sound of his voice. We're both elated and playful, but then I remember and say, 'Dad, I think this might be just a dream and really you're *dying!*' He hears me and his image breaks up a bit like a faulty transmission, but then he's still teasing me, pouring more love my way, and looking younger than ever.
>
> "Then I'm outside at nightfall. Above me stands an old blue house set up high on a bank above a big lake (Michigan?). I'm starting down a winding trail through shrubs and scrubby trees to go swimming when a woman comes out of the house and calls to me. She looks old-fashioned in her dress and apron and reminds me of Dad's mother, Grammy, though she's too far away for me to see clearly. She's looking for

her little boy, she says, because it's time for him to come home. I tell her I'll watch for him. As I near the beach, I meet a man and a boy coming toward me on the trail. The man appears Jamaican and the boy, reaching up to hold his hand, is only about three years old. Yes, the man assures me in gentle accents, they are heading for the house right now."

In the morning, I know this wasn't just some ordinary dream. That's why, as soon as I can, I write it down. I recognize the dream house up on the hill: it's the weatherworn house of my ancestors from my NDE, the waystation between worlds, only now it's set high on a hill by a large lake. My father grew up near Lake Michigan and has often compared its vastness to an ocean. I also recognize the old-fashioned woman calling him home as his mother. But who was the Jamaican man holding my child-father's hand?

Back at my parents' house, I meet Dad's overnight hospice caregiver, Tonn. He's Fijian – not Jamaican – but his accent, to my untrained ears, sounds the same. He tells me how Dad woke up last night around midnight wanting coffee – which to me comes as a great surprise. Dad always wants *wine*, especially at night. In any case, Tonn reports how he wheeled Dad into the kitchen and the two of them drank coffee together watching late-night TV. Each time Dad wanted to change the channel, he would first ask Tonn's permission, a touching courtesy, Tonn thought. When Dad was ready, Tonn helped him back to bed.

By this morning he's slipped into a delirium. All the next day the family sits with him, nodding and smiling while he says things that make no sense, chuckling when he appears to think he's made a joke. My brother administers morphine through a dropper, though I later reflect we should have given him alcohol. Much of his delirium may be due to withdrawal, but somehow none of us think of that. Now and then his mind clears. At one point he lifts his hand and clinks his wedding ring – fifty-nine years – with Mom's. At another, he focuses on me, standing at the foot of his bed. "You're beautiful," he says quietly, his last words to me.

That night, I dream again.

> "My dreams were filled with anguish and regret for all I'd not done or loved in this precious life. I can't describe the intensity of loss, of mistaken waste. I'm driving through a desert where the banks of dry earth have somehow formed into church bells, the cliffs bulging out in smooth curves. Now they're ringing, filling the open desert air with a beautiful clang full of longing, full of beauty, and with all my heart I wish I'd not left the Catholic Church! I love it! I know it so well! The bells' clanging, resonant sound is so pure and transporting, but I cannot embrace it because I, stupidly, misguidedly, turned away in my youth. What a fool I was!
>
> "Then a white guardrail beside the road – I'm driving fast – eclipses the hills from sight. Is it too late, I wonder, to make up for my choices? Yet it wasn't, I object in my own defense, a choice. I *wanted* to respect the church but I *couldn't*. It simply did not make sense to me, did not mesh with my scientific understanding

of the world, which I loved as much as anyone loves religion.

"Why oh why did I not answer those emails from my friend Jerome! I should have let him know I did love him! [Dad never made up with his bullying older brother, Jerome. I, on the other hand, received emails from a Jerome running an in-home shop, so my dream substituted him].

"I arrive at the monastery where I once lived, hoping to be admitted, but all my belongings have been cast out on the ground by an angry nun. 'Take your stuff and get out of here!' she says. I stoop to gather what is mine from the dust and see, as a final insult, that they have stepped on my reading glasses and crushed them. My books, my studies – they tore me from God. My heart aches with rejection and sorrow."

I wake from this dream at 4:00 AM knowing I've channeled Dad's inner emotions. I was not myself in the dream, I was he. Wasting no time, I throw on clothes and drive across Seattle in the predawn light, anxious to see him. Mom's asleep upstairs. I ask Tonn if I may speak with Dad alone. Gently Tonn points out that Dad has never regained consciousness and can't hear me. I know, I say, but I still need to talk with him. Tonn gives us the room.

I take Dad's hand. "God loves you, Dadda!" I tell him quietly but urgently. "God loves you *so* much! God is *not* the

Catholic Church! *People* made the church. No one is angry with you. No one is disappointed. You've filled your life with love and goodness – and that's all god wants from any of us. Let the church go! Let god love you! You are a good, good man!"

His eyes don't open and his squeezes of my hand are tremulous and random, but part of him is hearing me. I sense a vast reckoning going on inside him. This is intense work he alone can do, coming to grips with the choices he's made in life. He's like someone far behind on daily chores finally doing them all in a flurry of effort. Decades of alcoholic denial – he regrets every day. Every day he told himself he would drink less, and every day he believed his own lie, but King Alcohol got the better of him. And now, life is slipping away and it's too late.

Sitting on the edge of his bed, I realize nothing I can say or do will help him cross. Unlike Adelyn, who had embraced Jesus throughout her long illness and stood on the brink of a free-falling faith, my father has denied his own spirituality since college. For him this is the labor of dying. I remember the woman who came out of the old house – his beloved and loving mother. I leave to her the work of bringing him home. Grammy will guide him.

Tonn's cousin Sara takes over for the day shift, perched in a far corner as the whole family sits gathered around Dad's bed. A social worker from hospice pops by the house in the early afternoon. Our bedside watch has lasted so long that a new visitor seems exciting. Someone asks, how long does he have? Oh, she says, there's no telling. She's seen patients linger on this way for weeks.

Expertly she flips Dad from slightly on his left side to slightly on his right so he won't get bed sores. As soon as she does this, I know his left lung has been accumulating fluid and now weighs heavily on his already feeble heart. The shift will kill him. Should I tell her and the others to flip him back, or shall I let be? Guilty as I feel for not "saving" him, there's no point in drawing out his dying. I resolve to say nothing.

The rest of the family goes with the social worker into the kitchen, where they sit chatting around the table. I'm alone with Dad and Sara, who has a magazine. I sense Dad's getting ready to cross. I feel the same amping-up I felt with my sister, though I don't "see" any fog of light this time. His crossing is nonetheless imminent, and I feel a misplaced excitement.

The light! The light! Maybe I'll get a shot of it again. Oh, I hope so!

How horrible I am! I pray, God, I'm sorry for being so selfish! I can't believe my own father is dying and here I am excited for the light like it's some kind of carnival ride! What's wrong with me?!

The voice answers. It's definitely the voice, right there as soon as I pray, but he's cracking up again! How can this be? I know he's never bought into my drama (*Yes, we can do stuff!*) but laughter at a time like this is completely unexpected. *Oh, little one!* His tone is amused yet still loving. *You are human. Selfishness is part of the deal. Don't beat yourself up!*

Dad will cross any minute now, he tells me, but all is well.

I ask Sara to please call the family in; Dad's going soon. Sara doesn't even lower her magazine. From behind it she reminds me the hospice worker just now explained that Dad's likely to linger. "It could be weeks," says Sara.

"No," I say. She's surprised, meeting my eye as I say, "It's gonna happen now." I know what I know.

Sara does as I've asked and the others return to encircle Dad's bed. They search confusedly for some sign of imminent death – why did she call us in here? – but there's none. The social worker leaves. Dad breathes slower... and slower. I'm pretty sure all we need to do to "save" him is flip him back to his left side, but my angel does not urge it. I stay silent and let the spirits do their work.

My sister and I sit near the head of the bed and tell Dad again what a wonderful father he was. We recall the times he took us out in our little motorboat at the summer cabin. We'd fly across Puget Sound, wind roaring in our ears. "We'd shout, 'Faster, Dadda! Faster!' And then you'd go faster, and we'd love it!"

Dad exhales a final time. He's gone.

Though I try to sense my father's presence in the room, I pick up nothing. I do not feel light. Rather, I sense that he is intensely busy, that he must review his whole life in the light of spiritual honesty. A few hours later as his body is carried from the house where he'd lived for fifty years, I feel something grim in the air, though it may be only my own sense of how Dad's earthly personality would view this moment. I don't worry for him – that he might be blocked. His whole life was centered on love and service – just not *sober* love and service. Addiction had cheated only him.

That night I dream of a huge, powerful grizzly bear in the family living room that rears up so high on its back legs that its head and shoulders burst through the ceiling. Later, I see it pacing heavily around the yard outside the house. It's Dad – his fighting spirit! He's frustrated at his own death, feeling his power but regretting his mistakes.

Months later, though, when I pray at night for him to him to help me through a particularly dark fit of self-loathing, he appears to me in another dream as that same young, teasing self I saw on the first night of hospice. He conveys to me without words that he absolutely adores me. His love is such that it warms me. I know his goodness is powerful.

What I Think Now:

By this time, I'd come a long way from the confused girl in Manhattan who fearfully rejected her NDE. I understood that Dad's experience was "leaking" to me. I understood that blood family – those from whom the spark of life has been handed down – are close on the other side. I had an eye open to Dad's tidelands between the land of life and ocean of spirit.

Spirit energies surround the terminally ill for several days before they are to pass. Christopher Kerr, a hospice doctor who has interviewed over 1,400 terminally ill patients, has documented that the vast majority reports visitations from dead relatives. Dad never indicated he saw anyone, but his mother was looking to bring him home.

Dad was busy, I know now, because he had his whole life to review. A life review is a spiritual evaluation of significant moments of one's life. What constitutes a significant event from an afterlife perspective doesn't align with what we consider significant events here; key moments when we chose to be compassionate or cold are what determine our degree of success. Were you loving? Were you kind? Where did you fall short? The newly dead person is shown something resembling a movie of these moments in compressed time and from as many as three perspectives at once: their own, the other person or animal's, and god's. It's a little like their life is being graded, but at a Montessori school. No one is angry. When the newly dead person mourns regretted behavior, so do all the spirits looking on.

Roland W. was shown a time he held a glass door closed to shut his childhood friend outside after telling the friend to whap a bees' nest with a stick. In his review, Roland felt the countless bee stings, his friend's terror, the emotions of the friend's parents when they heard his screams, and even the anger of the bees themselves.

I believe Dad's life review began only once he left his body. What I was experiencing in these shared dreams were the spiritual struggles surrounding his death. First Dad's higher self, the one beyond this individual incarnation, visited me in the dream at the kitchen table to reassure me all was well despite the bumpy road home. Then I experienced the moral wrestling my father was in the thick of.

The strongest regret in the shared dream was that the beauty I'd perceived in Nature, the beauty of all things, was actually rooted in the beauty of the church as those bells' ethereal sound filled the landscape. To have loved Nature's expressions in place of the Catholic Church had been a tremendous mistake. Dad believed he had insulted the church by leaving, so the church was angry, God was angry, as symbolized by the indignant nun who had thrown all his belongings on the ground. She'd stamped on his glasses to show she disdained the pursuit of book learning that had "stolen" his love for the church.

All this emotion my dad experienced as he lay dying. All of this I felt and dreamed as I lay sleeping five miles away. Keep in mind that I, Louisa, don't care a hoot about any church, Catholic or otherwise. Churches are human creations. But for Dad, the church was the true path he feared he'd wandered away from in youth. Based on childhood reverence, the church represented his original idea of God, just as the Sun had done for me.

Dad died June 10, 2008. I might add that in the days and weeks following Dad's death, both my sister and I witnessed odd behavior from small animals. My sister saw a squirrel tracing the perimeter of my parents' house and trying to get in, particularly at the glass doors. It didn't want food; it wanted in. Then, across town few weeks later, a robin became obsessed with getting in *my* house through the windows. It would go from window to window, fluttering its wings against the glass, sometimes for ten minutes at a time. It left marks of robin spit. This was in mid-summer, not a time for nest building, and continued for over a week.

"What do you want?" I'd ask it. But it would answer only, "I want in! I want in!"

I've never seen such intense and odd behavior from a bird – before or since.

Chapter 11: Vanessa

What I Thought Then:

It's June of 2010 and I'm planning a big bash for my 50th birthday. I've made a celebratory video, *How to Turn 50, Bitches!* and rented out a park clubhouse venue for a big alcohol-free karaoke party. Among the AA friends I've invited, I haven't heard back from one I love most – Vanessa.

"Vanessa's pissed at you," my friend Val tells me on the phone. "She says she always comes to *your* parties, but you blow off hers." Specifically, I didn't attend Vanessa's housewarming party. At 26 and just a month away from being certified a journeyman, she's purchased a house about thirty minutes south of Seattle. The trouble was, her party fell on a Saturday night when I was on Whidbey Island seeing my boyfriend, so missed it. She'd wanted me there, I realize now, to celebrate this milestone in her sober life.

A runaway in her teens, Vanessa lived for years as a vagrant in Seattle's University District, buying, selling, and using drugs. When she landed in AA, she was what we call stark-raving sober. She'd recently been arrested for standing outside the University Bookstore and revving a chainsaw while wearing a red clown wig. She also swallowed swords and spit fire. Even sober, she gave off an onslaught of exuberance at first completely untempered by self-control, which made her appear a loud-mouthed attention hog.

Back in 2005, I was stuck in a medical waiting room when I got a call from her. I had no idea how she'd found my number. My level of dread ticked upward as she described a rift with her current AA sponsor and hinted gradually that she'd like me to take over. I made up my mind to say no. I'd cite the number of sponsees I already had, being a working mom, and whatever else made me too busy to take her through the 12 Steps. She was a lotta bit crazy and I had no doubt that if I let her into my life, she'd suck up all my time.

But damn it! Aww, dammit! Here came that voice again! Why was he snooping in my business?

How is she any crazier than you were? Help her as others helped you.

I was dead set against it. I argued with the voice that this street girl would inundate me with self-centered drama. Barely 21, she had a funny Munchkin voice, an elfin smile, and the metabolism of goddamn Tazmanian Devil. No – I couldn't let her into my life! Absolutely not.

She needs love. You have love to share.

Really? You're serious?

Just love her!

Oh, man. Here it came:

"…so like when I heard you sharing on Step 7 and stuff, and plus all your other shares, too, which are rockin', I was like, 'Damn! This woman is righteous!' You know? So I was wondering, maybe, if you could, you know, like… be my new sponsor?"

"Sure."

Did I just say that? Did I really just say that?

And yet, my heart knew the voice was right. Almost from the get-go, I loved Vanessa. As others would say at her funeral, she showed up as so unapologetically herself, she gave you permission to do likewise. She'd call me from diesel mechanic school in tears: male classmates poured coffee on her chair while she was in the bathroom, then laughed once she sat in it that she was "lookin' pretty wet down there!" Every week it was something. But I'd remind her of her focus, her power.

By the time we wrapped up the 12 Steps some two years later in 2007, both of us had grown into wiser, more compassionate women. Her powerful exuberance never left her. She'd sing in public at the top of her lungs and high-five strangers on the street, yet as a welder and journeyed diesel mechanic – or *almost* there – she performed exemplary work building the new Tacoma Narrows Bridge. By June of 2010, she had a different sponsor, but we remained close friends.

That's why now Val's words, "Vanessa's pissed at you," mean a lot. I realize I've been self-centered and thoughtless toward someone who has always shown up for me. Almost immediately I phone Vanessa, apologize, and ask if I can please come over to see her new home. We agree I'll come over the following day, a Friday, for dinner.

As I drive down I-5 toward her house, tired after the work week, I get that North Star feeling again. It's the voice saying, *Yes, yes. This is good.* The feeling doesn't fade as I pull up at Vanessa's SeaTac rambler, her dog rushing out to bark at me and my dog. I feel it still as I'm greeted in the junky side yard by Vanessa's hipster boyfriend, who tells me Vanessa will get home soon from work soon. We wait out on the deck so she can be the first to show me the place.

Her car pulls up – a newish Subaru – and she gets out in coveralls; she doesn't give a rat's ass about this "stunning beauty" bullshit she hears all the time. She wears no makeup; her long, dark hair is in pigtails. We hug and she greets my dog, then quickly changes out of work clothes to show off her house.

I marvel at each room. She's brimming with pride, both immersed in and bashfully aware of it. We go to a basement room where she tells me burglars broke in through the window last week and stole mostly music equipment (she plays guitar) but also some of her tools. As soon as we're in the room, I pick up a vague dark feeling. She keeps all her welding stuff down here, tools of her trade as an almost journeyman. Look at this biggest fucking wrench in the world! She holds it up and for added effect, scoops up her welding mask and puts it on. She's the same chainsaw clown, for sure!

That's when I really feel it – something dark, not good. It's not *evil* – just about loss. The giddy humor we've been sharing leaves me. What could it be? My eyes go to the broken window, still taped up with cardboard. Maybe they're coming back to steal more? I'm not sure, not ready to warn her of I-don't-know-what. She's getting iron bars installed next week.

Vanessa has brought me fancy vegetarian take-out: eggplant parmesan and salad. The three of us share a meal, our dogs playing. But it's Friday and she's bone tired. We marvel at her advanced age of 26 and mine of almost 50. "By the time I hit your age," she says, "I'll be tore up from the floor up!"

We hug goodbye. We say, "I love you."

The following Thursday morning, a text from a friend tells me Vanessa has "passed on." I become angry at what must be false rumors and call Vanessa, but her phone goes to voicemail again and again. This can't be. It mustn't be. But it is.

She'd finished a weld, stood up, and was struck in the head by the huge steel hook of a building crane. It dashed her brains out. A novice operator brought the crane around without the spotter required. Walled off by her welding mask, Vanessa couldn't see the hook coming.

Three days later, I go to an AA meeting of about 200 people in a large church basement where Vanessa chaired just two weeks before. I've heard that some people complained about her share as too long, too showy, too flippant. My love for her merges with indignation as I tell the group what an authentic, accomplished, and kind young woman she was, a runaway drug addict who trained in a man's field despite relentless harassment, all the way to journeyman.

I've made my point. The room is silent as I resume my seat.

After the meeting, I'm still standing near my chair when Kelly, a young woman I faintly know, approaches me.

"Can I tell you something kind of weird?" she asks.

"Of course," I tell her. "I'm all about weird."

"Well, you may not be into this, but I have this thing where sometimes I can see energies. I see, like, spirits and auras and stuff."

I nod. What has she seen? Vanessa?

"Okay, so – you have a really powerful spirit that hangs out with you. I could see it above you and to your left."

My heart jumps: she's seen him, the voice!

"And like when you were sharing about Vanessa, the more intense you got, the bigger it got. I mean, it was fucking huge. This oval energy field," she gestures, "like ten feet high."

I confide in Kelly about the voice, how it talks to me sporadically and I'm starting to think it's male. "Did you get any sense of who it is – male or female, anything?"

She had not. "It was just light, a shimmering. It lingered a while after you finished, and then it faded."

What I Think Now:

Egnacio brought us together, Vanessa and me. Left to my own selfish thinking, I'd have told her no, then written her off as a hot mess narrowly avoided. But he pushed me. With Vanessa, as with all my sponsees, I reaped the bounty of helping another person grow – which inevitably helped me do likewise.

But Vanessa seemed special. She was so damn candid, so real. Often, as we read and discussed AA's Big Book, I expounded on stuff with words that surprised me – the perfect ones for her to hear. This aptitude went on even when she'd call unexpectedly years after we'd completed the steps. Egnacio was always right there, helping me help her.

Once I learned I'd hurt her feelings by skipping her party, Egnacio urged me to call her, go visit her, and tell her face-to-face that I loved her. There was dark potential around the welder's mask, but I mistook it for bad energy left by the burglars. He did not intervene.

Kelly's description of Egnacio as a huge spirit confirmed what I knew intuitively – that he was old, powerful, and connected to my frequency. Now I had, essentially, an eye witness. It wasn't just *me* claiming some presence was with me. Kelly had seen him.

What our angels love is Love. They want us to grow it, to nurture it, to share it with one another. When I spoke of Vanessa in front of those 200 AA people, our collective love manifested in Egnacio, who grew bright.

There's a lesser-known Shiny Toy Guns song, *Sky Fell Over Me*, that reminds me strongly of Vanessa, in part because it's sung in a weenie doll-voice a lot like hers, and in part because the lyrics say exactly what I know she'd want to tell me whenever I grieve her death. She was welding outside on a barge afloat along Seattle's waterfront. It was about 10:00 a.m. on a beautiful, clear June morning. When she stood up and her life flew away from her, I like to think her spirit shot into that perfect sky much as mine did, and that she thought,
"Rad!!"

It's funny how randomized playlists can que up a certain song at just the perfect moment. I'll always remember a time I was running in my neighborhood, tears streaming for the loss of that girl, when the song came on, Vanessa's doll-voice seeming to flow through my ear buds to remind me – death is not death!

>
> *Leave me here.*
> *Now I'm with the angels.*
> *And don't you say*
> *It's not fair.*
>
> *Please don't think the world*
> *Has taken the best*
> *Of you or me.*
> *I know the love that's in your eyes*
> *Was there when the sky*
> *Fell over me,*
> *Yeah, when the sun*
> *Came over me.*

Chapter 12: Intimate Mind Reader

What I Thought Then:
It's the fall of 2010 and I need lumber for a project, so I head to Home Depot. As I pull into a parking space (toward the lot's north end but facing south), I think of my friend Josh. He's a gifted painter who works construction to pay the bills and, in 2003, built a deck for my house. I'll bet he comes here a lot, I think, putting the car in park. My thoughts drift, bringing a wave of affection for Josh and his fellow-artist wife, Ryly. I've known them ten years, since she was pregnant with their firstborn, who later played with my son. When their second child arrived prematurely, I sent a huge bouquet to the hospital and got to see their unbelievably tiny daughter in an incubator. Now, as I grab my purse and list, I think, I bet those two still have a damn good sex life, even after all these years and with kids and all. I bet they still really enjoy sex if they can somehow get away, just the two of them. In fact, I bet it's *hot*!

An image flashes into my mind's eye: It's Ryly lying naked on her stomach and looking out from the foot of big, fancy bed, her chin propped on one elbow, her gaze sultry. Her long, blonde hair, usually up in a bun, now flows to one side, covering one eye and shoulder as I have never in my life seen it.

I rear back mentally, appalled. *What*? Oh my god! What am I thinking? Why would I imagine such a thing? I'm a total perv!

I jump out of the car. No, I've certainly never thought of Ryly that way! I saw her so clearly, looking so hot and at the center of that whole scene, like a centerfold or painted nude – a frontal Ingres' Odalisque.

I try my best to shake off the image and get back to business. Discombobulated, I walk into the store and, thinking I'm at Lowes instead of Home Depot, head to where they keep the lumber. Eventually, I realize my mistake, backtrack to the cashier area, and start toward the other end of the store, passing displays and registers.

Who's this coming the other way? Why, it's Josh himself. Goodness! Such an awkward coincidence.

We greet each other with quick hugs.

"How funny! I was just thinking of you!" I say guiltily, actively *not* saying "and picturing your wife naked and sexy as hell." Instead I ask, "How's it going?"

"Re-eally good," Josh nods, grinning widely. "Ryly and I, we just got back from a weekend away. We dropped the kids off at Grandma's and spent a night at a bed and breakfast." He nods again, meaningfully. "It was…" unable to restrain his grin, "*much* needed!"

I laugh at his thinly veiled reference while he continues to beam. I say things like, "That's great – I'm so glad for you guys!" I ask where they went. I pretend to listen. Inwardly, I'm knocked for a loop. An astounding Weird Thing has just happened! This one was so vivid, so personal, and so none-of-my-business that now I'm even more embarrassed. I've just read a man's private, lustful, romantic thoughts of his wife. He was thinking of her as he parked at the other end of the lot, with no idea "spying" Louisa would snag the image clear as a centerfold. I want to tell Josh what's happened but, recalling Wendy Lee's furious indignation, I hold back.

A few months later, I'm mopping my kitchen's linoleum floor. This linoleum appears to have been installed thirty years ago or so. It's worn down, full of nicks, and never really gets clean anymore, so this chore is particularly unrewarding.

Scrubbing the mop on a stubborn spot, I think, Man, I hate this old linoleum! But you know who hates their old linoleum even *more*? Ryly. She *really* hates their kitchen floor. In fact, she hates it so much, she's getting it replaced. She's already made that decision. It's going to be bamboo – like that ex-sponsor of mine got installed. That's gotta be pricey!

A few minutes later, my landline rings. It's Ryly.

"I'm gonna ask you an extreme favor. I'm totally desperate, but you're the person who came to mind. So... here goes! I'm getting my kitchen floor replaced."

"That's great!" I say instead of, "I know. I just picked that out of the air same as I did your romantic getaway."

"Yeah, well, Josh doesn't think so. It's gonna be a bamboo floor, it's gonna be lovely, but the installers are showing up first thing in the morning – and I'm not ready. I'm still painting the cupboards! Wait – it gets worse! Bridget has a play performance tonight."

Bridget is the kid born prematurely.

Ryly rolls on frantically, "And if I miss it, Josh will never forgive me. He didn't want the new floor, he hates the mess, everything piled in the dining room, he hates all of it. If I try to paint later and drip on the bamboo, I'll be on his shitlist for life! So I'm asking, I know it's crazy, but can you possibly come over and please, please finish painting my kitchen cupboards *tonight*? Like, right now?"

Within twenty minutes, I arrive at their house, which is indeed in chaos. Everything from the kitchen is piled in the hallways and stacked on the dining room table. Josh is well-dressed and grumpy. Ryly is putting on earrings while she shows me the paint, the brushes, the yet-to-be-painted cupboards.

"We're LATE!" Josh yells in a monotone.

"Just go!" I say, waving them away. "Go! Go! Go!"

Soon the house is silent. I play unknown music on their boom box and crane my neck, standing on countertops to reach way back in their old corner cupboards. Hours pass.

By the time the family comes home, I'm all done and starting clean up. Bridget has performed like a rockstar, I'm told.

On the side, Ryly whispers, "You just saved our marriage, I swear!" And the new floor, as they both will show me later, turns out really nice.

What I Think Now:

How psychic connections work is, of course, a total mystery, but it does seem that we're on a closer "frequency" with some people than others. At that point in our lives, Josh, Ryly, and I were on similar wavelengths.

Strictly speaking, this was my first experience with clair*voyance* – clearly *seeing* the image that Josh was calling to mind – whereas the other knowings were clairsentience. Because he's a painter (and now successful musician) Josh's memory assembled a detailed image, one he wanted to remember as a whole, meaning all its components travelled to me intact: the old-fashioned bed posts framing Ryly herself, the wallpapered background. Somehow, all this travelled across the Home Depot parking lot into my consciousness.

Along the lines of the "diamonds of orderly precision," I want to point out the timing that let me run into Josh face-to-face. If I had walked correctly to the lumber section of the store, I would not have crossed paths with Josh and would never have known where the image of Ryly came from. I'd have just gone around forevermore ashamed about being a private perv toward my close friends. Instead, I went the wrong way, covered half the length of the store while Josh was getting out of his truck and walking through the contractors' entrance, as he was accustomed to do. We met smack dab in the center – in front of the paint department.

I've noticed that, aside from the Wendy Lee incident, most of my accidental telepathies have occurred when I'm feeling some form of love, affection, or belonging. The initial thought of Josh, I expect, arose from his proximity, but I *greeted* it with love for both him and Ryly. When I'm in a state of loving, my god-phobic sheath becomes more permeable. The only thing that can reach me when it's at full strength is Egnacio.

I think the moment I got a knowing about Ryly's new floor was the moment she thought of me as someone who could help her. I received no information about her being in a jam. I just knew about the bamboo floor and that the replacement was already in the works: "it's going to be bamboo." Considering that Josh and Ryly were not-quite-starving artists (he worked construction while she taught kindergarten) it seems unlikely they would shell out that kind of bucks for a fancy floor. In fact, I was surprised they would do so: "That's gotta be pricey!" In other words, my knowing contradicted what I knew of their circumstances.

Since these two episodes – which I did eventually share with them so that Josh attended my first NDE share – I've not picked up thoughts from either. Perhaps our frequencies have shifted. Perhaps we've done for each other what, as some NDErs maintain, was needed this time around in our incarnations.

I don't know. We'll all remember once we cross.

Chapter 13: International Association for Near-Death Studies

What I Thought Then:
It's a few weeks before the Home Depot / bamboo floor incidents, and I'm stuck in a looong Memorial Day Ferry line, waiting to visit my then-boyfriend who lives on Whidbey Island. I'm half listening to NPR as usual when an interview comes on that snags my full attention. They're interviewing some guy named Jeffrey Long about his new book, *Evidence of the Afterlife*. Evidence of *what*?! Turns out he's an oncologist who's never had an NDE himself, but someone he knew and intrinsically trusted had, and after hearing her story, he was hooked. He interviewed many NDErs individually, organizing recurrent features of their stories, then set up a website where they can post their own NDE accounts. Thousands of NDErs have taken his survey and posted their stories.

Whatwait. Thousands? *Thousands*?

This is the first time I've ever heard a credible, science-oriented person addressing Near Death Experiences. Before now, the only relevant public discourse I knew of was a book that, to borrow Holden C.'s phrase, made me puke all over myself: *Embraced by the Light,* by Betty Eadie. An AA friend gave it to me after I shared with her a little of my story. Evangelical Christianity was drilled deeply into Eadie's skull at a board n' brainwash school for stolen Native American children, so her god manifested as Jesus. Fine. Trouble is, she wrote about everything in her NDE literally, as if the figures and events she witnessed were *physically* present. I didn't know much about this stuff, but I did know nothing in my NDE had been physical. Reading Eadie's book, I felt embarrassed for her. If anything, the book further steeled my resolve to never, *ever* tell people about my NDE and Weird Things because I didn't want to be lumped in with a bunch of kooks.

But now on NPR, listening to Long feels entirely different. He's smart. He's talking about the spirit leaving the body as a form of conscious energy that's able, for instance, to witness and report on details in the operating room. He recounts the case of Pam Reynolds, a woman who, during brain surgery, was put into a state similar to brain death, eyes taped shut. She left her body and was able to describe visual details of events surrounding her body, including the case of blades for the surgical saw. And there's the cardiac surgery patient who saw his surgeon flapping his elbows as if imitating a chicken because, in fact, the surgeon's hands were unsterile and he meant to direct without touching. Long summarizes the classic NDE journey, how the spirit passes through tunnels or analogous transitions to reach other realms, experiences an ineffable light described as intense love, perhaps encounters deceased family members. His tone is cautious yet factual, which suits me. Most thrilling of all, he mentions "aftereffects" like clairvoyance and telepathy, both of which he calls "common" abilities among NDErs.

Common? Thousands? This is life-changing stuff!

Maybe I'm not a grandiose psycho after all. Maybe my 1982 experience and all the paranormals that have freaked me out since then are "common"! Dr. Long also names Near-Death support groups that sound a little like AA meetings for the used-to-be-dead. Maybe I should look into those!

But I don't. I have no time. Not only am I a single mom working one horrid part-time job after another since losing her university post in 2009 and adventuring with her emotionally immature boyfriend on non-parenting weekends, I'm also in the middle of writing my addiction memoir, which includes baffled anecdotes about my Weird Things.

Picking up the image of a naked Ryly from Josh's thoughts, however, that's somehow the last straw for me. It's too jarring, too specific, too *orchestrated* – that whole business of going the wrong way for perfect timing to run into Josh – to let pass. I *have* to tell others about it. I have to learn what's going on with the voice and my other Weird Things.

Hmm. What do you Google when all you know is that you died and came back and that, ever since, all sorts of crazy shit has happened to you? In 2010, it took me a while. "Died and came back," "Crossed over," "Paranormal gifts." Before long I hit the International Association of Near-Death Studies (IANDS) website, but they're located in North Carolina, clear across the U.S. Finally, I land on a low-budget page for Seattle IANDS, a local chapter of the bigger organization. I learn that meetings occur once a month.

I could easily slip in and say nothing. I could say I was there for a friend.

But I don't go, not that month or the next. The meetings fall on Saturdays, when I'm either parenting or off on mountain adventures. A year slides by. More than a year. Little Weird Things are still happening, but nowadays they feel kind of normal for me. At an AA meeting, if I know who the speaker will be before they're introduced, or if, talking with acquaintances, I know some mistaken phrase they're about to say, or if on a hike and not wearing my glasses, I "recognize" someone from 100 feet away – y'know, this stuff happens to me. Knowing who's calling before the phone rings – that's pretty standard, isn't it? Mental caller ID?

Still, I can't seem to make it to a single meeting. Then, in the fall of 2011, I break up (for the first time) with my emotionally immature boyfriend after he repeatedly ditches me on our 1,000-mile bicycle ride to San Francisco. Now, every other Saturday when my son's at his other mom's house, I find I'm lonely. And sad. And it's raining.

What was that not-dead-anymore support group, again? Where do they meet?

Walking into my first Seattle IANDS meeting at the Douglass-Truth Public Library, I appear casual, perhaps mildly interested, while the bulk of my attention is focused on scanning for dorks. I fear these people might all be dumb or crazy. They might want to indoctrinate me into their – I don't know – freaky woo-woo ceremonies. My inner cynic is barking like a chained dog, OMG! Crazies! Crazies! Get us out of here!

About a hundred metal folding chairs are set up in a large room, maybe half of them occupied, with well over half of those occupants being white-haired elders. At 51, I'm among the youngest. I speak to no one. A good fifteen minutes past the time the meeting's slated to begin, Kimberly Clark Sharp and Greg Wilson, Seattle IANDS Chair and administrator, take up their mics at the front of the room.

Greg reviews housekeeping points, then hands off to Kim, who recaps the nature of an NDE before introducing the speaker.

Lovingly yet in the tone of a standard spiel – because indeed she's grown this meeting, the first NDE support group, for almost thirty years – she speaks into a microphone words that ring ever-so privately true and answers that have eluded me since Manhattan in 1982. I am spellbound.

An NDE, she says, is defined as a set of memories from a time span when a person was clinically dead – i.e. without pulse or breathing – or when death was imminent. They may or may not include an Out of Body Experience, during which a person views their own dead body from an outside perspective and/or witnesses nearby activities. They may or may not feature some sort of transition, perhaps a tunnel, to a realm of white light that immerses the person in an indescribably powerful love, a love a thousand times more potent than any on Earth. The person is home. Even so, for a variety of reasons, they may choose to return to their body, or they may simply be sent back without a choice.

She's ticking off like a shopping list ideas and memories I've stuffed down for thirty years in fear of being crazy.

Next, Kim explains that NDE memories do not fade with time. Spirit memories, she comments, are not recorded in the same way as cerebral ones – unaware that, for me, in a matter of seconds she's just relieved three decades of wondering why I can still remember my NDE as if it happened yesterday. Additionally, people who have left their bodies often come back gifted with a range of psychic powers. They may experience or develop an ability to see spirits, foreknow future events, hear spirit voices, and/or read others thoughts.

Oh my freaking god. I'm not crazy. I'm not crazy.

I haven't moved an inch, but my whole reality has been transformed. I'm blown away. My heart is pounding. I'm sweating. "They," she keeps saying, not "Louisa." But now I truly know how poor Wendy Lee must have felt! It's almost as if this Kimberly woman has been spying on my whole life from inside my consciousness.

Now she touches on details I can scarcely believe. Some NDErs experience electrical issues. For example, they quickly kill the batteries in their wrist watches.

SHUT UP! I flash to the poor jewelry repair guy at Fred Meyer who eventually took to fleeing to the back room whenever he saw me coming, knowing I'd have yet *another* inexplicably "bad" battery – and the receipt for it. I was determined to wear a watch given to me by a friend who died, but after four battery changes, the repair guy would high tail it from his post and other sales staff would come forward to tell me he'd just taken lunch. So I gave up.

But there's more. The belief systems of NDErs, Kim notes, undergo radical change. Many divorce or experience family rifts because of changed attitudes, particularly those whose families embrace organized religion. I think of my "religion" – atheism – and how I've told no one in my family I now reject it. But, as Kim wraps up, most NDErs struggle for years to accept and integrate the disruptive implications of their experience – with the average delay being seven to ten years.

Okay. Try thirty years, I think, but I should get an extension because I was shitfaced drunk for almost half of that and wobbling around in new sobriety until the spider thing. Wasn't the spider thing about seven years ago?

Anyway, I'm in the right place now. It's just like AA all over again, that same amazing identification and explaining of what had seemed inexplicable. I'm not a freak. I'm not delusional. I'm just an ordinary, garden variety NDEr – exactly as I'm just an ordinary, garden variety alcoholic.

Kim asks for a show of hands from those who've experienced an NDE. Forgetting caution, I shoot my hand up like I wanna be line leader. Twisting in my seat, though, I'm disheartened to see behind me only about a tenth of the audience raising hands. I thought we were *all* NDErs! Then Kim asks how many have had woo-woos or spiritually transformative experiences (STEs), and almost everyone raises a hand. A few others are grieving the loss of a loved one. Still, I'm used to AA where just about everyone identifies as an alcoholic. Getting used to this might take me a while.

This month's speaker turns out to have been paralyzed from the neck down after he broke his neck diving into shallow water. A teenager at the time, he died not during the accident itself, but when a mechanical cot meant to flip him malfunctioned for long enough that he smothered to death between mattresses. In the midst of darkness, utter terror, and helplessness, he merely "popped through" into a realm of powerful white light – no journey, no tunnel – where calmness and bliss instantly quelled his fear. He experienced a sense of being loved beyond description. But then, just as swiftly, he was pulled back down into his paralyzed body. The orderlies had somehow gotten him out and performed CPR, much to his inner anguish.

While he never regained use of his limbs, the guy clearly enjoys a fulfilling life today: he has a beautiful, loving wife here with him and an award-winning career as a mouth painter, one who mentors fellow quadriplegics in the art.

At this point, Kim comments that, unlike hallucinations, NDEs radically change lives, inspiring people to center their values on the primacy of love.

I reflect guiltily that I'd certainly not done that. Rather, I'd tried to seal off my NDE in a vault – though I knew in my heart it was *more real than anything back there* – so I could go on soaking myself in booze and chasing my imbecilic ideal of coolness. If it weren't for the voice, I'd have hidden in denial all my life. My angel not only shouted me awake but guided me, via the motorcycle dyke, to find sobriety. It was from AA teachers and the 12 Steps, not my NDE per se, that I'd learned the truths that transformed my way of living – namely, that a meaningful life centers on impersonal love. I've progressed slowly, but between the two influences – my angel and my program – I've built what I know to be a beautiful, joy-filled life.

When the sign-in sheet comes around, I check YES beside "had an NDE," so before long I get a call from Greg, the group's administrator, asking whether I'd be willing to share my NDE story – first, over the phone with him, and then, if he deems it genuine, in an upcoming meeting. Telling Greg feels like unwinding a spool of memory that has never seen the light of day. He asks all kinds of questions, but excitedly rather than skeptically. I'm slated to be the first Seattle IANDS speaker of 2012, just a few months off at the January meeting.

After talking first to Greg and later to Kimberly, I decide to go ahead and self-publish the addiction memoir I've been working on for the last few years. Rejected by a score of agents, I've felt pretty discouraged about it, but their support emboldens me. Yes, I am a weirdo, and yes, I will tell the world. Up it goes on the web.

Every December, Seattle IANDS hosts a holiday potluck featuring a big-name speaker. This year, to my surprise, the speaker is none other than Jeff Long, the same medical doctor I heard on NPR while waiting for the ferry a year and a half ago. He'll be addressing us in a venue much larger than the library – a local community center – to accommodate the larger audience.

I arrive early and a little dressed up, bringing a contribution of homemade cornbread because it's cheap and I'm poor. I set my cornbread where a volunteer instructs, then turn toward the many empty rows of seats. My intention is to go way down front for a close view of the speaker, but along the way my attention is drawn to a petite brunette woman in an aisle seat – or, at least, to the back of her head.

Sit next to her, the voice instructs me. *She's a nice person.*

Ha! Are you kidding? I've never so much as laid eyes on this poor woman, so, with literally a hundred open seats surrounding her, it would seem pretty weird to invade her space like that. How about I sit a few seats down?

No. Sit right next to her. She'll ruffle up, but kindness can slice through. She needs a friend.

He gives me the love I need for this. So now, entering the lady's row, I scoot past chair after empty chair to take the seat right next to hers. I make brief eye contact and smile as I settle in, and sure enough she looks disgruntled, shocked, any number of things beyond ruffled. I can't blame her!

Kindness, he said. So I smile again and say simply, "Hi. I'm Louisa."

Here's a second account of the same incident, but from the point of view of the "nice person," M.K. McDaniel, in her book, *Misfit in Hell to Heaven Expat*:

> Since my return from "the other side," the Voice seems to converse with me on its own terms. I don't need to sit quietly and await it; it speaks right up. The morning of my first IANDS meeting, I decided not to go. The Voice told me to get in the car. I continued to argue with the Voice as I drove north. An hour later, I found myself in a meeting. It was mildly interesting, but I did not feel connected. The speaker's NDE was wonderful and full of joy and angels and blah, blah, blah. I didn't fit in.
>
> Months later, an IANDS email reminded me that a famous doctor would be the featured speaker that afternoon, but I really didn't want to drive that far. The Voice insisted, "You need to meet a special person there, and you must attend." I half-believed the Voice to be a figment of my imagination. I told myself it was time to test [it] once and for all. Arriving early at the unfamiliar location, I walked down an aisle in the middle of a large vacant area and sat in an end chair. I counted seven empty rows ahead of me and seven behind. I waited, avoiding eye contact so as not to encourage someone to sit by me.
>
> Within ten minutes, my peripheral vision noticed a young woman at the end of my row. I looked down at some brochures in my lap. She

entered my row, walked past all the empty chairs, sat right next to me, and said, "Hi!"

It was fortunate I was already sitting down because I was flabbergasted.

…At the break, full of excitement and wonder, I turned to the mystery lady and fully expected to shock her with, "I was supposed to meet you here today!"

She didn't hesitate, only flashed a conspiratorial smile and calmly answered, "I know."

This was too much. I asked her, "How did you know?"

She smiled. "I was wondering where to sit when my Voice told me, 'Go sit by that lady; she's very nice.'"

I grabbed her forearm and asked, "Your Voice?"

"Sure," she said, "Don't you hear it?"

I nodded with my mouth agape.

I sound way cooler in M.K.'s account than I actually was, but other than that, it's true. I'm not sure she physically grabbed my arm, but it was that kind of shocked connection, looking into each other's eyes. Once we'd become friends, we promised each would come hear the other's story and sit up front as support. M.K. had been reluctant to share her dark NDE, most of which was in hell, but hearing the honesty with which I told mine heartened her to go ahead.

What I Think Now:

Yup. There's no need to keep dividing my narrative. I'd found where I belonged, and, finally, I had integrated.

Chapter 14: Going Public – In Safe and Unsafe Places.

Safe

For my talk, the library's meeting room was more full than it had been for either of the previous meetings I'd attended. This was in part because I'd invited quite a few people. In the audience sat not only M.K. but Josh, whose romantic weekend I'd seen, Tim Smith, whom I'd known would be walking down Olive Way. Also there were my friends Jesseca, who I didn't yet know had crossed over during a surgery, and her spiritually sensitive husband Chip. I'd arrived after picking up my friend Murphy from a treatment center in Kirkland, a rich white neighborhood that he was desperate to escape. "Ah!" he sighed as we neared the meeting's location in central Seattle. "Black faces, brown faces! I'm home!" Indeed, I felt at home in the IANDS meeting with these and other alcoholic friends there to hear, not my AA story, but my *other* story.

I was so used to full disclosure in AA meetings that sharing the more shameful parts of my story posed no problem. In fact, I over-shared a bit about my various addictions, in part because I'd been working so hard on my book. Yet the compulsions I'd suffered were relevant; I used the same practiced denial to shut out my NDE and Weird Things.

My inner skeptic was, despite extremely adverse circumstances, sharing the tall stool with me. At times I could feel its eye-rolling, finger gagging, and general disgust. Only once did it overwhelm me. As described in a previous chapter, I was telling about my sister's death and how I'd felt her presence, her energy of love hovering in the hospital room. Yes, I'd heard about aftereffects of clairvoyance, seeing spirits, etc., but I'd never heard anyone speak of a spirit hovering in a room. It sounded lifted from a movie or Casper cartoon. That's what Kimberly was there for, seated on a stool opposite mine. When she asked the audience how many had hovered or sensed hoverers, I remembered again: I'm in a safe neighborhood, just like my friend Murphy!

The exhilaration that follows such self-disclosure is beyond description. In the bathroom, women thanked me. One assured me I should not feel guilty for having been unable to prevent the death of my nephew, as she had known her friends would be in a horrible car crash. Others talked of their own denial, of how hard it was to "come out" as an NDEr. To be surrounded with stories and encouragement like this was a wholly new and long overdue experience. It was my first taste of the NDE/STE community so beloved to me today.

I showed up for M.K. in the same way when she first told her hellish NDE story. I was front and center, a known safe haven in the crowd. Though she'd considered herself a good Catholic woman, when she expired from acute respiratory distress syndrome (ARDS), she'd been blocked from the Light by the anger and resentment she harbored from the painful blows life had dealt her. No tunnel, no nothing. Just darkness, shrieks, something burning, and a deep, horribly evil voice in her mind confirming that, yes, this was hell.

Finding herself first in a war-wrecked city patrolled by demons, M.K. escaped by offering companionship to another refugee, only to find herself transferred to another "circle" of hell. Each time, some act of kindness or connection removed her, only to place her in the next scenario. After what she experienced as nine years of misery, she finally reached the beloved man she'd nursed through leukemia until the day he crossed. Now he greeted her lovingly at the entrance to the light but, directing her attention with irksome amusement to a huge open book of records on a stand behind her, told her she wasn't done yet. She emerged from her month-long coma, during which she'd flatlined several times.

After sharing her NDE, M.K. connected with a subset in the NDE community: dark and distressing NDErs. While 15% of people who die come back with memories from the other side, less than 5% of those are hellish. There's often shame with having gone to hell, even if only initially. People wonder what they did wrong.

My own theory is that their sheath of anti-god was fortified by too much fear and resentment as they strove to protect themselves from a world they viewed as hostile. Over time, the membrane becomes too thick for them to pass through, cutting them off from their reunion with god. In other words, hell is the experience of being outside one's body yet not reunited with one's source, leaving the lone soul vulnerable to all the dark flotsam and jetson of demons and similarly unhappy souls.

Victor, a man in his 20s, had such a dark experience when he died from the flu at age eight. A troubled Korean foster kid who believed himself unwanted and unlovable, he found himself clinging to a rope above a barren, blighted hellscape populated by demons. After hearing M.K.'s story, he bonded with her despite their markedly mismatched demographics. I myself had a Weird Thing involving Victor – a time I knew I would see him with a homeless friend on a traffic island. He would be on the far side of a wall I was about to U-turn past. It was twilight, and I was on my way to an AA meeting. But I looked especially, saw Victor with the homeless guy, honked and waved. After that, Victor came with me to some AA meetings, but alcohol had never been his problem. He developed increasing paranoia about being judged by his Catholic church and eventually fled Seattle.

M.K., too, had continued attending the Catholic Church after her NDE, but once she'd shared her story and found her people, she was outta there. She now speaks frequently online, sharing her changed view of God and spirituality. I like to think our respective "voices" or angels worked together to help us both gain courage. She remains a dear friend.

At the *next* holiday speakers' meeting in 2012, the speaker was none other than author Betty Eadie herself, the one whose book had turned me off. I felt a little ashamed for not loving and revering her as so many did, or for mentally flagging a contradiction in her intricately beaded Native garb and loyalty to the textbook religion shoved down so many tribal people's throats, supplanting the most beautiful belief systems known to me. Yet Eadie deserved credit. She was first. While I was busy getting shitfaced and stalking the cool boy, she'd put out *Embraced by the Light* in 1992, addressing a scoffing, unreceptive world she hoped to change. Still, I felt what I felt – and *didn't* feel. By the date of her appearance, I'd heard ten more NDE speakers in monthly meetings, and each time hearing them had triggered in me a living memory of the light, a reverberation, as if they'd brought a spark of that same loving energy into the room.

Now, standing near the back as Eadie talked, I sidled over to one of these NDErs. David, who'd drowned in his thirties when he was thrown from a white-water raft and held under the rapids in a swirling current, is much taller than I, so at first I wasn't sure he heard my stage whisper: "I'm not getting any light off her."

David kept his eyes on the speaker and let few seconds tick past before he shook his head slowly. "Me neither," he murmured. "Nothing."

"It's like she's just saying the words, not going there."

"Right," he said, but with empathy. "She's just told it too many times."

David understood me. He was right there with me, not feeling light. Imagine the freedom, after so many years in doubt and secrecy, of being able spontaneously communicate my experience (I'd yet to hear anyone speak of what I now call "getting a freebie") and be readily understood. Yes, I had found my people.

Unsafe

In the year between these two holiday speakers, I readied the manuscript of my addiction memoir for Kindle publication, a process that entailed far more work than I'd imagined. I first reread the manuscript, cutting words and trying, somewhat unsuccessfully, to catch typos. I learned how to format it for upload in a system far more finicky that of today. And I hired (for pittance) a graphic designer friend to craft a cover image.

Her idea was to use a still shot from the birthday video I'd made, *How to Turn 50, Bitches*. In that video, I transform from a frumpy old lady to a corset-clad vixen who strides confidently around downtown Seattle. My friend loved it and told me the corset-clad me conveyed everything the book contained about evolving into my own person.

"You just look so free!" she said. So we went with it, publishing in September of 2012. Unfortunately, not everyone saw the corset-clad, striding Louisa as free. A lot of people just saw her as... what is this? Burlesque?

My AA community didn't mind, though. An alcoholic's "story" is essentially a cautionary tale meant to highlight the depths to which our disease can drag us before we hit bottom and open our hearts to a transformative power through the 12 Steps. The story's happy ending may be simply that the teller is alive and coherent enough to recount their tale, or they may have evolved into a worthy and happy human being. Many in my community had already heard a few of my Weird Things; some knew about the voice saying *This is the last time I can help you* or *Don't go*! But this was my *whole* story, following the AA template, "What it was like; what happened; and what it's like now."

I sold fifty ebooks in the first two weeks. One woman who owned a recovery-based bookstore hosted a book reading: about fifty people attended. There was no book to sign, but I'd made post cards of the corset-clad, striding Louisa and signed those. Former addicts began to seek me out, asking if the out-of-body experiences they remembered, such as watching from above as others tried to resuscitate them, were NDEs. Other readers commented that they felt less alone in their histories of compulsive self-destructiveness, or more confirmed in their sense that religion had little to do with spirituality.

I felt terrific about the book. So terrific, in fact, that about two weeks before Christmas I called up a family member and told him I'd just e-published it. I expected my family to be happy for me, but probably not to bother reading it. After all, they'd shown no interest in my recovery for eighteen years; why should they start now?

Let's just say I couldn't have been more wrong.

Let's just acknowledge that every person has their own memories of what their family was like, and that these memories often conflict.

Let's just consider how no one in my family knew the format of a typical AA story, so they assumed I must be bragging about my depraved, obsessed, compulsive behaviors. Why else would someone parade their dirty laundry in public?

Let's just remember that in thirty years, they'd heard hardly a word about my Weird Things, so the paranormal gifts I described seemed be coming out of nowhere, as if I were just plain making shit up.

Several family members bought Kindles, read in outrage, and responded with condemnation in a barrage of flamer emails, Facebook mockery, and 1-star "reviews" meaner than I'd never dreamed possible. They mailed me a certified letter with bullet points of cuts and changes I must make or face legal consequences. Day after day I cried, shook constantly, lost sleep and almost sanity, but set to work making the edits they demanded.

My Al-Anon sponsor coached me not to engage with my siblings until they had "calmed down," so I refrained from trying to defend myself. But her advice backfired. They pictured me as smugly ignoring them, not deigning to answer, so their emails grew even *more* irate, more frequent, and more abusive. Eventually, just the sight of my laptop triggered panic attacks. I had to auto-forward their messages to a trusted friend who agreed to screen them and pass along anything of substance.

There was nothing, he said. Nothing but insults and outrage.

About one month into this circus, I learned I had breast cancer.

Of the two ordeals – breast cancer versus family hating on my book – the latter was far more traumatic and scarring. The addiction memoir was my first experience in trusting enough to pull everything out of the vault. I meant to help others overcome experiences just as painful. My family's reaction – How dare you?? This is disgusting!! – awakened the dragon I thought I'd slain long ago: deep shame for who I was.

Rather than rehash the pain of my particular journey in sharing my story, it might be useful to consider a 2006 research paper, "Six Major Challenges Faced by Near-Death Experiencers," by Stout, Jacquin, and Atwater, to see how my family's response fit the general pattern. Here, the authors characterize a component of Challenge #3, Sharing the Experience.

> *Coping with Negative Reactions.*
> [Respondents described] the traumatic and isolating effects of having told this experience

> to doctors, family members, or trusted friends who were dismissive, misunderstanding, patronizing or otherwise negative. Eighteen respondents (78 percent) described a very painful and/ or lasting consequence of having shared the experience with someone who did not want to hear about, believe, appreciate, or understand what happened. ...The fear, isolation, and loneliness felt by those who... had shared with someone who reacted negatively was one of the biggest challenges that participants described. Typical comments included "My family didn't want me to talk about it," "My spouse discounted me," "My husband started making fun of me in front of his friends," and "My son was embarrassed when I talked about my NDE." Eighteen respondents (78 percent) reported feelings of alienation, isolation, or depression over the problems associated with not being able to share the experience.

In other words, even my trauma at having my story rejected was garden-variety. While we're looking at this study, we might also consider an excerpt from Challenge #5, Adjusting to Heightened Sensitivities and Supernatural Gifts.

> ...In addition to these heightened sensitivities following an NDE, 19 respondents (83 percent) said that they had developed one or more supernatural gifts as a result of their NDEs. The gifts mentioned included intuitive, auditory, or

visual knowledge of what was or what was to come (17 respondents, or 74 percent); ...mediumship (3 respondents, or 13 percent); and telepathy (3 respondents, or 3 percent).

While many people may embrace these gifts, that was not necessarily the case with participants. These gifts could surprise and disrupt the experiencer's customary thought processes and actions. Some learned to adjust to accept the gifts, while others described praying to be "left alone." One respondent said, "It drove me crazy because I didn't know what to do with it, so I shut it down." Another said, "Initially, it was frightening." Still another commented, "I worked hard to get rid of these sensitivities and psychic gifts."

Choosing Confidants.
Afraid of sharing, one respondent kept the NDE, which had occurred at age 14, entirely suppressed for 36 years, while another kept silent...for 42 years. Neither had shared the NDE even with family members. Others also described decades of silence.

It was to address this prolonged silence that Seattle IANDS' Kimberly Clark Sharp organized the first-ever NDE support group back in 1982 (the same year I died). Initially, four NDErs met informally around a coffee table and each shared their experience. All were well aware of the risks of doing so publicly. A hospital social worker who professionally counselled many

NDErs, Kim was at that time a well-known public speaker on the NDE phenomenon, yet for decades she remained closeted. She explains in her book, *After the Light*:

> ...In my numerous lectures throughout the state of Washington, I had not once revealed to an audience that I myself had had a Near-Death Experience. I could not fathom being that intimate with a roomful of strangers. Besides, I still feared such a revelation would undermine my credibility as a serious health care professional, and as a result, undermine my work. I wasn't surprised when the other three [group members] agreed. We had all long ago realized it was prudent to keep quiet on this subject to protect ourselves and our loved ones from other people's ignorance, prejudice, or condescension.[9]

NDErs would likely *still* be pathologized were it not for the advent of the Internet, which has enabled us to find one another and meet, both locally and internationally. Today almost every U.S. state has at least one IANDS chapter, and many more exist abroad. Back in 1982, when I had my NDE, there were no official groups. In 1987, when I saw the ghost, or even 1997 when my sister passed – still nothing! For this reason, I can't truly regret having kept silent about my NDE and Weird Things for so many years. There was nowhere I knew of to go, no one to tell without sounding insane.

---

[9] Sharp, Kimberly C. *After the Light*. (New York: Authors Choice Press, 2003), 141-142.

Chapter 15: Guidance from my Angel

By this point in my life, as you have surmised, I was a full-on loony-tunes woo-woo, so as a transformation tale, the book could end here. But if you've read this far, you probably wouldn't mind hearing about more Weird Things, as I still affectionately call my aftereffects, and Egnacio, as I affectionately call the voice.

A lot of other things happened in that year between holiday speakers Jeff Long and Betty Eadie, but let's back up even further. Years before, as mentioned, I'd lost my position directing the university's Writing Center when my department's budget was slashed during the 2008 recession. My job played out for another year on the previous year's funding, and for a while so did my unemployment benefits and health insurance. I admit, outside a few sporadic, horrible part time stints, I used the bulk of my time to write my addiction memoir.

But by 2011, I found myself without health insurance. The Affordable Care Act had passed as legislation but wasn't up and running. Washington State offered a Medicaid plan of its own known as Basic Health, but its waitlist ran over two years.

Mind you, I had plenty of ego around my health. At 51, I was taking intermediate ballet three days a week, not trailing but up front in the class. I'd soloed the Wonderland Trail, a 100-mile wilderness loop around Mount Rainier. Clearly, I'd be fine without health insurance – an astronomical expense for someone as financially strapped as I was.

But not according to Egnacio.

If you thought angels don't concern themselves with matters as mundane as health insurance, think again. After weaning my child, I'd developed an infected lactation lobule. It hurt, swelled, was obvious. Twice I saw doctors about it. Twice, Western medicine being what it is, I underwent a barrage of tests to rule out cancer. These came out clear. It was "only" an infection. But no one would treat that infection! "It'll go away," I was told repeatedly.

But it didn't – for four years.

If you read up on cancer, you'll find the only thing it plays in more happily than sugar is inflammation. Inflammation thins the hydrophobic membranes between cells, making it easier for healing agents *and* bad guys to pass through them.

So I'm just hanging out one time, and apropos of nothing, Egnacio says, *You need health insurance.*

What? No, I don't! I'm super healthy, and besides I'm super poor. I can't do that. Sorry!

Day in, day out, *Get health insurance. Get health insurance.* The guy is nothing if not persistent.

Now, if he'd warned me I was going to get breast cancer, I'd have hopped right to it. But he didn't. He waited until I was perusing Facebook, when a post from a young Goth woman drew my attention. We were longtime acquaintances in both AA and Al-Anon, but we'd gotten closer grieving Vanessa's loss. A modern-day Morticia Adams, she was one of those who stay "cool" after getting sober, so I was surprised to learn she was an administrative assistant in a huge bureaucracy: Washington State Healthcare Authority.

Ask her for help.

How awkward! Plus I know what she'll say. I'm on the Basic Health waitlist already.

Ask her for help. Ask her for help. Get Health Insurance NOW.

He was starting to yell.

So I texted her on Facebook Messenger. With her black fingernails, she texted back that a new alternative had just become available – I can't recall the name, but I'll just call it Basic Plus. Unlike Basic Health, it charged premiums – about $280 per month.

Wow. I thanked her, but said no thanks, that was way beyond what I could afford.

Get health insurance!
Get health insurance!
You can pay that much!

Yep. He's yelling again. He never yells unless it's a big deal, so somehow, I've got to pull this off.

I texted her again to say I'd changed my mind, and without batting a heavily blackened eyelid, she emailed me an application. I paid the $280 a month by check. It hurt every time. You know that little span of time when you're excited about a little extra money in the bank – and then you remember a stupid thing like this? That happened, again and again. Sometimes I had to ask my mom for help, but I wrote the checks dutifully every month, feeling Egnacio almost watching over my shoulder.

I got a mammogram. It came back clear. What a frickin' waste of money!

One of the worst jobs I took during my post-recession unemployment crisis was as a seasonal extra for Crate & Barrel. Colleges weren't hiring. I'd taught one Composition course at a pilot school (not recommended) and another at a community college where I kept kicking misbehaving students out of my classroom. I did some editing work and put up a few tear-off fliers around town offering one-to-one coaching, but nothing came through.

One way to stop liking a yummy restaurant is to work there. Things went the same way for me at Crate & Barrel. It's not that the products were bad or the people mean, but the Christmas season is do-or-die in retail, and the managers viewed all of us seasonals as disposable stop-gaps. Long hours, boring tasks, endless dusting and cleaning – it just wasn't fun. My pay was $10 per hour, or $9 after taxes.

Yet, when January 2012 rolled around, I outright begged to be kept on. I'd keep working at the seasonal rate; I'd work all weekends; anything – just don't let me go!

They let me go.

Around this time, however, I got a nibble from one of my flyers – a hospital administrator who couldn't move up the hierarchy because of her language skills, especially her thick Czech accent. For privacy's sake, she had me meet her in her high-rise apartment. She liked the lesson, paid me $35, and scheduled a second the following week.

Driving home across the Aurora Bridge in the tinted shades of dusk, I was marveling at how easily I'd just earned in an hour what would have taken me six hours at Crate & Barrel. It could make a nice little side-hustle, this coaching stuff!

Start your own business.

Uh-oh. It was him again.

What are you? A financier?

It's your best future. You'll succeed.

Do you *not* know me *at all*? I'm terrible at business. I know NOTHING!

I will guide you.

I drove, thinking, weighing, stressing. *Start your own business.* I knew beyond a shadow of a doubt that this idea could never come from me, because the prospect seemed *Start your own business* absolutely impossible and terrifying to me. I would fall on my face.

Okay! Never argue with your angel! By the time I got home, I was full of ideas on how to proceed and whom I could ask for help. Longtime AA friends built me a website for almost no money, shot staged photos to display on it as in exchange for my writing stuff, and posed as clients in the photos just for a coffee; I posted ads on Craigslist, Thumbtack, Tutors.com. I ran all over town tacking tear-off flyers onto coffee shop bulletin boards.

My mother gave me a lump sum "loan," to get started – in other words, to cover my mortgage until I could pay it myself. Starting off was hard. I had no business plan, no marketing strategy, nothing. I went on Food Stamps. I'd drive all over Seattle at any time of day or night, especially on weekends, to meet with all types of clients. Gradually, my clientele grew. After about six months, I went off food stamps and, with the help of a basement tenant, became solvent.

It's now been ten years – and I love what I do. I still don't advertise or do anything businessy other than good work that earns me word of mouth commendations. Most of my clients work for big tech companies, and since the pandemic, all my classes are online. The funny thing? I used to accidentally read clients' minds when sitting next to them, most often with them to my left. If an editing client was struggling to explain themselves in a personal essay or cover letter, perhaps in a second language, they'd often go happily bonkers as I typed their thoughts, saying, "Yes! Exactly! How did you know what I wanted?"

But as it turns out, I accidentally read clients' thoughts over the computer, too.

> ME: "Give me an absolute phrase about Robin Hood. Remember, noun plus modifier."
>
> IN MY HEAD: Ha! He's picturing Errol Flynn and gonna say, "His green tights sagging..." That's so funny!
>
> CLIENT: "His green tights sagging, Robin Hood jumped on his horse."

> CLIENT, sharing screen as she takes an interactive parts of speech quiz, hovers cursor over the word 'Cousin.'
>
> IN MY HEAD: Oh, dear, she thinks it's a pronoun. She's thinking how it refers to a person without their actual name.
>
> CLIENT: "Pronoun!" [Sees it's a noun.] "Oh!... I was thinking how it names a kind of person, but not their name."

IN MY HEAD: Don't say, "I know!"

I learned I had breast cancer the same way most women do. My next mammogram was flagged, and the biopsy came back positive. Originally, I started attending Al-Anon meetings in 2011 after I broke up (the first time) with my emotionally immature boyfriend, but once I started getting panic attacks from the duo stresses of a cancer diagnosis *and* raging family, I went more frequently.

It was an ordinary Saturday morning in December of 2012. I wrapped up my usual Al-Anon meeting on top of Seattle's 500-foot Queen Anne Hill. Afterwards I dashed through the rain to my twenty-some-year-old Honda Accord and, my mind full of thoughts from the meeting, started home. I had just enough time to grab some lunch and then head downtown to get my hair cut and colored. Leaving the parking lot, I turned sharply right and braked. Everything felt normal. But the next time I touched the brakes, rounding a corner as I approached a steep hill, I noticed they felt a tad soft.

You have no brakes. Pull over.

Oh, come on! They're fine. It's pouring out. And I have a haircut appointment. So, no.

Pull over now.

It's raining! I'll swing by that brake place tomorrow, okay?
They will fail on the hill.

What? Fail? What? That can't just happen like snap! Like, maybe I need new brake pads? New disks? I'll take care of it.

You have nothing! Stop NOW!

I can't do that. I know Dravus is steep, but I'll use the hand brake if anything goes wrong. One thing I'm *NOT* doing, though, is cancelling my hair appointment from a month out and standing in the rain because my *ANGEL* thinks my brakes are bad!

He didn't answer. I thought I'd won.

At that point, what looked like a black and white street sign on my left grabbed my attention. When I went back later, I'd find it was nothing but the back side of an ordinary "No Parking" sign for the oncoming traffic, but in that instant it clearly bore the words ARTERIAL TURNS above a black arrow pointing right. I'd seen this sign literally hundreds of times, but, wait – here? I suddenly felt dizzy. My thoughts blurred. I couldn't— shouldn't this sign come up a block further ahead? Or was this where I turn?

It's here! Yes! Just turn! Turn!

So I turned right.

Immediately, I realized two things: first, that I never meant to turn onto this narrow, unconnected little side street. Second, that I had no brakes whatsoever. When I depressed the brake to turn, the pedal went to the floor with zero resistance and the car's momentum stayed so strong I could barely pull in the arc of the turn. Instinctively I pushed the brake over and over as I coasted down this side street's shallow dip. By the time I was rolling up an equally shallow rise on far side, Egnacio seemed to be tapping his foot.

I steered to the curb and gradually, oh-so-slowly, came to a stand-still. I moved the gearshift to park. The wipers still kept rapid time on my thickly spattered windshield as if nothing mind-blowing had just happened. Other than that, all was quiet.

"I'm sorry!" I sighed out loud. "Thank you!"

I killed the engine and sat there a while, processing.

A few minutes later, I found myself walking in the pouring rain toward the nearest bus stop, down the series of steep hills. That hand brake idea? It would never have worked. I'd barely kept control of the car turning onto the little side street. What could I have done if I faced a drop? At the bottom of West Dravus Street, several cars were lined up at a traffic light in front of a bridge over a six-lane arterial. Not a good landing for a no-brakes car.

I caught a bus. I texted my hair stylist, not that my *angel thought* my brakes were out, but that they were in fact out.

I had the car towed to a brake shop near my home. When I went to pick it up, the mechanic had saved a broken rubber tube from the brake line to show me. "These old cars' rubber parts last only so long. It can just take one sharp turn or a bump and, crack! There goes all your brake fluid. Your system was empty."

So, yeah, Egnacio was right. Again.

That's the only time, to my knowledge, he's actually taken matters into his own angel hands, so to speak, using his powers to scramble my thinking – (the dizzy, blurry feeling) and creating an illusion (ARTERIAL TURNS) to save my life and those of others. Why I merit this kind of intercession, I do not know.

I can be such a brat, can't I? But he loves me. And I learned my lesson that day: *DO NOT* argue with an angel. He knows the future, for chrissake, and he doesn't butt in unless it matters. I've never argued with Egnacio since that time.

Whining, however, is a different matter.

Shortly after the brakes incident, I got two pieces of good news. First, the "expensive" health insurance I'd started just over a year ago at you-know-whose insistence would cover all my cancer treatments, because that clear, healthy mammogram I'd gotten right off the bat ruled out any pre-existing condition. What's more, the tumor had been caught very early on. It was less than a centimeter across could be removed via a simple lumpectomy. The date for my surgery turned out to fall exactly on my sobriety birthday – Monday, January 29th – when I would be turning 18 years sober in Alcoholics Anonymous.

For each of my last seven sobriety birthdays, I'd thrown a huge whoopee party, both to celebrate the re-beginning of my life and to create a bright spot for alcoholics depressed and lonely during Seattle's dark, rainy winters. These were a huge deal: scores of AA friends crammed into my little house, spilling onto the back deck and smoking in the front yard, for a party a lot like those of our drinking days, but without the drinks. Colored lights, loud music, dancing, tons of food, photos, games, clowning, etc. Over the years, my January parties had become a thing.

About a month earlier, I'd posted the event on Facebook and sent out invites to a zillion people. When I learned I had cancer, I lost all interest in what would become of it. For one thing, parties take a lot of work, and for another, between cancer testing and my siblings' rage, I was continuously frantic. So, the event had stayed up.

Then I learned the good news: no mastectomy, no chemo. I felt so grateful, I changed the Facebook event name from "18 Years Sober" party to "Get to Keep my Boob" party. Friends who'd been following my posts about the cancer diagnosis talked to friends. Carpools were arranged. Dishes, drinks, and desserts were planned. In the end, my friends created a huge party that involved little work on my part. Someone made a huge felt-penned mural-card on the wall of me beating cancer and everyone signed it with loving notes. At one point, running up to my bedroom to grab something, I stumbled on twenty people in there playing Cards Against Humanity.

When everything was in full swing, someone decided the time had come to sing and cut cake. The music stopped and those who could whistle did so, others yelling that everybody was going to sing. I stood with my son in front of a cake homemade for me and lit with eighteen candles. To my left, out the French doors to the living room, stood a sea of people looking on. The song began. Cameras flashed.

"Happy Birthday" can seem like a reea-lly long song when you're feeling super awkward. I'd been in such a nervous state these past few weeks, I sailed right past awkward to mortified with embarrassment. My siblings came to mind, all their email flamers, their condemnations and reviews. I thought, They're right! I'm a narcissist! Why else would I create a situation like this to make myself the center of attention?

I hated myself, book, cancer and all.

At this point, I felt Egnacio – whom I still thought of as only "the voice" or "my angel" – swoop in. He was laughing again, shaking his angel head. I could *feel* his amusement. He conveyed: *Don't be silly, little one! This is the whole point of life! As good as it gets! Just let them love you.*

Let them love me? – Me?

Never argue with your angel. I had to give it my best shot.

To reverse the trajectory of my feelings took a huge push, like Superman stopping an asteroid and shoving it back toward outer space. That sheer effort, I would say, took me halfway through "happy BIRTH-day, dear Louisa." But by the time everyone sang the song's last line, I was looking into their eyes and marveling at the beauty of their faces, their kindness, their caring. I'd been going to AA meetings for eighteen years, the last ten primarily to help new people. To this party I'd invited an often-homeless but currently-sober Native American guy with a heavily scarred-up face and hardly any teeth, a brand-new-to-the U.S. Korean guy in his first sixty days sober, and a few folks from my home group that I'd just met. Also present was a former convict I'd picked up during a crisis and driven to a mental health center, sponsees I'd taken through the steps, and many long-time friends – all members of my tribe, many of whom looked toward eighteen years' sobriety as the life they wanted. Love was in their eyes, their smiles, their off-kilter singing, and I let it fill my open heart.

The next day, looking at photos friends had taken with my digital camera, I noticed that, in the cake-singing photo, a large orb appeared beside my head. Initially I thought nothing of it. Sure, I'd heard some woo-woos believed spirit energies could show up in digital photos as "orbs," but I wasn't into that. A dust mote caught in the flash, maybe some nick on the lens, a trick of the lighting – it could be anything.

As the morning progressed, friends began posting their photos from the party online. I was clicking through when I saw it: a large orb just above my head in a photo taken perhaps one second after the other.

Two digital cameras. Two moments. Two angles. Same orb. How could that be?

I recalled this had been the very moment when my angel

communicated with me. As usual, he'd seemed to speak from my left, just as the orb appeared to the left of my temple in these photos.

Taken with my camera

Different camera, angle, moment. Same orb.

I expanded each photo. In the one from my camera, I could see orbs within the orb, circles resembling craters on the moon, most of them small but two quite large and distinctive with little splash-like edges. The photo posted online was less distinct, but without question, its orb had the same features, the same two larger craters. The orb had risen a few inches in the second photo and rotated in flight, as shown by the new placement of the two craters.

I was looking at photographs of my angel. This was his energy caught in the act of addressing me, then moving away as soon as his job was done.

I stared. I marveled. I grabbed my phone.

I texted Rachel, the woman who had posted the second orb photo, to ask her if she could email me the original with greater resolution. But she didn't respond until late afternoon, when she told me – nooooo! – she'd already deleted all the party photos from her camera.

Let them love you. That advice comes in really handy when you're a single mom estranged from her blood family and undergoing a lumpectomy. Two days later the ex-con picked me up at 6:00 a.m. and drove me to the hospital, where an old friend from grad school met us (she's not even an alcoholic!). She stayed until I woke from surgery, then another alcoholic who had called me almost daily when she was going through a divorce drove me home with to-go containers of pho. Inside my house waited still more friends who had picked up my son from his other mom's house and taken him grocery shopping to pick out all the food we'd need that week.

Love carried me.

Radiation treatment sucked, getting nuked five days a week for six weeks, and when I finally reached my second-to-last day, I was in bad shape. Arriving home exhausted, I saw that a new 1-star review of my book had gone up. This one was from someone in AA, a folksy guy who'd hoped the book would contain pointers but was sorely disappointed that it amounted to little more than a sordid monologue of all the twisted things the author ever did. I threw myself on my bed and sobbed for quite a while.

But wait. Wasn't "sordid monologue of twisted things" a line from one of my siblings' emails? I checked. It was. So they'd bought yet *another* Kindle to post yet *another* review.

Family wasn't fixed yet, but that was okay. I'd met a mentor in Al-Anon, a fellow cancer survivor who also happened to work as a manager in Amazon Books. Family, she said, were barred from writing book reviews, good or bad. All I had to do was send in their names, email addresses, and proof of our relation to the complaints department and all their reviews would be promptly removed. I did and they were.

I began healing, but lung damage from the radiation burns still plagues me as a mountain climber ten years later.

By the way, after I filled out reams of paperwork, the local hospital forgave me $70,000 in charges my lousy state-funded health insurance hadn't covered. And a few years after that, the state refunded every check I'd ever written to pay those monthly premiums. A Washington judge ruled that the Healthcare Authority should have expanded Basic Health to fill demand, so the premiums were collected unlawfully.

Pretty much, I had cancer for free.

Chapter 16: Disregarding My Angel

In 2006, I fell in love with a man I met through my clean and sober mountaineering group, OSAT. Gerard was gorgeous, smart, funny, and amazing in the wilderness, with oodles of feats to his credit. He'd free-climbed Early Winter Spires, soloed the Pacific Crest Trail long before anyone else had heard of it, navigated with a compass to difficult peaks without trails – no big deal. He could check out a tall stack of books from the library and return them two weeks later, practically memorized. He fixed electrical systems on enormous jet planes, drawing from immensely complex schematics he carried around in his head. He could do this in part because he was "on the spectrum" for autism – which also meant he had difficulty imagining others' emotions or processing his own. He'd had no friends outside work before he joined OSAT.

We had five wonderful years together, climbing everything in sight, through-hiking for weeks, and pursuing indoor activities.

But the good times lasted only so long. When he moved to a rural island, he also stopped participating in both OSAT and AA. Before long, he relapsed in secret.

I knew it, but I didn't want to know it. I broke up with him in 2011, then got back together late in 2012. Many were my misgivings about the relationship. Many were the moments I sensed he was lying and unfaithful. But sensing is not the same thing as acknowledging. I wanted so much to recapture our golden days and hoped so much he'd get sober again that I denied the obvious.

After two years of my pretending everything was fine, however, Egnacio yelled at me. It was a beautiful morning. Gerard was at work and I was home alone at his kitchen table, sunlight beaming in through the large window. His property adjoined the rolling hills of what was once a 140-acre dairy farm, later turned loganberry farm, now preserved as in a land trust, so I could gaze out at its lovely meadows and woods as I sipped my morning tea.

My eyes had just drifted to the stack of mail by the windowsill when Egnacio said, *Everything here is lies and corruption*. He was not talking about the mail stack. That's just where my eyes happened to be resting when his message came through, so the moment is seared into my memory mail stack and all. The feeling he gave me – wrongness, sickness, barrenness, almost filth – unfurled like noxious smoke. I looked quickly back out at the countryside, but my mind felt like it had been shoved into a VR headset where I could not escape that awful feeling.

I pulled back hard. I said, No it's not! It's lovely here. Everything's lovely.

I wouldn't call this *arguing* with Egnacio. I was just rejecting the knowing, choosing to believe in Gerard's goodness – because I loved him.

Later that visit, I was looking for scotch tape, pulling open all the kitchen drawers, when at the back of one I saw a neat stack of iPhones – four of them. I knew which one was newest, the one he'd only recently discarded.

Take it!

It's locked.

Just take it. We'll cross that bridge...

I scooped it out of the drawer and tucked it into a side pocket of my computer bag.

Later that night, we were planning to go see a movie in town. I volunteered to look up the showtimes on Gerard's iPad. He was shaving at the bathroom sink at the time, and I could see his profile through the open door.

"What's the code for the iPad?"

He froze, razer poised. One beat. Two beats. Then he gave it to me – four random numbers – and resumed shaving. I said them over and over to myself to memorize them.

When I was heading home the next morning, I asked him, "Isn't there something you forgot to tell me?"

He looked momentarily at a loss before saying, "I love you."

As soon as I got home, I started charging the phone's battery. That evening, I stood at the kitchen counter and tried the iPad's code on the iPhone.

Nothing. It didn't work. I sighed.

But Egancio showed me:

5343 – *swap the outer two digits* – **3345**

I tried it. It worked. The phone unlocked. The whole process took less than ten seconds.

His phone was filled with hundreds of salacious texts with multiple women that told me all I needed to know – a years' worth of exchanges about drinking and screwing during visits carefully timed around mine. I found them not that night but the next day, sitting in my car outside a café where I would meet my next client. One girl from his work was roughly his daughter's age and completely caught up in recreating *50 Shades of Grey* scenes. There were no naked photos, however, perhaps because she was quite overweight.

Now I knew how Jenna must have felt when she read my journal full of fantasies about the cool boy. I seemed to see through the phone down a deep shaft to a subterranean pit, where far below the light of day naked bodies writhed à la Hieronymus Bosch. I felt immense shock at each crass word Gerard had sent. At the same time, some little bird seemed to fly from my chest into the bright spring day. *You're free! You're done!*

I didn't feel free, though. Letting go of that relationship was extremely tough. I'd never have been able to do it without seeing the lies and corruption for myself.

Did Egnacio think it wrong of me to secretly take someone's phone? Apparently not if it's their means of deceit. He was all for it.

I shot photos of some of the grossest texts with my own phone, sent them to him without comment, and mailed back his iPhone. A week later, I wrote him a long letter, the gist of which was that he'd chosen alcohol and I'd chosen sobriety, and there was no way we could bridge that gap. Two years after that, we met for coffee and a walk to nearby park, where we sat on the grass. He apologized that he couldn't look me in the eye, so he held my ankle while he spoke his apologies and cried his eyes out. His touch frightened me, though, because I had once loved it so. Now it felt like a cross between a crack pipe and a snake.

All my rage went into my journal, incensed at him, never the various girls, whose numbers I now had. I'd learned too much the first time around with my lesbian partner's infidelity to believe venting anger at anyone would help anything.

Mostly, I was angry with myself. The cheating had gone on for two years when he was travelling for work and on weekends when I was home with my son. I'm frickin' clairvoyant! Why hadn't I known?

At the deepest level, I had. But I was just as caught up in being addicted this relationship as I had been to drinking. The addictive reward circuit seems to wall out spiritual sensitivities, and I was powerfully addicted to my *idea* of him, which I adored.

So Egnacio had to yell again.

About a year and a half ago, I called Gerard. I'd heard from his sisters that he was skeletally thin and shaking too much to sip from a cup when they met him for coffee after the pandemic. Retirement had left him with no shield against the call of alcohol.

"Sweetheart," I said, "you're dying."

He'd been driving his pickup truck on the island and pulled over.

He tried to sound cheerful. "Everyone has to die!"

"Yes," I said, "but to die before you're even sixty is a waste of life. Don't you want to live?"

There was a long, long, silence. He would always put his thumb over the mic when he was sobbing. I think just hearing me call him sweetheart again tore his heart.

"I don't know," he said with difficulty.

About year ago, I visited Gerard in treatment for alcohol addiction, where he was sweet and hopeful, shuffling around the center's cafeteria in the mooseskin moccasins I'd gotten him many years before. I gave him *A New Pair of Glasses* and felt a mournful love.

Just a week ago, we exchanged a few texts in which he bemoaned yet again his poor choices back then.

Just a few days ago, in 2023, his daughter texted me that he'd collapsed and died in his home from alcoholism. He hemorrhaged internally on his sixtieth birthday, alone with his puppy in that lovely little house. So he didn't die before he was sixty.

His daughter spoke to an elderly great aunt who remembers how, after a catastrophic stroke left his mother half paralyzed and unable to speak when Gerard was eleven, he began binge drinking. His father was a hard, cruel, Type-A engineer, never home. In 1974 in their tiny Eastern Washington town, no counselors, no antidepressants, no way to ease his pain existed except to drown it in alcohol. He impaired the development of his teen brain, and addiction got its hooks in deep.

I have his mooseskin moccasins now. I have some of his ashes, which I will soon carry up the mountain he used to specify and scatter off a thousand-foot cliff. Three Fingers. It's the mountain we climbed for our first adventure in 2006, when kisses were new and love grew fast. I admit that, as codependent as I was, always wanting *more* of him – more attention, more time, more love – it's weird to hold his ashes and know I have all that's left on Earth.

Yet I hear from him now much more than I did in those eight years apart. It's safe to love him again: I don't have to worry about going back. He has such regrets. My heart breaks for him because I know firsthand how it feels to flounder amid the quicksand of addiction and the depravity it ushers in.

There but for Egnacio go I.

Chapter 17: Miracle in the Wilderness

In August of 2018, I hiked Section K of the Pacific Crest Trail in Washington State. As seasoned PCTers know, it's the toughest section outside the Sierra, and I did it solo after my hiking partner injured her back. Solitude in true wilderness is a far bigger experience than words can convey. The transformation that occurs when you're hitting up against your physical limits every day is likewise hard to describe. I walked 127 miles through spectacular mountains, climbing and descending 26,000 feet, crossing the roadless expanse between Highway 2 and Highway 20 at the height of wildfire season.[10]

Immersion in a place where Nature's still boss, as she is in the half-million acres of Glacier Peak Wilderness, sets you back to who you are at your foundation. You feel the flavor, the shade, the tone of your lifelong consciousness – your simples "I-ness" apart from all the tweaks we effect in society. It's an incredibly humbling state. At its base, I have found, my awareness is an ignorant, bumbling instant of "what?" in the midst of all that's becoming. Hang out with that.

No phone; no data. My only companionship was Egnacio and god itself amid all the ancient peaks, eager greenery, and dutiful trees I passed.

---

[10] See videos of this trip: https://youtu.be/1YEUM1huzUI and https://youtu.be/McRi8zbW0TY

Here the years, centuries, and millennia roll in and out like ocean waves with the storm-etched peaks standing witness, a time scale in which my own lifespan feels like a gnat's. I can't say my ego was *gone*, only that I lived mostly outside it, loving everything while sort of rolling my eyes at my own inescapable self-interest and Louisa concerns, which struck me as endearing foibles.

Day after day and night after night, I talked aloud to my angel with a sincerity that triggered tears frequently enough that I quit noticing them. At night when I prayed in my sleeping bag, I felt a gratitude so big – holding all my angel and god had done for me – that the tears would trickle from under my night hat and find their way into my ears.

One afternoon I was exhausted beyond exhaustion to the point where no view, however spectacular, could raise even a blip on my aesthetic gauge. At a certain point, aesthetics just go. My pack weighed over thirty pounds; my feet had at least four blisters, and I'd just crested 6,000-foot Fire Creek Pass. In front of me was a 180 degree view of countless peaks, some edged with snow to the north, all skirted with evergreens, overlapping one another to the horizon. Very nice. Starting down this snow-patched glacial cirque, I could also clearly see the trail's switchbacks a thousand feet down. It looked like a skinny, meandering dust-snake.

Listen to me! This is where you FALL!

Right. Right. It's him, my angel. He feels pretty excited.

I responded: Duly noted.

But all I could really think about was my next campsite, Mica Lake. It was a couple of miles off and about a thousand feet down, though I couldn't see it.

I'm serious! I'm serious! You FALL!!

He was shouting again, no question about it, and if he'd been using English words, he'd have said "fucking serious." I knew that. And I wasn't going to *argue*, but I sort of wanted him to calm down. I was just too damn exhausted to care about *anything*.

I'll be careful, I promised. But I wasn't happy about it. Being careful felt a lot like the time I waited at green light, because descent, after hours of struggling like a laden beetle up, up, and up, is a hiker's green light: down, down, down!

I slowed my pace, but it still wasn't enough for him. He wanted baby steps. He wanted me to not even lift my eyes from the trail.

Never argue with your angel. This was a time to honor my maxim.

Feeling like the most dutiful, obedient, unquestioning angel-hearer ever, I took ridiculously small baby steps, one foot barely clearing the previous. I kept my gaze glued to the trail, the steeply sloped rocks, fine gravel, the ruts carved out by rainstorms. I knew all these were hazards. I knew hiking alone out here was extremely dangerous. And I knew I was fatigued and vulnerable. But it still seemed like overkill.

Never argue with your angel. Baby steps. Little flowers either side of the trail.

Are you happy now? I asked.

He was.

After about fifteen minutes, I reached a big granite slab I had to turn around to downclimb, one foot fishing for the ground beneath it. Past that, I pulled my phone from its sandwich bag and took some pictures. I'd just started up again when it hit.

HOLY SHIT!!

Pain forked down the inside of my shin and threw my face into crazy gymnastics.

OH MY GOD!! HOLY SHIT!!

If I'd been moving when that struck, I'd have tumbled. And if I'd started rolling with that heavy pack, I could not have stopped. And falling head over heels amid granite boulders, I would have died.

Once the pain subsided, I offered a ton of gratitude. But I also told myself this flash of agony had been only a passing fluke. I did NOT want to be injured. I was trying hard to rule that out. Why? Because I was already sixty miles into this hike, and I had more than sixty left to reach Highway 20.

Once I reached the level patch that was camp, I experienced one more mini-shot of nerve pain as I stood up from filtering glacial melt at Mica Lake. This one hurt way less, at least, so I told myself overnight rest would fix it.

Two British boys joined me toward dusk, Ed and Nick. Ed was hiking the PCT, but Nick had been so tantalized by the photos his brother sent home, he'd flown out from London to join him. That's why they didn't have beards like every other PCT guy. We chatted and joked, knew the same crazy Israeli hiker, and traded some food. Even though they set up their tents literally ten feet from mine – flat rock being scarce – I loved them both.

In fact, by the time I was snuggling in my down bag and loving their low-pitched voices so close, I'd forgotten all about the flash of pain. So I just prayed, as usual, to my angel and god beyond him: "Thanks, you guys, for this amazing life, this amazing world and my getting to be in it! I love you!" I thought of my addiction, breast cancer, and the fact that I was 58 years old and yet strong enough to be here, and pretty soon my ears were tickling. Gratitude tears.

The next morning dawned gorgeous and clear, the wildfire haze having blown off. Ed and Nick were long gone when I finally got rolling around 9:00 a.m. To find the trail down without falling off a cliff took me a few tries, but I did. I was feeling super happy, super grateful, with seventeen miles and 2,000 feet down ahead of me to reach my next camp.

I was talking to the plants, remarking how great it was for them to finally be out from under the snow. I passed some gnarled little fir trees, severely stunted from the high altitude and bent over or broken by yearly snow burdens into weird, humpbacked shapes. To them I thought, I know it's tough, but here's where you are. Isn't that all god asks from any of us, that we try our best with what we're given?

I was striding along full steam, happily singing some ear worm, when—

HOLY SHIT!! HOLY FUCK!!

This time the pain zapped both ways, nerves screaming up my inner thigh and down my calf. I made a noise. I stared wild-eyed at nothing, half bent over, my heart racing as the pain eased up. This time, at least for a second, it hit a nine.

Let's not panic. Let's not panic. We're okay. We're fine. Let's take a lil' step.

HOLY SHIT!! HOLY FUCK!!

The thing was shrieking like a fire siren in your ear. I tried stepping another way.

Z-A-A-A-A-P!!! Dentist drill inside my knee.

Nothing worked. I was still in the same spot, no way to get anyplace else.

My mind groped for a plan. I scanned up the open mountainside for somebody, anybody. But what could anyone even *do*? The next trail junction, I sort of recalled, was nineteen miles ahead and it led lord knows how many miles to the next dirt road, which led lord knows how many miles to remote pavement. I was fucked.

I gathered all my will, all my intention, and I prayed desperately: "*Please* help me! *Please* take away this pain!" I tried another step, just a gingerly attempt, and back I went to making noise and bugging my eyes at nothing. My leg could not bear any weight at all.

I had my friend Rob's InReach in my pack's outer pocket. I'd used it just last night, as I did every night, to tell my loved ones where I was. But it also had a rescue beacon. Rob had taught me the steps to send an S.O.S., as one should in my predicament. I knew full well if I did this that and the other thing, the beacon would send a signal to the nearest InReach station where someone would figure out the ranger station nearest me and send it my coordinates. Rangers there would assign a Search and Rescue team, probably via helicopter because this cirque was so steep. I'd sit here for six hours or so, finally hear it chuffing over the nearest peaks, and then I'd be horribly embarrassed while they got me up there somehow and choppered me out.

"No," I thought with distaste, "I'm not doing that."

For any normal person shocked with nerve pain like a frickin' taser every other step and sixty miles from anywhere – sixty miles of steep, rough trail, that is – the InReach would have been the only choice. I knew that. But it wasn't *my* choice. I felt a strange impatience, a contempt something like I'd have felt for a BuzzFeed article: "Top 10 Things to Do When You're Crippled in the Wilderness!"

What did the plants know? They were with me. What did my soul know? For two years, by this time, I'd been interviewing NDErs and writing up their stories for the Seattle IANDS newsletter. And almost every month, I'd gone to hear speakers who told of amazing things that actually happened to them – one car passing through another, a drowning man hoisted to the surface by bow rope that tangled in his legs, help offered by expert people who turned out not to exist.

Miracles, I knew, could happen at any time.

But such miracles, I thought, my hopes sinking, were not for me. I wasn't pure enough. Wasn't it my big fat ego that had gotten me here to begin with? When friends would look askance at the words "127 miles" and "alone," hadn't I inwardly smirked with pride? Wasn't I, Louisa, even at 58, still one bad-ass bitch?

No, I thought. Bitches with big fat egos don't get miracles.

Now, for the first time since saying goodbye to my friend at the trailhead, I felt lonely. Profoundly, deeply lonely. Lonely not just for company, but as a human being, a spirit locked inside a body. I'd traded words, looks, and touch with various people, but had anybody ever really *seen* me? Known me? Loved me?

I had no somebody. Empty, I did nothing.

At the switchback just ahead of me, a rib of alpine trees clung to the steep slope, all of them stunted – except one. My sight singled out a grand fir with a trunk over a foot thick. Really? How could that happen way up here, unless the thing was centuries old? Through my thoughts flashed memories of research I'd read on the hidden life of trees. Ancient trees like this were matriarchs; they nurtured the young and weak trees around them with an altruism science could not fathom. They sent water, sugar, and minerals in direct contradiction of Richard Dawkins' selfish gene. They lived in the spirit of agape, not competition.

Standing there, I recognized my someone.

"You," I thought. "I choose you."

It took a while, but I hop-limped toward her and up the shallow bank to her trunk, her roots underground as with all grand firs. I placed my palms on her rough bark and, closing my eyes, touched my forehead to the surface between them. I sent out simply, Are you there?

Something came back, faint but not me: *I am*.

My heart leapt. I knew in that moment, I was not alone.

Eagerly, I sent her this: You've stood here for centuries of dawns and dusks, turning sunshine into life with god's help. I'm just a pesky gnat, but can you help me? Can you ask god... to help me?

Her response was instant, the single note of a tuning fork: *Each life must ask directly... Each life must ask directly... Each life must ask directly...*

Here was a truth I'd always known, awakened in me by her intent. She meant that I had to ask god *myself*, from the font of my livingness; that's how life works for every living being.

I understood, but I still felt too tainted by my deeply flawed self. I feared failure, which would leave me nothing. So I blurted out in thought: But see, I already tried praying, and it went nowhere 'cause I kinda suck, so I was hoping you...

Each life must ask directly – she was fading.

I knew she was done. I thanked her. I kissed her bark with reverence, tears streaming. Cautiously, flinching at each nip of pain, I made my way slowly back to the trail. But just a few gingerly steps later, ZAAPP!!!! Blinding pain. Again.

Okay, fine. I gave up.

Here I was, a miserable sack of ego, but I had nothing else to show god, nothing else to offer, like the freakin' little drummer boy. *Ask*, she'd intoned. *Ask directly*. So, standing there, eyes open but on the trail, I prayed in thought:

God, my angel, I know I'm here because of vainglory. That's a funny word, but it fits. I got myself into this, and I know you can't change facts. But *you* also know how much I *love* this, all of your artwork, and how dearly I want to finish. (*Ask directly*.) Please, can you give me some guidance?

Guidance. The instant I sent that thought, my mind began whirling with input – knowing, knowing, knowing – more than I could parse.

First came love, a beautiful wave of it. *Little one, we love you! Don't be so hard on yourself!* Even my flaws, to them, were endearing; I was a thoughtful spirit toddler with the mashed yam of ego smeared on both chubby cheeks.

Next came information. The problem was not in my knee as I'd thought, but my inner thigh. I'd strained it so it had tightened protectively. That tightness was pulling my knee out of alignment just enough to pinch a nerve.

What? No way! My inner thigh was dandy!

It's not. Remember this?

My angel highlighted a moment from the night before when, shifting about in my tent on my knees, I'd felt it twinge.

Now I was to place my foot atop the nearest right-sized rock or log and stretch it. Gently.

To my amazement, my right adductor was so tight, I could scarcely get my foot up onto a rock the size of a basketball. Crazy! I had to start slow as I stretched it, and I knew to repeat this same stretch every 200 feet or so. The only trouble with that, my skeptic objected (yes, it had tagged along), was that I was *incapable* of walking 200 feet.

But I did it. And as I stretched again, I got the next knowing.

Remember this? I was with a physical therapist from years back who'd had me kneel on a rolled-up washcloth to stretch something under my knee cap. *Hold your trekking pole across that spot,* said the voice, *and pull.* This, too, I was to repeat every 200 feet.

I'd walked quite a ways pain free and was starting to think I might have run out of miracle guidance when my angel dropped the pièce de resistance:

Remember this?

He brought to my mind the little Velcro loop I kept being annoyed to come across in my pack because I was sure I'd put it on the "don't bring" pile back home. Why did I bring this thing? I'd click my teeth and re-tuck it somewhere.

Here is why, little one! Remember this? I was with the same physical therapist on our final visit, when he taped my knee with kinesthetic tape. "No one knows quite how this stuff works," the PT was saying. "There's no overt benefit, but it's thought the sensation itself acts like a beacon of sorts, signaling the brain where to send more blood and healing."

Yes, said my angel. *But this time, it will act as a beacon for ME. I will send healing. I will set it right, little one. You will be strong and...* I could feel his effusion of joy at this gift he was bestowing... *you will finish!*

I don't argue with my angel, but I did respond, Finish? Sixty miles? Are you freakin' nuts? Isn't the goal just to get me out?

Trust me. I will make you strong.

Right there, right then, I heaved my pack onto the trailside bank and started pulling everything out of it, food, raingear, hat, first aid kit overflowing onto the ground. Where was it? I'd seen it just the other night. Shit – did I lose it? No, here it was.

What should I do with it?

You know.

I laced it just under my knee cap and tightened it – how tight?

Just so we can feel it.

"We" meant me and him. I felt absolutely starstruck, blessed beyond my dreams. Why was he doing this?!

I reshouldered my pack. I understood that now I could go 500 feet between stretches, then quarter mile, and so on. Got it.

Maybe a mile later and a thousand feet down, the jig appeared to be up. A six-foot-thick tree had fallen across the trail, with the walk-around above its huge roots climbing a steep, muddy bank. I stood and took a good, long look at that steep, slick path – the muddy slides where people's feet had slipped down the clay, the spindly ferns they'd clutched at, the thick roots they'd stepped over.

You're so screwed! said my skeptical mind. Prepare to feel some intense pain, because no woo-woo angel bullshit is gonna to get you up and down those fifteen slick-as-shit feet! One slip and you're toast!

Trust me, little one.

I started up, one step, another step. Nothing gave; nothing slid. I raised my bad leg over a large root. From the top, I looked down at a slapdash chute of slick roots and muddy skid tracks dropping to the trail. I focused on just this handhold, just this foot placement, and the next thing I knew, I'd alighted on the trail. Ha! My hands and legs were muddy, but who cared? I could have danced.

My skeptic slunk back in its cave.

I reached Milk Creek, which the trail crossed at its lowest point. Snowmelt pounded down this steep channel, stern, silty, and loud. A fresh wooden bridge had been built across it, and there I sat down to eat and wash up.

I looked up the mountainside I'd just descended and tried to guess the spot where my leg had gone out, the spot with the tree. I imagined a Louisa who had chosen the sensible alternative of the electronic beacon instead of woo-woo nonsense of the spirit world. She was still stuck up there. In fact, she had at least another five hours to sit there, crippled, bored, and defeated. I imagined, once the rescue people found her, the humiliation she'd suffer at having caused such a fuss, her embarrassment watching the land recede below amid the rotors' deafening throb. Her journey was over.

But not mine! No sirree! Instead I'd talked to a tree – a tree! – and she'd answered me. Acting on tree wisdom, I'd *asked directly* from a place of humility, and my angel showered me with miraculous grace! He told me I'd finish! So much love I felt for him.

I washed the mud from my skin with frigid water. The bridge built before this, and the one before that – so much laughter and human affection the work crews had shared; I could almost hear them, just as alive as me but in the 1930s and '40s. Before them, the true stewards of this land, the Sauk and Suiattle, had probably known of gentler places to cross. I loved them all. I hailed them joyfully from this tiny floating leaf of a gnat's life, this little zizz of time while I breathed and felt. Now I was gonna eat this string cheese in a tortilla with precious mayo, lie back on this here pungent wooden bridge, and float my thoughts in this white-water roar, alive. But first, to document this miracle for all my life, I took a timed selfie of me sitting on a rock with my huge pack and little black knee loop.

From that low elevation, mile after mile, I walked a miracle. I climbed three thousand feet that day, feeling stronger than I had since starting out, and made camp at Vista Creek. I'd meant to go further according to pre-miracle plans on my map, plus I'd learned from fellow hikers that I needed to take a fire detour and catch a bus back to the trail, which added even more mileage. Still, something told me not to push it.

The next day proved the hardest, longest day I've ever hiked in my life. To catch the bus I needed to get around a wildfire, I hiked twenty-three miles to my next camp, gaining and losing over five thousand feet. I woke early the next morning and, hoping to catch the 10:00 a.m. bus from Holden to Lake Chelan, all but ran the last eight miles. The way was rife with roots and mud. My feet became pancakes of pain, but my knee – jarred again and again on the rocks, catching my weight as I jumped, moving, moving, moving – it held.

I trusted. And after what seemed like forever, I heard a British voice call out, "Hey Yahd Sale! You made it!" Yard Sale is my trail name. It was Ed and Nick, of course, beckoning, ready to hug me. From the hotel cafeteria where we ate ourselves halfway catatonic, we stumbled out and, joined by others we'd met on the trail, caught the bus to the boat to the bus that collectively skirted the wildfire.

At noon on the eighth day, I emerged from the woods right where I'd said I'd be, 127 miles from the place where I'd started and about 63 miles from the spot where my knee gave out. Every device and spare battery I carried was dead. The night before, sharing a campground with a black bear, I'd slept deeply and peacefully. I'd lost seven pounds in seven days. And I was flying in happiness. I knew my full powers for the first and perhaps only time in my life, and that was a wondrous feeling.

The next year, I came back with my hiking partner to show her just the most beautiful stretch of Section K, which of course included Mica Lake and the grand fir matriarch. Since I'd told her my story, my friend was eager to see this tree.

There was only one problem, though. We couldn't find the matriarch. All the trees on that part of the trail were – as they *should* be so high up – small, slim, and spiked with low branches.

I don't know what to tell you about whether the tree was "real" or how she manifested or what. I just know I need to go back there one more time and look for her again. It's a few days' hike in, but I have to find out. Maybe, if I'm alone, she'll show up again.

Chapter 18: Intentional Medium

In November of 2019, I communicated with my father, who, as I wrote above, died in 2008. I loved my father deeply, but I'd hated watching what alcoholism did to him toward the end of his life. He was unkind to my son, his namesake, jealous of the attention my mother lavished on her little grandson. He continued to make "being drunk is funny" jokes with me long after I had ten years sober. He angered recreationally, usually at TV newscasts or the newspaper. All this because he was in pain, both emotionally and physically.

But I still loved him. I take after him in countless ways; he handed down a life to me laced with the same ingredients that seasoned his consciousness. I also learned a great deal from him – much more than atheism. Self-sufficient frugality is a way of life for me, a point of pride. I eat expired food and fix broken things the same way he did.

This rainy weekend, I was at our family's summer cabin – one of his favorite places. It's on Anderson Island in south Puget Sound, rustic and a century old. Of course, as cabins tend to do, it not only smells cabinish but is constantly sinking into disrepair, so my dad, who grew up during the Great Depression, *loved* keeping busy there with chores, maintenance, and makeshift fixes.

All day Saturday, I was following his example, replacing the toolshed's thickly mossed, rotten shake roof. It had needed replacing for about fifteen years, but the need became more pressing after a fallen tree branch poked a hole through and broke off an eave. In the in the pouring rain, I pulled the old shakes off, stapled on new tar paper, and began layering it with asphalt shingles. Above me, wind shifted in the tall fir trees. I heard raindrops hitting my hood.

I kept feeling my father's presence as I often do when I'm fixing stuff there, as if he were looking on, pleased with my efforts. But on this day, the sensation was keen. I felt steeped in his presence and approval, which I loved and missed. Nothing paranormal about it, I thought. Just that sense we all get at times when memory and fondness mix.

But what if there *was* something to it? What if Dad *was* around looking on?

A few months before, at the beginning of September, I'd attended an annual conference of the International Association of Near Death Studies (IANDS) just outside Philadelphia where I was chatting in a hallway with a medium I'd heard speak. I described to her some of my experiences – knowing some aspects of the future, accidentally reading minds, and hearing my angel. She beamed at me and said, "You're a medium, honey! You just haven't developed it."

Since then, I've believed she's right, but who has the time to "develop" their mediumship skills? Not me. I can't even meditate most mornings, and I'm always just a teeny bit behind schedule. Medium school? Maybe someday.

Still, I made up my mind as I was nailing shingles, starting to smile and murmur to my father, that the next morning I would sit quietly and at least *try* to reach him.

I was up early as usual. The friend staying in the second cabin would, I knew, sleep in late. I drank my tea, sitting at what used to be Dad's place at the table, facing a row of windows that look out over Puget Sound to a distant shore.

Eyes shut, I focused on the crackle of the fire and my own breathing. Doesn't that sound like what you should do? I thought so. So I just sat there, and whenever I'd start getting bored or my mind would wander, I'd try to call up that closeness I'd felt on the shed roof in the treesy rain.

Maybe ten minutes of that. Then it seemed the next step would be to address him. That's what they do in movies, right? "You're a medium, honey!" So I gave it a try.

I thought: Dad, please say something to me. I want to hear from you.

Nothing happened. The fire crackled.

Please come to me. Please speak to me. I am ready. I am listening. I love you. Please.

More nothing.

I repeated this a few times with more nothing in response. Time seemed to drag on for ages, though I'd guess only about five minutes passed. I was sure he could hear me. The trouble had to be my reception: I couldn't hear him. From all the NDE interviews I'd conducted, I knew there was a veil separating us, something keeping me deaf to him. It might even be my own impatience. Finally, trying just one more wording among the many I'd already offered, I asked, Is there anything you'd like to tell me?

WHOOSH!!!

He was there. Not the Dad I was expecting, but the father I'd known as a child. Was I surprised! I could feel him! Just as clearly as you do when you're staring into the eyes of someone you love, I could feel his way, his presence.

Not only that, but I'd been hoping to make contact with the weary, depressed, alcoholic father I'd known for his last fifteen years. I'd all but forgotten how he used to be. There'd been one afternoon I was about five when we shared the chaise lounge after I "helped" him edge the front walk, mostly playing with the sod blocks, and we'd shared a beer in the low sunlight. That's when I'd loved him most intensely, with just a hint of Electra complex. Nothing weird; I just thought my dad was super handsome and cool.

Here I was 59 years old, and he'd brought all that back to me in the whirlwind of his arrival.

Next, I became aware he was already in the midst of showing me an image: something white with squares of fine wire mesh. Was it the old crib? I hadn't thought of it in decades, but it was a weirdly designed one he and Mom used for all four of us kids. Instead of wooden bars it had large rectangles of bug screen, along with a foldable top that would keep bugs out – though we lived in Seattle with relatively few insects. I saw it now at closer range, and now closer still. We were walking toward it, approaching it in his memory. I was in his mind and he was knowing, in this memory, that his baby girl, Louisa, was in the crib, though he stopped just short of where I might actually see myself. Huge amounts of love radiated from him for that infant, *huge* love. There was pride and gratitude that I'd entered this world via him. It was a sacred honor to him – then and now – that I had come into my life through his.

Blown away as I was, sitting there transported into Dad-ness with my eyes closed, it took me a few seconds to realize that he was using this image to answer my question of a moment before – whether there was anything he'd like to tell me. Yes, there was indeed, and it was this:

All of you was there then, all of you in that tiny form — and when I lived, I loved THAT!

I still faltered to grasp his meaning, so he added, *You didn't have to do anything.*

Now I understood! Oh – ! There was something he wanted to *correct*. All my life he'd pushed me to excel. If I got anything less than a straight A on anything, he'd pretend to get quite grave about it – a joke, yet not *really* a joke. "What happened here?" he'd ask, pointing to an A-. When I decided not to get a PhD, when I came out as (temporarily) lesbian, when I left a tenured teaching post, always I'd run up against his urging, however subtle, that I do and be something more. What he'd crossed the veil to tell me was that it was all untrue. He had loved me with all his heart just for being, whether I was 48 (when he died) or the flower bud of me in that crib.

I understood. I sent him my deepest love and told him how grateful I was to be his daughter. But then my fucking asshole skeptical mind butted in. Even now, it's got to poke its socially conditioned, conformist, materialist nose into my first intentional medium experience. What kind of nuttiness was this – communicating with our dead dad?! Who do you think you are? You're making stuff up!

So I asked him directly, Dad, I need something. How do I know this is really you?

Without a beat, with no time at all, he emphasized the crib again, but this time, from where we stood, we could see into the opposite corner of it. There sat brand new Teddy bear of bright pink, luxurious plush. It struck me as a bit garish, nothing more, until Dad said, *This was the first stuffed animal we got you.* Oh! Now I recognized it as the faded, one-eyed, much-loved and laundered Teddy bear I'd had as a child. This was when he was still new, from a time before I could remember! Dad finished, *...and you named him "Áha."*

I did! I did name him Áha! That's right!

With that, he was gone, his energy vanishing just as suddenly as it had arrived.

Áha! I'd not thought of that name in forty or years or so, but I remembered it! Áha held special meaning for us because one of Dad's morning routines for years had been to make my sister's and my beds, then set up little pageants in front of our pillows with carefully posed and balanced stuffed animals. There was always some drama suggested with various toys or props. Áha might have on a Halloween mask and be scaring a bunch of fleeing stuffed animals; he might be seated with a little Beatrix Potter book reading to the others; Áha joined Toady at a little table with toy foods. Morning after morning for years, Dad poured his love for us into these little scenes. I'd preferred Toady myself, but Dad always gave the leading roles to Áha. Now I knew why: Áha was first.

I had plenty to contemplate long after I left the cabin. The succinctness, the iconic efficiency, the directness of each image was flabbergasting. I guess on the other side, prep time to choose the perfect vehicle is not an issue. A parent myself, I knew the feeling he shared via his memory of the crib – that immense love for one's baby. And to counter my skeptic, he needed no time at all. I, too, can remember toys once important to my now grown son. But how did Dad's spirit manage to select an image only he and Mom could know – the brand spanking new Áha – and connect it not only with my memories but to a specific *name* I couldn't have recalled without his reminder, yet instantly knew was right?

Once again, my skeptic slunk away into hiding.

It brings me great comfort to know my father has shed the burdens of his human life and shines bright as a powerful spirit. My mother, at 97, still hasn't accepted my experiences. She rolls her eyes and says, "You have your.... beliefs, I know."[11]

I've gone back to the cabin several times since this incident and tried again, but without that sense of his presence as a precursor, I can't tune in. I tried to reach my older sister and got only somewhat curt *Be an aunt to my kids*. We have family divisions, it's true, but I'm trying. I'm really trying. Somebody's going to have to fill Mom's throne when she vacates it.

Maybe someday I'll fit mediumship school into my schedule. But just looking at my track record, it probably won't happen anytime soon. You'd think if someone had an opportunity to converse with the dead, they'd put it ahead of their day-to-day work. I'd think that, too. But then I look at my bank account. Teaching syntax pays the bills and, unless you're a Tyler Henry, mediumship doesn't.

---

[11] My mother died shortly after I wrote this. Among her last words were, "And my sister's here!" – a sibling who had died five years earlier.

Chapter 19: Life as a Happy Full-On Woo-woo

Woo-woo paranormal events will continue throughout my life, I'm sure. They bring me joy, reminding me there's far more to this world than meets the cerebral cortex. Energy never vanishes. Life has meaning. God's up to *something*.

Egnacio plays charades

Our culture is highly aware of adolescence and puberty, when the body is rapidly changing, as difficult and emotionally fraught stages of life. But it scarcely recognizes the transitions of aging, when the body is rapidly changing *again* in unwelcome ways. It's a phase equally difficult and fraught.

At 63, I am three years too old to run for village leader in rural China. Thankfully, I don't live in rural China, but if I did, they wouldn't want me. Apparently, enough people think I'm likely too doddering mentally and/or physically for the job. Ouch.

I still climb mountains timing myself. I still do strength training. Overall, aside from the irradiated lungs, I'm in better shape than I was in my thirties. But that doesn't change the label: senior.

At the end of 2020, after dating yet another guy I'd met through Facebook who, after a couple of months, revealed a severe mental illness, I let go of dating. This was my last addiction. Like food, romance can be either a healthy staple or an addiction, a crutch. For me, *needing someone* – a counterpart to witness, validate, and appreciate – had haunted me all my life. Candidates to fill that role are all over the internet, dressed up by one's imagination. But a person I could truly love and be loved by? Clearly out of my hands. So, at this juncture, I became ready to give up dating, suffer a withdrawal from hoping, and be okay with just me. Best decision ever.

At the same time, I was crawling out from the aftermath of a severe case of original, non-variant COVID 19 contracted right off the bat. In March of 2020, I was training yet again to climb a glaciated volcano, carrying a 30 lb. pack up and down a 300-foot staircase near my home. Lots of other people were training as well on this rain-free Saturday when some kind of traffic jam forced a bunch of us near the top to stop. What was up, I never found out, but all of us stopped and, like coils of a slinky, caught up with one another, blocked from going both up and down. Clumped together on this narrow flight of stairs, everyone was breathing hard from exertion, fogging up the cold air around us. Masks were not yet a thing. I tried to hold my breath, but I was far too winded.

Five days later, I came down like a falling tree. It was bad. And even after my flooded lungs had drained, it stayed bad for about seven months – horrid headaches the day after exercise. I lost my strength. I developed crippling arthritis in my hip. My badass mojo was gone. On top of this, I was alone during lockdown.

Oh, and my dog died. Really. Like everybody else, I became weepy, tense, lost in loneliness.

For years, the voice / my angel had been urging me to write this book, but, as with mediumship, I never had the time. Without dating, I thought, I might open more hours. So I *tried* to strike a deal with my angel, something like this: Okay. I promise

I'll pour every spare minute into writing the *Die Hard* book if *you'll* promise to send me the perfect partner after I finish. Deal? ...Deal?

Sometimes my angel is markedly silent. No deal.

Soon after, I became curious about past life regression and decided to hire a hypnotist who could lead me through one. A friend recommended a medium in California, whom I called to ask if she could perform regressions over video chat. Everything, by this point, had moved online, so I figured it couldn't hurt to ask.

No, she told me, she preferred to be in the same space as she guided clients because not all the energy transmits remotely. She was sure I could track down someone in Seattle who—

"WOW!" she interrupted herself. "Who is that with you?! Oh my god, he is a powerful presence. Masculine. Very masculine and very, very old!"

She was all excited. I confirmed he was my angel, and I started telling her about how, when I first began to formulate my AA concept of a higher power, I wanted a feminine goddess, a feminine guardian angel. I figured angels had no gender since they had no bodies, so I could assign it either. But as our culture is beginning to understand, masculinity and femininity have far more to do with energy than they do with anatomy. Before long, though, I realized no amount of lesbian reluctance was going to change the energetic timbre of my angel's voice, which was unmistakably masculine.

As I said, I *started* to tell her all this, but she was far too excited to let me speak more than a few words.

"He's old, old, old. I'm thinking – no, not Mesopotamia – maybe Atlantis!"

And right there she lost me. I can get only so woo. I'm sorry.

Remember how, when Vanessa died, I asked Kelly, who saw my angel as a large aura, whether it was masculine? She'd had no sense about it one way or the other – but *I* did. That's why I asked. So for ten years, I'd sensed the voice's masculine energy, and now this medium was fairly frothing at the mouth as she confirmed it over the phone.

After this I think, in my loneliness, I might have developed a crush on my angel. Here's an excerpt directly from my journal:

3/2/21 – 5:00 a.m.

> "I realized this morning that my angel has loved me since before I was Louisa.
>
> "I had a scary dream last night of demons trying to take possession of me, but I called out for god, for goodness, for their protection from evil. It worked, but I woke up kind of freaked. It was 2:30 and couldn't get back to sleep. So at 4:00, I got up planning to work on the book as promised.
>
> "Thinking of my angel as I dressed, I realized I always call him 'MY angel' when, really, he's not mine at all. So I should just call him 'Angel,' which struck me as a somewhat cheesy name/noun compared to who he is.
>
> "Who he is. That stopped me. He is *someone*. A door began to open. I asked him to tell me his name so I could call him by that. Nothing came

back. I told him I'd ask in meditation as soon as I got downstairs.

"Meditating, I remembered the psychic message from my dad, how I could feel his intense love for my essence, that baby in the white crib. That's when I realized my angel loves my essence because he's known me since BEFORE I was that baby in the crib.

"We go way back! And I think he misses me because in this incarnation I've forgotten who I really am and who he is. HE knows what I've been before Louisa. HE knows how our spirits have connected over the millennia. When he held me in the light and poured love into me, it was actually a brief reunion.

"I want to know his name! I want to know who we've been to each other in past lives. I want to know why I incarnated without him, and what it is I set out to do that I've not done yet. Am I his daughter? Sister? Wife? Lover? Heck – am I his son? Father? Mother? There's no knowing.

"I love you, Angel! I cannot remember who we've been, but I love you always!

6:08 a.m.

"I got quiet and asked... and asked. At first, nothing, then something like a sigh, maybe an eye roll, and then he told me he's had sooo many names in sooo many lifetimes, *and none of them are in alphabets that you know.*

"Shit. I'd forgotten all about that. I figured 'Gabriel' or some saint's name or something. Peter. Anthony.

"But he started. He showed me, hanging in my thoughts, a capital 'I' and next to it a small 'g.' I was totally at a loss – all I could think of was Iggy Pop! I told him that, I said I don't know any 'Ig' names, but all he did was show me a faint 'E' hanging under the 'I.' Finally, I asked, 'Ignacio?' I felt assent from him, like when you're close in charades but not quite there yet. The 'E' in my mind's eye grew brighter.

"'Eg-nacio? Is that even a name?'

Affirmative

"So I looked it up. Wikipedia says it's the Etruscan origin of the Spanish / Gaelic name Ignacio, meaning 'born from fire.'

"That's my angel's name: Egnacio. He's born from fire – that elemental – so it makes sense that he was *in the sun* when I met him. It makes sense that the medium said he was old, old. Eturia developed in 900 B.C. He's probably far older. Neolithic? Chinese? Egyptian? But his Etruscan name comes from a lineage closest to my current life, so that's the one we rolled with."

What I didn't record here was how much I whined, "Please? Please? I want to call you *some*thing!" before Egnacio reluctantly gave me the letters, and how happy all this made me, just to know

Egnacio is someone ancient and that he loves me. It was all I needed.

He conveys that I'm silly to insist on a name, such labels being pointless in his telepathic realm, but he gets it. Most things humans do are silly, driving about in these little round brains and meat-coated skeletons like bumper cars on the fairground track of this life, smashing into each other, getting stuck for years against the outside bumper but too flustered to find reverse. Silly but cute. It's okay.

Past Life Regression

A few months ago, I engaged in an online past life regression hypnosis session with NDEr Zach Tavcar, whom I tracked down after seeing his YouTube interview with Jeff Mara.

Hypnosis is an odd experience. You're somewhere else yet, at least in my case, simultaneously aware of where your body is. You feel sort of normal and yet time is different. I was sure the session had lasted about an hour when in fact it lasted three.

Throughout the session, my rapid eye movement was off the charts. The same thing had happened to me last time I'd been hypnotized, more than thirty years earlier by a psychologist. In my addiction memoir, I referred to the REM experience as "popcorning." That is, my eyes were bouncing around so much and so fast, it felt like they wanted to fly right out from under the lids, making it impossible to keep my eyes closed.

I told Zach this was happening, and he instructed me to simply ignore it, but that's easier said than done. I kept seeing an intrusive stripe of daylight and occasional glimpse of the mirror above the mantlepiece as I lay on my couch. This battle to keep my eyelids shut became a distraction that to some extent limited how deep I could go.

Two of the four past lives I revisited related to resonant memories or feelings I've had in *this* life. That can mean one of two things. Either my feelings have stayed strong for these places because they were linked with past life memories, or I was just imagining past lives based on my present-day values.

For each life, Zach guided me from a neutral landscape to focus on a specific day when something happened – something important, something meaningful to me.

In the first life, I stood in an abandoned mountain village. Looking down, I saw I had hairy male calves and sandals. I'd come back to see the home where I used to live with my aunt after my mother's youthful death, which I considered quite normal. The roof was terra cotta, the house small and situated near many similar ones. I was standing in the doorway, looking across to a stone hearth with a stool beside it. But the place was empty. I was the only person there.

Zach asked, "Where is everyone?"

As soon as I tried to answer, I burst into tears – which utterly shocked Louisa on the couch. Heartbroken, I sobbed, "We heard they were coming, they were close, so we had to leave, we had to go!" Zach asked who was coming. "Their army! They'd kill us or take us, so we had to leave everything..." Yes, I knew, we'd succeeded; yes, we'd eluded the invaders and most of us made it to the city below, poor and displaced but not killed or enslaved. But the happy community I'd loved here for decades, to which I'd just now made a dicey, difficult pilgrimage to honor someone or something, was lost forever. Here I stood. I wept with a profound sense of loss and wrongdoing.

Zach guided me out and onward to another life. This time, I was boy of about thirteen. I fished with all my uncles and cousins – but today I'd made clear I was best at diving under the boat. There I'd free up our nets if they caught on the sea floor and otherwise got tangled, so my uncles didn't have to bring them up unnecessarily. I was slim and pretty much naked, with perfect brown skin. My sisters and aunts onshore cleaned and grilled whatever we caught. I loved to dive! I could swim like a fish, so at home underwater and proud of my abilities – of the role I held in my family and the praise I got from elders.

In the next one, I wore a thick, heavy snake bracelet that wound up my forearm – made of gold so pure it was pliable. It didn't belong to me, but I wore it whenever I danced in ceremonies conducted by our priestess, as I'd just done – a great honor. I was a girl of perhaps 19 and lived in a place where women held power. Elder women ruled, carried out rituals, and enjoyed more powerful esteem than men did – and I could feel it. I was pretty dang cool to be doing what I did. (Yep, even in past lives with the coolness thing.)

In the next and final lifetime, things became very strange. I was a businessman in New York, perhaps fifty-five, and I'd just closed the deal of a lifetime. I was super tickled about all the money I'd made and couldn't shut up about it. I told Zach I'd told others I could close this deal – I kept seeing the black and white Warner Brothers concentric circles – but I didn't express how nobody had thought I could. "And now," I said proudly, "I'm set for life!"

I, Louisa, lying on the couch with eyes popcorning in REM, experienced something mind-blowing. Whenever the businessman spoke, he *PULLED* my voice toward its lowest registers; I experienced physically his will to speak in a certain way. My throat kept shifting. I couldn't stop it!

Surviving Death, a Netflix special, had featured a medium whose voice changed to its highest and lowest registers depending on whom she was channeling, but when I watched it, I'd felt horribly embarrassed for her. She was clearly faking, I felt, pretending with her piping high voice for one spirit and her deep low voice for another. Why oh why, I'd thought back then, did they even put her on the show? Now we spiritualists look like idiots! No one will believe us!

As the business man kept pulling my register down, I fought to keep it in my normal range, so I ended up warbling absurdly – and was astounded. He'd draw out my vowels, too, into snooty old-fashioned tones. I fought for normalcy here, too, but as soon as I relaxed control even a little, I'd form words as if I were in an old movie. I realized I owed that Netflix medium a mental apology: it does happen.

Furthermore, I had contempt for this man – who I used to be! All he cared about was money! He was looking out a big picture window in his high-rise apartment at the Manhattan skyline. He thought it was the coolest place ever! I knew, as him, that my friends teased me about my resemblance to the Monopoly character. Apparently, I looked and dressed a lot like him, paunch and all. So I, Louisa, felt alienated from him as from none of the others. I hate Manhattan. I hate business. I hate anybody's glee surrounding deals and money. Talk about shallow!

Unexpectedly, business man knew of my attitude and turned on Louisa-me – aware of my judgment and not okay with it. Here's a transcript.

> **Zach**: What do you see?
> **Deepening voice**: New York. I've done [warbling between low and normal] something important...
> **Louisa voice**: I don't know what it is but I'm happy about it, and I'm a man again. I made something happen.
> **Zach**: Where are you in New York. New York City?
> **Louisa voice**: I'm in New York City... It's maybe 1950 and...
> **Deepening voice**: ...and, it's a very important time and place, I believe. And I feel, I feel I'm very important.
> **Louisa voice**: Ha!
> **Zach**: You're excited?
> **Louisa voice:** No, this is Louisa laughing at this person!
> **Zach**: Oh. Why?
>
> [Silence...wrestling between identities]
>
> **Zach**: Is he dressed funny?
> **Louisa voice**: No. Takes himself so fucking seriously!
> **Zach**: Oh. Like a business man?
> **Louisa voice**: Yeah. And...and he only likes men. Not gay. I mean I only respect men. And I think I am [warbles] super smart and...

Deepening voice: ...something I've told other people I would do [seeing Warner Brothers] and I.... I'm just really pleased that it happened.

Zach: What was it? What was it that you did?

Deepening voice: It's a business deal. Big connection between my company and another.

Zach: Gotcha. What were you dealing with in your company?

Louisa voice: I don't know, but I keep seeing the Warner Brothers cartoon thing. I had [warbles] something to do with that. But all I know for sure is that...

Deepening voice: ...I've made the deal come through ...and now I'm set for life! But, boy, Louisa doesn't like me!

Zach: Why doesn't Louisa like you?

Deepening voice: She thinks I'm pompous and believe in stupid things. But I'm extremely enthusiastic about them, I'm very... if you choose your ladder, and you climb that ladder, and you do it well, that *is* honor and that *is* discipline – and it takes sacrifice. There's a whole lot behind what I made happen! I'm deeply proud of it. And, you know, er... [faulters] ...fuck her if she thinks it's trivial!

Zach: For *you*, that was important. It was part of *your* journey.

Deepening voice: [pleased with Zach's response] Yes! She wasn't there! She doesn't know [strong emotion] how *hard* it was to make that happen.

Zach: The sacrifices you made.

Deepening voice: [likes Zach] And I believed in myself. [Seeing view] It's very exciting to be here! Very exciting! I see the skyline and... who would have thought that New York would grow up into this... this fantastic collection of citadels and sky-scrapers! There's I-beams and concrete – it's like a symphony of human achievement. That's where I wanted to be; that's where I wanted to make things happen; and [choking up] ...I made them happen! I did it!

Zach: That's definitely something to be proud of. You took the passion in your heart and manifested it, and that's an honorable and high achievement.

Deepening voice: [bitterly] Well... Louisa doesn't think so.

Zach: Everyone has their opinion, and that's okay, right?

Deepening voice: [under his breath] Yeah.

The business man had other thoughts that I didn't bother to vocalize. He, in turn, had contempt for the romanticism of Louisa's mountain climbing. He wanted her to recognize that the spires of New York were every bit as beautiful as the peaks of any mountains, and that he had "climbed" them just as determinedly as she reached summits. Louisa thought only nature was awe-inspiring; I – as him – thought the works of mankind were. Louisa thought the ascent of challenging peaks was admirable. He countered that he'd chosen a different challenge, a different kind of "ladder," but that the qualities required to move up it drew from the depths of one's character, even if the reward was lots and lots of money instead of standing on a summit.

The long round of hypnosis exhausted me that evening, but the next day I looked up Warner Brothers in the 1950s. I found the greatest blunder Jack Warner ever made was to underestimate the value of Looney Tunes, Merry Melodies, and all the other cartoons containing Bugs Bunny, Daffy Duck, Elmer Fudd, Foghorn Leghorn, etc. Jack Warner considered them worthless because movie audiences had already *seen* them. So, on February 12, 1955, Warner Bros. sold the TV distribution rights to 191 of their black and while cartoons to Guild Films for $2 million. The cartoons proved a gold mine. In the first two years alone, Guild Films made $10 million leasing out them to TV stations across the U.S.

That was the deal "I" closed. And while I may have been "set for life," my life certainly didn't last much longer. A fat, meat-eating cigar smoker, I must have died before June of 1960, because that's when I came back as Louisa. Just as well, because the company I'd worked so hard to build up dissolved amid financial scandal in 1961.

What I learned from my past life regression session is that values don't transfer from one life to the next, but certain loves and memories do. When I visited Greece, I *had* to go see

Knossos, and while I was there, I felt a great sense of sacred belonging, of identification – as if I'd once lived there.

When I was three years old and travelling through Singapore with my family, my father would give me coins to throw into the water for the boat people. Among my earliest memories is watching the young boys dive for them. At three, I remember feeling intense jealousy for the way onlookers praised them for this ability, because I knew I was better at it. I could out-dive all of them, I was sure – though I didn't yet know how to swim. Of this past life, I'm quite confident.

I'm also confident of my life as the Guild Films guy, even though he and I disliked each other. When I graduated from college, I *had* to go live in New York City, I found a job in the publishing district near the Empire State Building, the area where my former self probably worked and lived. I felt the thrill of this bustling metropolis and its history, but alcoholism got the better of me, leading first to my NDE and later to severe panic and depression.

I couldn't hack New York in this lifetime. It wasn't the same place, and I wasn't the same person.

Microsoft Voices Guy

In the winter of 2021, I visited my friend Jesseca in Texas, who, as I've mentioned, had a Near-Death Experience during surgery for a collapsed lung and who experiences so many paranormal knowings, visions, and messages, she often feels like a courier. In fact, she's had to ask her angels to please filter the flow. When we're together, we not only revel in the joy of each other's goodness, but experience synchronicities (speak of a person from way back just before getting a text) and trigger electrical disturbances (TV system cut out, thermostat jumped to 80 degrees in the middle of the night, etc.).

When I was flying back to Seattle, feeling that paranormal stuff was pretty normal, I sat with an empty seat between me and a slightly scruffy guy in his early 30s who was busy on his laptop. For the first hour or so we didn't speak, but after he'd closed up shop, some interaction with a flight attendant got us started. Somehow, he ended up telling me that as a small boy, he'd had severe epilepsy and could speak only a few words by age five.

"Did you ever die during a seizure?" I asked, nudged by Egnacio.

With surprise he told me he had, more than once, needed to be resuscitated. I asked casually if while he was dead he went anywhere or brought back any memories, but he said no. His "no" should have ended the topic, but I sensed something he wasn't saying.

"But did the experience *change* you in any way? I mean, since then, have you had any paranormal experiences?"

"What do you mean?"

"Like, do you ever hear a voice, or know the future, or read people's thoughts?"

He paused, quite still, hovering over something. So I told him about Egnacio.

"Well, I don't have any *names* for them," he remarked, as if that were kind of kooky, "but I have three voices. For most of my life, there were only two, but recently there's been a third now and again."

I knew it! I just knew it! I was so excited!

He unfolded his story for me, how when he was little the voices had come into his consciousness as loving influences who taught him to speak, comforted him as a stigmatized special needs kid, and became his mentors for life in general. "I made amazing progress. No one understood how I was doing it, but they taught me layer after layer." He aced tests and eventually nailed job interviews, guided by them. They helped him excel at coding. Now, he was a senior manager at Microsoft. That his voices *began* after the times he died had never occurred to him, but so they had!

"What they help me to do now in my job is understand people. They'll tell me what someone's thinking, what I should say, what that person needs. It makes me a really good manager. I mean, I've turned teams around! Basically, when your people feel heard, they want to excel."

"So, in a one-on-one, you have several conversations going on at the same time?"

"Well..." he paused. He was searching for words to describe a knowing. "It's not *words* I get, you know? Not something I *hear*, per se. I get the whole thought – but it's not from me. And each of the two has their own distinct voice; I can always tell which is which. This third one was only recently about... it's a long story."

He would occasionally glance about nervously to be sure we weren't overheard.

At this point, I told him about IANDS, that there were plenty of people who heard voices after coming back from the other side. I explained that we held monthly meetings in Seattle, met yearly for an international conference, had many websites, and were always welcoming new people. Though he was clearly intrigued, the more I said, the more his barriers went up, defenses like electric car windows gliding shut.

When I asked for his email, he apologized and politely refused. "I'm actually kind of high up in the organization. I mean, in my division, I... Let's just say have a high profile and, trust me, it would *not* go over well if my people heard about this stuff. I've never told anyone."

"No one?"

"I mean, I told my mom when I was little."

"Did she believe you?"

"Of course not. I was a kid! She assumed, you know, imaginary friends. And it's not something –" He waited while someone passed by. "It's not okay to talk about. I feel strange even hearing myself say these things out loud." Clearly, he did. "I'm sorry, but just I can't see myself wanting to... get involved."

He was truly spooked. He wouldn't even enter Seattle IANDS' web address or email into his phone. I had to write them in pen on a napkin and hand it to him. Pocketing it, he told me he was set to retire in a few years. "Maybe then," he said, nodding, "I'll look you guys up."

I never got his name or saw him again.

A Quick Display from Egnacio

Nine months ago, I got my hip replaced in a day clinic. I woke up in the recovery space. My opening eyes showed me a large square window to the nurses' station – their backs, shelves, and screens.

For about ten seconds, I experienced perfect clarity. I recalled I was doing the "Louisa" thing. My body had just been repaired. Love was here, filling the room, filling my consciousness. And on a two-foot-high swath of blank wall above that window to the nurses' area was something I should attend. Up there, Egnacio was presenting visually what he wanted to tell me, what he'd already been telling me for some time.

Look.

It was my current life as a projected image. A ring of circles surrounded a central circle, each containing a portrait alive with subtle movement and connected to the central circle as if by two-way sun beams. The people in these portraits were connected to my life, my doing. I couldn't recognize individuals, but I knew they were friends, relatives, and clients – each a person with whom I shared a genuine, reciprocated fondness. The inner circle represented me, but without an image.

Egnacio pointed out that pretty much all the connections converging from the outer circles were virtual, not in-person. These exchanges of good will, humor, fondness, and trust – in other words, the stuff of life – all happened online or over the phone. The inner circle became an aerial view of me in my little Ballard house. Egnacio depicted me as a pencil line that scribbled in many small zig zags and loops, retracing over itself, making a darker and darker tangle of lines.

To stay here is wasteful/harmful.

I was unsure quite what he meant. I do trace and retrace the same little paths day after day as I have for twenty-four years. But also, the air I breathe is dirty; car exhaust from a busy arterial behind my yard's back fence and trees lays a sooty film everywhere in just days. Crime has risen: recently a madwoman physically assaulted me on those same exercise stairs where I once caught COVID 19, and a homeless man brandished a 10-inch sickle knife at Beverly, my little dog, as she passed him on a park trail. People have pulled apart the chicken fence to enter my back yard. The time to leave arrived some time ago.

But Egnacio's message was more about missed potential.

Go where you can do more.

I agreed to get moving on moving somewhere else. He'd help me figure out where.

Between states of consciousness, I felt huge love for all the people who would recover in this same spot and pity for those who would see nothing. I resolved to tell the nurses they must hang framed photos and artworks on this amazing swath of wall for the unfortunates who did not receive visions there. It was such a great idea! I was really going to tell them!

Then I'm not sure what happened, because my ten seconds of clarity ended as my physical brain came back online, clouded by anesthetic and pain meds. I became a loopy, post-op fool. Fortunately, I did remember that visions are taboo – not something we're allowed to talk about – so I said nothing to the nurses about the wonderful wall.

Chapter 20: Lessons from Egnacio (and others)

What follows is a list of all the things Egnacio has said to me and a few reflections on what they imply.

1. More real than anything back there.

Our culture presents real/unreal as a binary. Something either happened or it didn't. It's fact or it's fiction. Even if no two witnesses of an accident report the same scenario, our culture maintains that *something* real did happen. Its realness exists independent of flawed perception. It simply is.

But Egnacio said *More real*, as if there were some kind of continuum and the reality I experienced *back there*, in my earthly life, was inferior to the one I was experiencing now, with him.

Remember from Chapter 2 the idea of our "reality" experience as a hologram our brain projects based on nerve input from our various sensory organs. Recall that the hologram is concerned exclusively with what's relevant to our survival. Consider also that we're social beings whose survival rests with the group, so we have elaborate apparatuses that help us interpret the behavior of others and gauge our standing among them.

The vast majority of our thoughts and concerns are simply meaningless. We enmesh our thinking in the games our species has created – economy, politics, history, science. Death reminds us that all such concerns are trivial.

Egnacio's use of the comparative "more" implies levels of reality, which reminds me of Emanual Swedenborg's levels of heaven. The closer we get to god, the more real stuff is. This can happen in life, too. You can have a petty rivalry with a friend occupying your thoughts, but if you learn they're dying, you might jump to the higher level where all is forgiven. Loving beauty and goodness on Earth is more real than worrying about the stock market. Being kind and useful to others is more real than self-absorption.

Still, in this realm, we can get only so real. The scale continues in spiritual realms. That's what Egnacio, I think, might have been saying.

2. *You can't stay; you're not done yet.*

I had objectives Egnacio wanted me to accomplish, so he, as an extension of god, made the executive decision, you're going back – despite my having ingested more than a lethal dose of lidocane. Some people get to choose and others don't.

Excerpted below are a few NDErs return stories:

> Jóse H.:
> "My father looked me in the eye and said, 'You need to go back.' I refused. He said, 'You *have* to.' I felt this pulling sensation from my back, and I was back in my body. I opened my eyes, surprised the doctor doing CPR. Then I went back to my father, right back to our debate. Finally he said, 'I'll make you a deal. If you go back, I promise you, when your time comes, I'll come get you.' I said okay. Instantly, I felt the pulling at the back of my neck, and this time I was fully in my body. My first thought was,

'Wow – this wasn't such a good deal!' The pain was tremendous and I couldn't breathe."

Jodee C.
"God told me, 'You have an opportunity to go back to your body.' And God started trying to get me agree, saying, 'You need to go back and help people.' And I still said, 'No way. Not going. Forget it.' So God took me to the ceiling of Cucina! Cucina! café in South Lake Union of Seattle. My brother Sam and my cousin Randy were in there talking up these two girls. I said to God, 'They're picking up two chicks!' and God was like, 'Yes, they *are*! Go back!' With that, I passed through the same realms I'd come through. The next thing I knew I opened my eyes; I was on life support, and I started vomiting."

Kris W.
"At the same time, I was given a vision of the Earth from space – the actual from distance a little closer than the moon – and a revelation came to me that the whole Earth was groaning in pain. I was told that if I went back, I could help alleviate some of that pain. So I turned back and mentally connected with the father god and mother goddess, and I told them, 'I want to go back.' My answer pleased them, I felt it with every fiber of my being. Instantly, I was back looking down at my body, and it looked even worse. My thought was, 'Really?!

Getting me back in that thing is really going to take a miracle!' The next instant, I *crashed* down into my body."

Norma E.
"On the other side of the stream were hundreds of people, all of whom I was excited to see. I stopped at the edge, and my aunt, who had recently died, stepped in from the other side to greet me. Using what seemed like a net, she tried to clear some sort of moss from the surface of the stream. She worked intently at this, but each time she managed to create a clear pathway, the two sections of moss would merge again. Finally, she looked up and told me: 'I'm sorry, but you cannot cross now. You must return.' With those words, I found myself falling as if from a great height until I plunged consciously back into my body. Excruciating pain hit my consciousness."

Tony C.
"I recall seeing a bunch of images, a collage on a wall showing high points and low points of my life, and I accepted that I had lived them, but I was ready for whatever came next. I wanted to go wherever the Light-river was taking me. All of a sudden, like someone flicked a switch, BAM! I was back in my body. I was pissed. I felt, 'Nooo! I don't want to go back! Don't make me go back!' But, lotsa luck: you don't get to decide. I was suddenly in darkness and hurting like hell. I was scorched where the

lighting had hit my face and where it left through my foot."

Brian M.
"I could see my body on the ground, but the picture was frozen. I began to realize I *wasn't* going to be able to change the world the way I'd thought: God was *right*, and it was going to *suck*! I was shouting, 'No, no! I don't want to go back!' ...So then my mom comes out of the light. She'd died of pancreatic cancer when I was twenty-one. On her deathbed, she'd said, 'Promise me you'll leave this world a better place than you found it,' and I'd promised her. Now she says, 'You *promised*! And, sweetheart, this is part of the difference you're going to make! You won't remember all of it, but God will give you synchronicities and dreams and new senses. Know I'm always with you, but... you're gonna go back!' Then light expanded and came around me. So... Shwoooh! I go back into the body."

Tricia B.
"I heard a voice, not male or female, but booming. It's a telepathy that vibrates from within, not through your ears. It said, 'Look down!' So I looked and I saw this river with all these souls that I knew would be my students. God said, 'These souls need you; they need to be reminded of their connection to the light.' I could see some of the souls trapped in bubbles of fear, or maybe anger, that cut them off from

the light. But I didn't like the idea. I said, 'No, God, I was born a feminist. I don't want a traditional woman's career like nurse or teacher, and I want to make a lot of money!' God laughed at that, and, as silly as this sounds, I feel like I was kicked, or maybe hurled, out of heaven. The darkness surrounded me, and I was back in my painful body, knowing I had to be a teacher."

Zach T.
"Then, all of a sudden, I felt myself getting sucked back like a vacuum, a vortex, like going down a hose really fast, and I popped back into my body. I could hear, 'Zach, Zach, Zach, are you okay?'"

Alma B.
"I begged, 'Please, can I come in?' I felt my grandmothers on either side lower their hands to my elbows as if they were finally about to escort me. But the orb responded, 'Continue to do what you have been doing.' Then everything went silver gray except the orb itself. I wondered 'What's going on?!' But it zoomed away from me, and I saw… the ceiling of the hospital. I cried, No, no! – filled with deep grief. But in that same moment, an overwhelming joy spread over me like a beautiful blanket. I'd never felt anything like it – joy and grief at once. I looked to my left, and I could turn my neck! My neck hadn't turned in over six years!"

Karen T.

"I knew I couldn't let my children grow up without their mother the way I'd grown up without my father. I said, 'I have to go back!' He said, 'You may. You'll be allowed to remember enough of this to make certain you know it's is all true.' I woke up in the recovery room with my husband and kids. In that moment, I had two levels of consciousness. One was my physical brain still confused from anesthesia, wondering why my whole abdomen was stitched up. At the same time, my spiritual consciousness was sharp as a tack, holding all the details of my journey and still feeling that divine love around me and filling me."

As for ***not done yet***, consider David B.'s (the guy who drowned whitewater rafting) self-realization that he had not finished.

> "Of the many things I learned, the most significant was that love is the key to all, that it is the power of the universe—God's power. Love is the key power we all come here to learn and use to overcome adversities. Judgment of others, I perceived, is simply wrong-headed. We're here to accomplish different things, each under a variety of different circumstances in order to facilitate their learning and accomplishment.
>
> "I came to realize that this life was one of many I'd lived. I had come this time to accomplish

aims that I'd determined before I was born. I realized that for me to move on by dying would be perfectly fine, but I also knew that I would then have to come back in another life to accomplish those same things; I viewed it much the same as having to repeat a grade in school. So far in this life, it appeared to me that I'd been a poor student. In that realm I knew clearly the goals I had meant to fulfill on Earth, but I knew I wouldn't be allowed to remember them if I went back.

"I was on a spiritual precipice; I was presented a choice and had to make a decision. I didn't want to go back, yet I knew it was the best choice. The instant I decided, I was back in my body, floating limply down the river."

3. *Implications of the ghost*

From the ghost I learned the danger of obsession with a particular outcome. Haunting, it seems to me, is a form of addiction. As a ghost, I want so much to change something that happened, whether it's my own death, another's death, or something else I can't accept, that my spiritual development halts. I repeat the same addictive cycles over and over, choosing repetition over reunion with god and openness to repurposing in another life.

I can easily do the same thing on Earth without dying. In refusing to grow, I become ghostlike.

4. *This is the last time I can help you.*

Egnacio was cutting me off, basically. He was saying, No more rescuing. If you insist on driving blind drunk, from now on you will suffer consequences. Go ahead and throw away your gifts, your future, your life!

From this, I gather there comes a point with any addict when, if they are truly bent on self-destruction, it's right to let go – no matter how much you love them. Free will is free will.

5. *You DO know right from wrong.*

Right and wrong exist. This is huge. And to throw away one's life on ego, fear, and addiction, whether to drugs, shopping, or social media, is wrong in the sense of waste; it goes against our purpose. In the Old Testament, the original word for sin is "khata," meaning "to fail" or "to miss the goal." When we endlessly chase safety, pleasure, or relief, we miss the goal of life, which is to extend the reach and power of love – i.e. god.

Here's an account from David M., who found himself in a dark place after swallowing all his cocaine because he imagined the police were coming through his second-story wall:

> "I could see my body lying on the bed and I rose up from it. I could see my essence, my spirit, coming out of my legs. From there I descended to a deep, dark place. I felt startled, frightened, confused. I was moving very fast downward, deep into total darkness, until I came to a place with an enormous stone slab; and lying on that slab was my lifeless body. *I* could move about – my essence or spirit – but that body was not

going to move. I went into a panic – no idea what was going on.

"So much of life is paradoxical. My choice in that moment was the opposite of what I was experiencing, which ended up being the right choice. I did *not* want this outcome, and with that choice, I began to hear distant voices trying to guide me. Later on, after the experience, I recognized them as the voices of loved ones who had passed. They guided me up from the darkness, until away at a distance, I could see the light coming toward me – or maybe I toward it. The light grew bigger until I was engulfed in its presence. Everything became perfect."

David, who had used cocaine daily for over twenty years, never used drugs again.

6. *Call Allie; He has Goodness. Trust him; Speak to them*
Angels can work through other people.

If I hadn't connected with Allie as Egnacio urged, I never would have learned that a woman I'd always considered my spunky ally in drinking was dying from alcoholism, never would have heard my friend, whom I respected, credit a higher power for the incredible "coincidences" that had brought us together.

If I'd not reached out to Travis as Egnacio urged, I never would have gone to the international phone center, never would have connected with Bruce or Flintstones John or had any of the amazing AA experiences in Chania.

If I'd not reached out to art teacher John as Egnacio urged, I might have at worst gotten drunk from sheer loneliness, and at best never have seen the beautiful convent where my friend studied art.

In short, without connecting with these people to whom Egnacio referred me, I'd never have made it through Greece sober or have built a foundation for lasting sobriety.

7. *Help her cross.*

Like birth, death is a process, a labor, an intense transition to what's next. Egnacio's urgency suggests it can be easy or difficult. If we're held back by negative beliefs, anger, resentment, or self-pity, these anti-god energies can thicken our defensive sheath, blocking or complicating our re-integration with god. Love does the opposite.

This means *anyone* can help another being cross, primarily by surrounding them with love and assuring them the other side is sweet.

8. *Don't go!*

Angels can access any point on the time continuum and any number of potential futures. They know what's coming. And they're okay with affecting outcomes.

9. I'm here for you. You know why; Diamonds of orderly precision

God is everywhere, in everything that lives and in the intelligence that orients the laws of the universe. Anything can become a vehicle for god's intention. The spider became a conduit for god, just as Egnacio is a manifestation of god, and just as you are.

We have multiple levels of awareness. Our surface level pretty much equates to our chatterbox brains and whatever thoughts we're having. But we can step outside those thoughts and judge them from a higher level, or know something deep down without knowing we know it.

"Diamonds of orderly precision" calls to mind the clear, unambiguous angles and shapes into which we cut diamonds. God is in every detail, not as "fate," but as design.

10. We can do real stuff!

Spirits are constantly influencing what happens, allowing each spirit to actualize itself or fail and come back to try again. As William James noted, "Spiritual energy flows in and produces effects in the phenomenal world."

Many individuals are aware of their angels, some as a normal course of life. They can see in retrospect that they have been guided and protected. They can recall times when a voice inside, indistinguishable from their own thoughts, warned them not to do something they chose to do anyway. How much we hear our angels is only a matter of degree.

At a higher level, the entirety of humanity is guided toward progress. It may occur on a two steps forward, one step back basis, but occur it does.

Alma B. was hit head-on by a taxi while riding her bike. Though she survived the impact, her GI tract was destroyed to such an extent that an array of diseases left her crippled, plagued by seizures, and unable to think. When she left her body, the relief was a joy. On the other side, she approached a heavenly gateway but was unable to pass through it. Instead, she peered through its opening to where she saw the workings of the spirit world represented at three tables:

> "I was shown a glimpse inside the gates. I saw three tables of light, and there were saints – they had robes on – gathered around each.
>
> "At the smaller table, they were leaning over and saying, 'So she needs this; and for him we'll put this in place.'
>
> "At the next table, I heard them saying, '*They* need this; let's do this for them.'
>
> "The largest light table was behind the other two, a huge one with many saints around it. I couldn't hear, but I knew they were talking about the planet – how to help it. More than any of the others, these saints had to *allow*. They were so serious because of all they were letting unfold."

"Letting unfold" means we are free to render the planet uninhabitable for ourselves if we fail to learn. Conversely, if we are able to uproot the greedy, we can restore balance. Climate change has already reached such an extent that it's clear our entire way of life will collapse. But even in this unexpected course, we will be guided by divine influence. (And by the way, Alma is now a yoga instructor in her 60s.)

11. Selfishness is part of the deal. Don't beat yourself up!

Egnacio's laughing reply when I apologized for my selfish thoughts indicates we are wired as physical beings to be selfish in thought, but that's not what matters. It's the *choices* we make in our behaviors, the way we *act* toward others – that's where the spiritual rubber meets the spiritual road.

12. You need health insurance; ask the goth woman; Start your own business; You have no brakes!

When I asked my oncologist how long ago the cancer had started, she replied only, "Oh, years ago!" But I think Egnacio got after me to get insurance almost immediately after it formed. He's concerned with my well-being, not just my survival. At times, I feel as if I were his project. He *likes* to see me grow and thrive.

13. This is the whole point of life! As good as it gets! Just let them love you.

One can't ask for a more explicit message!

Self-loathing only traps us in self, blocking us from what friends want to give: love. My role in that moment was to "catch," not "throw." The exchange is what matters. So we're told in AA, our job is sometimes to be of service, other times to allow others be of service to us.

14. *Everything here is lies and corruption. Just take it.*

Angels don't like manipulative liars. It pains them when beings harm other beings.

The idea of private belongings being sacred clearly doesn't cut it from Egnacio's perspective. That principle is "less real" than the sanctity of honesty and truthfulness.

Egnacio knew everything that went on in that house, and, trust me, there was plenty. He let me waste two years trying to recapture the past. But at a certain point, he drew the line. It was almost the opposite of *This is the last time I can help you.* This time he essentially said, *I can no longer stand by.*

I had to see the lies in Gerard's own texted words before I could leave him. Egnacio knew that, so he showed me how to unlock the phone.

15. From the tree: *Each life must ask directly.*

Any being, as an expression of god, must reach out to converse with its source. Animals, trees, everything is in constant discourse with the unifying web of life. Our god-phobic sheath of fear and anger is permeable one-way: from the inside out (unless you have an angel who yells). It's up to us to call god. God'll call back, but it's never first to pick up the phone. We need to seek.

16. Remember this? This time, it will act as a beacon for ME. I will send healing. I will set it right, little one. You will be strong and you will finish! Just so we can feel it. Trust me, little one.

Angels can highlight memory as shorthand to accomplish something new.

My angel and others wanted me to finish. This wasn't just a hike. It was a high point of my life in body, mind, and spirit. He wanted to give me that gift.

The sheer frequency of communication I had with Egnacio during this episode is astounding. We were literally conversing back and forth. This doesn't mean Egnacio was particularly chatty, but that I'd arrived at a humble, happy, loving state of spiritual openness wherein I could hear him. I was no longer deaf.

Once my knee was working and I found myself among fellow PCT hikers avoiding the fires, I stopped receiving messages, but I still sensed Egnacio was close.

17. From my father's spirit: *You didn't have to do anything.*

What we love is the *essence* of another person or creature. Their current personalities and deeds may express that essence, but we should remember where the impetus comes from: a *being*, an incarnation of god energy. Their current form is secondary. Their accomplishments reflect rather than define who they are. And who they are is god. Love the whole in the particular. Don't exclude the whole to love only the particular – your little circle – defensively.

Tara Brach suggests thinking the phrase "We're friends" to express this love, whether to human strangers, animals, trees, or plants we come across. Doing this alone can change the nature of your world.

18. *I've had so many names in so many lifetimes, and none of them are in alphabets that you know.*

The more I think about this line, the more amazed I become. Not only did it come entirely out of left field, from my perspective, but it suggests Egnacio remembers a series of lives (none of them), each as someone who had a particular name in a particular culture.

In spirit form, we don't need names. Whomever I think of, you know.

Reincarnation is real. And it seems simplistic, but I'm just going to say it. Seems like we get incarnated again and again, learning more every time, and eventually we become angels, then more powerful angels. The Love all comes from god, but angels are big lumps of god cake mix.

19. From my business man self: *If you choose your ladder, and you climb that ladder, and you do it well, that is honor and that is discipline – and it takes sacrifice.*

I feel like I have nothing in common with the Looney Tunes broker, but here, he was trying to say what we *did* have in common. It's the quality of *yearning* in each of us that expresses our spiritual essence, that desire to bring things about as an expression of us.

One young woman whose NDE I heard at Seattle IANDS had gotten caught up in gang activity in East Los Angeles when, in the midst of a head-on car collision, she left her body. Her angel brought her to Jesus (who at first flinched away from hugging her because she was covered with resentment diarrhea). When that was gone, Jesus said he had something to show her.

In a different kind of time/space, he flew her all over the planet and showed her people baking cherry pies at that very moment. In each case, he highlighted for her the emotions of caring and craftsmanship in the people creating them – doing it lovingly, wanting it to turn out well, with honor and discipline and sacrifice, you might say. Each hoped others would enjoy it, but most of all, each took pride in their creation. Not selfish pride, but giving pride: Look at my beautiful cherry pie!

After dozens of cherry pies, Jesus flew her to the best. An old woman somewhere in Europe – was it Italy? – was just bringing her beautiful pie from the oven. She'd baked a LOT of pies all her life, but she took no less care. This one was for her grandchildren. She loved them, she loved the pie, she'd used her knowledge, experience, skill, attention, and most of all love to bring about this masterpiece.

"That," Jesus told the young NDEr, "is what makes a good life. If we send you back, we ask that you live in that spirit." My Looney Tunes broker felt that, in his own way, he'd made a damn good pie!

Chapter 21: On Contempt vs. Open-mindedness

Depression evolved, I have read, as a mechanism to conserve energy that might otherwise be spent on foolhardy, impractical exploits. It served survival for that reason, as a counterbalance to enthusiasm. If I thought, as an australpithecine, that I was going to climb a really big tree to get at its tantalizing fruit, but every time I got to a certain stretch, I couldn't get past it, I would need some kind of mechanism to tell me, "screw that!" My close relatives lacking a proper "screw that!" threshold and so trying repeatedly to get past the impassible stretch would more often fall out of trees or waste time that could have been spent eating less attractive fruit. With more falls and less food, they would less consistently survive and reproduce. In modern times, however, the "screw that!" mechanism has somehow expanded its purview to apply to life in general. Hence, a huge sector of the population is clinically depressed.

Contempt, I would say, is a variation of "screw that!" We feel a sort of disgust at the relatives so convinced yet again that they're going to get that tantalizing but out-of-reach fruit. They're wrong. They're dumb. We can apply the same feeling to any individual or group that differs culturally from our own. Why are they doing things that way? I can't relate. Screw that!

Intellectual contempt, a subset of the above, is a feeling that something is not even worth looking into. The Wright Brothers were mocked and ridiculed in the press as they continued to believe they could construct a heavy, winged object that could fly. Ridiculous! "There probably can be found no better example of the speculative tendency carrying man to the verge of the chimerical than in his attempts to imitate the birds," wrote Rear Admiral George W. Melville, Engineer-in-Chief of the U.S. Navy, in a 1901 *New York Times* article. He continues, "A calm survey of certain natural phenomena leads the engineer to pronounce all confident prophesies at this time for future success [of flight] as wholly unwarranted, if not absurd."[12] And George was far from alone.

Similarly, I've heard accounts from NDE researchers who sat on a scientific discussion panel with skeptics. After some sweeping dismissive statement by a skeptic, one of the NDE researchers enquired whether he had read their study – or, for that matter, *any* of the literature. "Of course not!" was the reply.

In other words, "screw that!" Across the board, NDE skeptics exhibit contempt prior to investigation. They point out that all the evidence is anecdotal. But why is there so much of it? Why are the anecdotes so consistent? Isn't such a striking consistency worth exploring?

As noted in Chapter 1, conspiracy theories abound online, and no educated person is going to devote time to delving into their "research." But NDE research is both conducted and documented according to stringent research protocols. The authors are qualified, vetted, educated, and consistent across the board in presenting their findings. The field's only shortcoming is that its evidence is primarily narrative.

---

[12] Melville, George W. "The Engineer and the Problem of Aërial Navigation." *The North American Review*, Vol. 173, No. 541 (1901), 820. https://www.jstor.org/stable/25105260#metadata_info_tab_contents

Furthermore, NDE research does not contradict mainstream science; it simply complements it, pointing to gaps in our knowledge and experiential phenomena that suggest an expanded model for the behavior of energy in the universe. In other words, we should approach NDEs and their aftereffects as evidence of *something* beyond a mechanical universe. Perhaps future technologies will produce a means by which to observe spiritual energies, but until then, we must not plug our ears, recite the alphabet loudly, and bark "screw that!" to the *people* whose consciousnesses are already able to sense them.

As Bruce Greyson observes in his book *After*,

> [My father] passed down to me not only his passion for science but also his awareness of the essential tentative nature of science. Science by its very nature is always a work in progress. No matter how well-founded we think our world view is, we have to be prepared to rethink it if new evidence raises doubts.... Studying things that fit our preconceived ideas helps us understand their fine points better. But studying things that *don't* fit our preconceived ideas is what often drives breakthroughs in science.[13]

I myself have a final little story to share with you about contempt. I would call this attitude "FOMO-Induced Contempt" (FOMO = Fear Of Missing Out).

---

[13] Greyson, Bruce, *After,* (New York: St. Martin's Essentials, 2022), 19-20.

In 2005, I had a cold and used the zinc drug Zycam, which I picked up at Safeway. Not bothering to read the instructions, I stuck the nasal sprayer up my nose, sprayed, and sniffed up the liquid from both nostrils. (Clearly, I need to be more careful about what I put up my nose!) For five hours I experienced excruciating pain. I didn't go to the Emergency Room for two reasons: I had no one to watch my four-year-old son, and I had bought the stuff at Safeway, so it had to be FDA approved, right?

Well, it wasn't. As a pure element, zinc did not need such approval. I had no idea that I was one of a tiny percentage of the population with an exposed olfactory nerve. In most cases, the olfactory nerve is sheltered between two large mounds I can compare only to butt cheeks. Some of us, however, have merely an open valley instead of a crack between mounds, so the zinc pools on the nerve and dissolves it. When I became part of a class-action suit, I was one of 1,000 people who had developed scent blindness as a result of using Zycam. The makers objected that we were supposed to leave the drops in our nostrils, not sniff. But who does that?

I am the only plaintiff I know of who has regained 99% of their sense of smell. As soon as I'd found internet accounts of scent blindness resulting from zinc in studies from the 1950s, I understood that my nerve had been burned through. I could smell nothing – absolutely nothing. Complications of scent-blindness are more involved than you might think. Not only do you have no clue about smoke, spoilage, or body odor, but you also can't taste food, because ninety percent of taste is smell. I tried at least thirty flavors of Jelly Belly beans and they all tasted exactly alike: sweet.

I designed myself an olfactory workout. I did it, I think, with Egnacio's help, or maybe it was my idea – not sure on this one. Anyway, I put every smelly thing I could think of in a plastic cannister, and several times a day I would sniff them all, one after another, and pray for the nerves to connect. "This is moth balls. Nose, find my brain. Brain find my nose. This is garlic. Nose..."

When I'd been doing this for two weeks, one morning I got the tiniest, faintest glimmer of cigarette butt smell. I called everyone, overjoyed. Scent-blind fellows have since asked me who told me to follow that routine. I reply it just made sense.

Several odd things happened to me during this period when I was scent blind. On Day 3, I was dressing in my room when a strange noise startled me. I stopped to listen, but the sound stopped, too. So I resumed putting on my socks, which turned out to be the source of the noise. The friction of knitted material on my feet sounded clear and distinct. Immediately after, I jumped at a rattly, rasping noise coming from the closed window. Once I looked out my front door, I realized it was a gardener on the far side of the street raking leaves from my neighbor's sidewalk. So loud! Jesus! Would he please knock it off?

As my day continued this way, I gradually realized I was hearing more acutely to compensate for not smelling. Remember the 40 – 50 bits of information per day our brain can process consciously out of the 11 million it detects? Well, my brain had made some executive decision to acknowledge more sound bits since we weren't receiving any smell bits. It just used the spare bandwidth to turn up the volume.

But even weirder things began happening to me psychologically. Scent is made up of sixteen different sensitivities, as taste is made up of four. These came back to me widely staggered, so for a while I could smell some things but not others. Because red bell peppers and gasoline smelled identical to me, I would often think about grabbing a salad as I filled up my tank. Shit and Starbucks also smelled identical, with similar associations. But more significantly, once I had *some* sense of smell but still major gaps in awareness, I began to develop contempt for those people reporting smells I myself could not sense.

At first, I wasn't aware of the low-level irritation I felt whenever friends around me remarked on a smell. It doesn't happen that often, so the pattern eluded me for a while. Maybe at a restaurant, maybe near some ripe garbage.

But one time my response was over the top contempt. I'd arrived early to a women's AA meeting in a church where some kids' event had recently taken place. There were children's chairs where our chairs belonged, so I changed them all out. In the process, I developed a headache. After about ten minutes, the next person arrived for the meeting. The instant she came in the door, she appeared painfully upset and called to me, "Oh my god! What *happened* here? It's awful! Open a window!" The next woman came in and went through the same OMG routine. As did the next.

It was bleach. Apparently, a kid had had some kind of accident, and someone had wiped down the entire kitchen with pure, undiluted bleach. The women propped open doors, struggled with sticky windows, but most of all, wouldn't shut the hell up about something THAT WASN'T EVEN THERE!! I grew intensely annoyed. My efforts to strike up normal conversations were bypassed for more talk about the goddam bleach. "Big deal!" I wanted to say. "You don't like the bleach smell! Can't you shut up about it?"

Here's the weirdest part. Somewhere at a deep level I could acknowledge only to myself, I suspected they were making the whole thing up. I sensed a bleach conspiracy, an Emperor's New Bleach where everybody was feeding off each other's hysteria and each trying to top the other in terms of how sensitive they were to this imaginary smell.

"Screw that!" I felt. I'm not playing their game.

Rationally, mind you, I knew full well the bleach must have been potent. I had a headache, after all, not to mention there was no reason whatsoever for a bleach-spiracy. But here's the thing: I felt left out. Even though I could smell quite a number of things now, I was lacking whatever these other women had – the notes for bleach. Therefore, some part of my ego wanted *them* to be wrong so that I would not be insensible.

Why? Because I'm human. My standard for what is normal is what feels normal *for me*. The gardener was inconsiderate to rake the sidewalk so loudly and the AA women must be exaggerating about the bleach because I wanted *my* perceptions to be accurate.

Basically, skeptics of NDEs and other paranormal energies are stuck in the same FOMO-Induced Contempt. Why should these NDE people experience love a million times more powerful than earthly love or possess an ability to read thoughts or receive spiritual messages – while they, the skeptics, have none? Are they missing a sensibility other people have? Are they lacking a sector of experience? Screw that! Their way of experiencing life is the legitimate way. The senses they have are the ONLY genuine senses. Anyone who claims otherwise is.... is.... WRONG.

For an NDEr to have their experience dismissed is roughly equivalent to my announcing to those women, "Friends, there is no bleach. Maybe you washed your clothes in some new detergent? Yes? Think about it. Maybe you applied some different moisturizer, and now you're just smelling your upper lip? That's more likely."

About a month after his 1998 NDE, John B. told his story first to himself in the mirror, just to wrap his head around it.

> "I forced myself to look at what it meant about the nature of reality. That night, I called a friend in Philadelphia, and when we met for dinner, I told him everything. I remember him saying, 'Are you *sure* it wasn't a hallucination?'
>
> "To me, that's as if you went to a dinner party and had a full conversation with the person next to you, but when you try to tell your friends and family about it, they say, 'Are you *sure* that wasn't a turtle? Maybe you saw one out in the garden earlier today?'
>
> "You want to shout, 'Of course not! I know the difference between what's reality and what's not!' It's insulting. I tried to tell a couple other people and got the same reaction. I reached a point where I just shut it down."

Human hubris. We point to Icarus as its representative, but what about the hubris of *not* flying, *not* trying, *not* exploring – because in doing so we'd become vulnerable? If I can't understand it, it must not exist.

The notion that our primate senses and brains would be powerful enough to grasp all the goings on of the universe is laughable, yet it's society's default. Yes, our senses are cool, but they developed long before we were even shrews, the common ancestor of mammals. Insects can see and hear. Earth worms can smell and taste. But there are also senses we lack. Bats and sea mammals can... actually, screw it; sonar is stupid. Migrating birds and butterflies navigate the globe with.... never mind what. Kelsey, my coyote halfbreed, knew the roofer was lying cause... she was, um, wily. I might add that Kelsey also ran to the basement, squeezed her way under a bed, and refused to come out about ten minutes prior to Seattle's 2001 earthquake...but whatever. Animals run to high ground before tsunamis...because they feel like it.

Our categories of understanding are likewise cool, shared by much of the animal kingdom and exceeded by some. Quantity, quality, relation, modality. There cannot possibly be any other ways of knowing. Might dolphins (including Orcas) possess telepathy? Absolutely not, and I can tell you why: because *we* don't. Furthermore, we can't imagine how such communication would work. Therefore, it does not exist. That huge part of their brain that we don't have, that extra paralimbic lobe? It's a stupid part. I wouldn't want it anyway. It's just... extra brain for mammals without hands.

Obviously, quantity, quality, relation, and modality can do more than optimize how we consume and reproduce. Our brains have grown. Applied to abstractions, these modes of thinking can organize a lot of information – more than enough to for humans to have collectively developed a complex technological society that spans the globe.

But are they enough to comprehend the universe? To think outside linear time and 3-D space? To understand the nature of life energy? The nature of consciousness itself?

Why would they be?

*   *   *

> *"To know that what is impenetrable to us really exists, manifesting itself as the highest wisdom and the most radiant beauty which our dull faculties can comprehend only in their primitive forms – this knowledge, this feeling is at the center of true [spirituality][14]."*
>
> ~ Albert Einstein, theoretical physicist and dummy

When I was an atheist, the universe seemed far more intelligible to me than it does now. But it also seemed hopeless. In 1981, before my NDE, I wrote a paper in which I summarized with great contempt Kierkegaard's third sphere of existence as follows. Briefly, the 1) aesthetic individual lives for pleasure; the 2) ethical individual follows rules; the 3) religious individual, as I wrote in my paper...

> "...humbles himself before God and accepts his trivial earthly needs... He is existing as a human individual trusting entirely in God's will. Here, simply embracing the belief that God knows everything best becomes the day-to-day act of faith."

---

[14] Okay, so he said "religiousness." But he *meant* spirituality!

I remember thinking, "What an imbecile that Kierkegaard is!" – struggling to suppress my contempt for his pathetic Santa Claus view of human existence at least enough to describe it without sarcasm. I would never, never be so blindly stupid.

And yet, at 63, I find these very words written so condescendingly by 21-year-old me accurately describe the way of life I now aspire to. Beyond that, if I worked for hours to craft the perfect wording, I couldn't better describe the state of mind I possessed preceding my miracle on the trail, when I was best able to hear Egnacio: I was one who "...humbles herself before God and accepts her trivial earthly needs...."

Life without faith in some form of goodness is unbearable. Will we blow ourselves up? Will we upset the planet's delicate balance too much to sustain ourselves and the magnificent array of life forms with which we share it? *Be a human,* Egnacio tells me. Live in trust.

Trust, however, does not mean complacency. *You do know right from wrong*! Where I see wrong, I must exert myself. "Where there is error, let me bring truth." "Grant me... the courage to change the things I can."[15] "Be the change you wish to see in the world." "Change does not roll in on the wheels of inevitability, but comes through continuous struggle." This is our job, our purpose as humans. It's why I was sent back, why so many NDErs are sent back. We're here to contribute.

I wrote this book because Egnacio constantly bugged me to do so. There is an error. It's been many centuries in the unfolding, from the dawn of monotheism through the contorted

---

[15] Saint Francis prayer, Niebuhr's Serenity prayer, Mahatma Gandhi, & Martin Luther King, Jr., respectively

growth of organized religions. It's time to stop the thinking in the dichotomy of either / or – either materialism or religion. Both are short-sighted.

Humans need to know god exists. They need to know love is paramount. They need to know every act of kindness is sacred and meaningful, from delivering disaster relief to offering a smile to a stranger. And they need to challenge and combat the greed and selfishness of the rich and powerful, heads of destructive corporations, a minority bloated with malignant symptoms of fear and aggression. This book, this tale of my own metamorphosis from skeptic to believer, is my offering, my crumb on the scales of change.

Also by Louisa P. available on Amazon:

A Spiritual Evolution: *How 14 aftereffects of a Near-Death experience helped cure my addictions and changed my life*

The Purpose of Gravity and Other Stories
Short fiction 1990 - 2005

Printed in Great Britain
by Amazon